P9-CQX-615

Advertising For Dummies®

Cheat Sheet

How to Buy Ads Successfully

- ✔ Determine the best publications for reaching your customers.
- ✔ Find the best sales reps who work for those publications.
- ✔ Be tough, firm, and fair.
- ✔ Uncover every available rate and hidden discount.
- ✔ Never stop negotiating.
- ✔ Use reluctant-buying and competitive-posturing techniques.
- ✔ Complain quickly and firmly, and demand make-goods when mistakes are made.
- ✔ Don't be afraid to use the "This isn't working" speech.
- ✔ Make your ad dollars go farther than your competition's.

How to Avoid Legal Hassles with Your Advertising

- ✔ Be truthful.
- ✔ Don't mislead.
- ✔ Substantiate your claims.
- ✔ Be fair to consumers.
- ✔ Make necessary disclosures clear and conspicuous.

Key Media Terms to Remember

- ✔ **Quantitative research:** The *number* of people listening to a given station.
- ✔ **Qualitative research:** The *kind* of people listening to a given station.
- ✔ **Cumulative audience:** The total unduplicated media audience accumulated over a given period of time.
- ✔ **Cumulative rating:** The reach of a radio or television program or station, as opposed to the average rating.
- ✔ **Ranker:** A report showing a selected demographic audience of each radio station in a given market, ranked from highest to lowest (for example, the number of women 18 to 35 who listen to each station in a market).
- ✔ **Dayparts:** Time periods throughout the day in which radio and television stations sell ads (for example, radio morning drive time from 6:00 a.m. to 10:00 a.m., or TV prime time from 8:00 p.m. to 11:00 p.m.).
- ✔ **Column inch:** A standard print media measurement; a 3-x-11-inch ad is 33 column inches (or a quarter page).

Advertising For Dummies®

Cheat Sheet

Why Customers Choose Your Store over Another

- **Image:** The image of your store is more in tune with the customer's own tastes and desires.
- **Personality:** The personality of your business is friendly and one they feel comfortable with. *Remember:* Personality begins with you and the people who work for you.
- **Convenience:** A convenient, accessible location with great parking and a bright and cheerful ambience is always a winner.
- **Service:** Market research shows that what customers want *most* from any business they patronize is good, old-fashioned service.
- **Uniqueness:** There is no more certain way to attract customers than to offer something they cannot get elsewhere.
- **Price:** If you're only selling price, you'll have to continue to lower that price, or come up with even better terms, on an ongoing basis in order to continue to attract new and existing customers. Make sure you're offering several other benefits to your customers beyond price.

How to Write Good Advertising Copy

- Make your ads relevant and memorable.
- Find, or invent, a creative hook.
- Write the way people think.
- Don't be ponderous or pompous.
- Before writing an ad, know why people buy your products.
- Remember that creativity is hard work; don't get lazy or discouraged.
- Deliver the same message across all media.
- Keep it simple; the consumer doesn't have time for complex copy.
- Deliver your message with clarity.

Reasons to Send Press Releases

- A promotion or new hire
- A purchase of a competitor's business, or a merger
- A community project your company has sponsored
- An industry award you or an employee has won
- The introduction of a new product or service
- A new location or the addition of a branch office
- A highly successful year or quarter
- A change in corporate policy or a new affiliation

For Dummies: Bestselling Book Series for Beginners

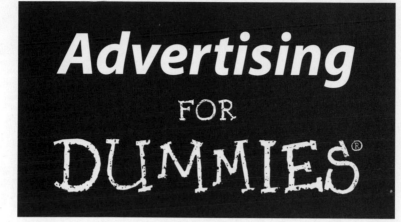

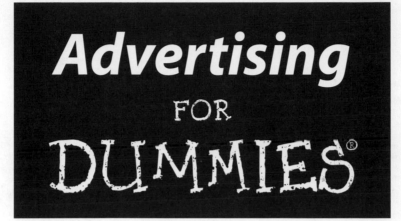

Advertising
FOR
DUMMIES®

by Gary Dahl

Wiley Publishing, Inc.

Advertising For Dummies®

Published by
Wiley Publishing, Inc.
909 Third Avenue
New York, NY 10022
www.wiley.com

Library of Congress Cataloging-in-Publication Data:

Library of Congress Control Number: 2001092743

ISBN: 0-7645-5377-1

Manufactured in the United States of America

10 9 8 7 6

About the Author

Gary Dahl is an award-winning copywriter, creative director, and advertising agency owner in California's Silicon Valley. His career spans 35 years, during which he has handled all facets of advertising for hundreds of clients. His agency, Gary Dahl Creative Services, in Campbell, California, specializes in electronic advertising. Dahl's ability to creatively capture the essence of a client's business in 30 or 60 seconds of clear, concise, broadcast copy is a result of having written and produced hundreds of television commercials and thousands of radio commercials for a wide variety of businesses, including financial, automotive, wireless, education, retail, high-tech, and yes, even dot-coms.

Gary Dahl has a unique understanding of what it takes to successfully convey a client's message to potential customers. As the creator of the retail phenomenon the Pet Rock — which still ranks as the fastest selling and most publicized novelty gift product in retailing history — Dahl has proven the extraordinary power of a creative idea combined with an effective, well-planned marketing strategy. He has been featured in *Time, Newsweek, People, Playboy,* and other major magazines; has appeared on numerous network TV shows; and has been interviewed by countless radio networks worldwide, including NPR, the BBC, and the Australian Broadcast-ing Company.

In 2000, Dahl won the Grand Prize in the Bulwer-Lytton Fiction Contest, defeating over 4,000 entries from all over the world to take top honors in creating the worst possible opening sentence to an imaginary novel. The contest, hosted by San Jose State University's English Department, is named after Edward George Bulwer-Lytton, a minor Victorian author, who wrote the infamous and oft-quoted opening line, "It was a dark and stormy night. . . ."

An accomplished public speaker, Dahl has made advertising/marketing presentations to numerous university advertising and marketing communications classes, advertising and civic organizations, and business and professional clubs throughout the country. He and his wife, Marguerite, live in the hills above Los Gatos, California.

Dedication

To Marguerite, my soul mate and the love of my life

Acknowledgments

First, I want to thank literary agent Carol Susan Roth, for encouraging me to write this book, and Hungry Minds Acquisitions Editor Holly McGuire, for seeing its value. I also owe an enormous debt of gratitude to Matt Fidiam and Kate Reynolds, whose insights and expertise aided me so much in completing the work. And a big tip of the hat to Michael Fineman, Diane Cimine, Andy Nunez, Stan Madden, Marjorie Cooper, and Lisa Canady for their help. Many thanks also to San Jose State University professor Scott Rice, who had the impeccably good taste to award me the Grand Prize in his wonderful Bulwer-Lytton Fiction Contest, notoriety without which this book would never have happened.

Finally, my heartfelt gratitude to my Project Editor, Elizabeth Kuball, who worked her blue pencil to a pathetic, little stub while making this book vastly more readable, and to Willie Baronet, whose technical editing kept me honest while reminding me to add much valuable information.

Publisher's Acknowledgments

We're proud of this book; please send us your comments through our online registration form located at www.dummies.com/register.

Some of the people who helped bring this book to market include the following:

Acquisitions, Editorial, and Media Development

Project Editor: Elizabeth Netedu Kuball

Acquisitions Editor: Holly McGuire

Technical Editor: Willie Baronet

Senior Permissions Editor: Carmen Krikorian

Editorial Manager: Pamela Mourouzis

Media Development Manager: Laura Carpenter

Editorial Assistant: Carol Strickland

Cover Photos: © Bob Daemmrich\Stock, Boston Inc.\PictureQuest

Production

Project Coordinator: Dale White

Layout and Graphics: LeAndra Johnson, Brian Torwelle

Proofreaders: TECHBOOKS Production Services

Indexer: TECHBOOKS Production Services

Publishing and Editorial for Consumer Dummies

Diane Graves Steele, Vice President and Publisher, Consumer Dummies
Joyce Pepple, Acquisitions Director, Consumer Dummies
Kristin A. Cocks, Product Development Director, Consumer Dummies
Michael Spring, Vice President and Publisher, Travel
Brice Gosnell, Publishing Director, Travel
Suzanne Jannetta, Editorial Director, Travel

Publishing for Technology Dummies

Andy Cummings, Acquisitions Director

Composition Services

Gerry Fahey, Vice President, Production Services
Debbie Stailey, Director of Composition Services

Contents at a Glance

Cartoons at a Glance

By Rich Tennant

page 7

page 59

page 167

page 187

page 229

page 259

Cartoon Information:
Fax: 978-546-7747
E-Mail: richtennant@the5thwave.com
World Wide Web: www.the5thwave.com

Table of Contents

Introduction

• •

*A*t first glance, advertising may seem complicated. Print, broadcast, outdoor, direct mail, collateral materials, Internet — each media has its own positives and negatives, its own mysterious production language, its own unique rates. How does a novice decipher this stuff? How do you know what to buy and what to ignore?

Yes, advertising can be complicated, even intimidating, but the good news is that it ain't rocket science. I've learned a few tricks of the trade in my 35-year career that will prove helpful to you when it comes time to design, write, and implement a creative, hard-hitting, memorable ad campaign for your business.

About This Book

You can read this book front to back, or you can simply refer to it as you would any reference book, dipping into the chapters you need right away. Whichever way you read it, you'll discover some shortcuts, insights, techniques, and money-saving facts that will get you the most bang for the buck while taking some of the mystery out of this all-important element of your business.

Think of *Advertising For Dummies* as a guidebook to map your way through the back alleys, side streets, and secret pathways leading to effective advertising. Advertising can be a very intimidating subject — it has its own language; it comes in a huge array of media choices; it requires, when done right, creativity, clarity, and solid production values to cut through its own clutter; and it costs a lot of money. But advertising is also essential to the success of your business. Use this travel guide to chart your course down the hidden boulevards of advertising, and you may discover that, indeed, the streets are paved with gold.

Foolish Assumptions

This book is not for the CEO of a major corporation with virtually unlimited funds for slick, glossy production, and mind-boggling amounts of cash for media buys. Instead, this is a book for entrepreneurs, owners of small to mid-size businesses, and professionals selling important services — in other words, anyone who is trying to drum up business and create a successful company with the help of advertising. This is a book for the rest of us — the people for whom an advertising budget represents an important percentage of gross income and, therefore, a drain on the old take-home pay that must be taken very seriously.

Over the years, I have helped numerous clients project clear, concise, creative messages within limited budget parameters. I used to dream of boundless production budgets with which to produce award-winning ads for both print and broadcast. I always wondered what it would be like to take a complete crew — cameramen, sound and lighting technicians, stunt drivers, fashion models, actors, makeup people, hairstylists, even caterers — to some exotic locale where I would have a one-month deadline within which to shoot a 30-second, $2 million spot. It never happened. My guess is that less than 1 percent of all professional advertising people actually work on the major national accounts, creating the ads you see each night during prime time — the ads produced with unrestricted budgets, which, sadly, still seem to miss the mark more often than not. The other 99 percent of advertising professionals are guys like me.

How This Book Is Organized

This book is divided into six easily digestible parts, and each part is divided into chapters. Here's the scoop on what each part covers:

Part I: Advertising 101

From the moment you get out of bed in the morning, to late at night when you turn off the television and turn out the lights, you are bombarded with thousands of advertising messages. Advertising is here, there, everywhere. And into this clutter you will now insert your own advertising. What you'll discover in this part are the fundamentals of effective advertising. Maybe you've considered hiring an ad agency — if so, this is the part where I tell you who the players are and give you the pros and cons of going this route. I also guide you through the creative process and show you how to generate ideas that will separate you from the herd. If you want to find out about the fun side of the ad game, or you're just starting out and aren't sure where to begin, this part is a great place to start.

Part II: Writing Great Ads for Every Medium

This part of the book is the longest because the depth of your media choices is simply mind-boggling (and new forms of media, both good and bad, are introduced nearly every day). In this part, I stick to the mass media choices of radio, television, print, outdoor, collateral, Web sites, and Internet advertising. I walk you through the steps of writing broadcast and print ads that will motivate and sell. I show you what goes into producing radio and TV commercials, as well as print ads and brochures, and I let you know what you need to know to build a Web site and advertise on the Internet. I also show you why *continuity,* delivering the same message across all media, is the all-important key to a successful ad campaign.

Part III: Developing a Plan That's within Your Budget

This part is important in helping you decide which media you will use and how much media you can afford. Here I help you identify your target market, set your sales goals, narrow your focus, and develop an advertising plan that will work. I delve into the complicated world of co-op advertising reimbursement, in which your ad dollars are augmented by others'.

I think you will be pleasantly surprised at the quality of media you can afford, even on the smallest budgets. Mass media may, at first glance, appear to be unaffordable. But regardless of the expense, when you consider how many people you can reach with mass media, it's the smartest way you can spend your money. What you *can't* afford to do is fritter away a limited ad budget on questionable media that is better suited to wrapping fish than it is to attracting new customers to your business. So in this part I help you plan an advertising strategy that will actually bring customers through your door.

Part IV: Buying the Different Media

This part gets down to the nitty-gritty — the actual spending of your hard-earned advertising budget. Here I take a hard look at negotiating with print media to get the best possible page position at the lowest possible price. And I let you know why buying television time isn't nearly as complicated as putting a man on the moon.

Here's the best part of these chapters: I give you the inside scoop on getting all kinds of free stuff (even vacations) as part of your media expenditures. The chapters in this part give you the information you need in order to maximize your ad budget by spending it wisely.

Part V: Beyond the Basics: Making Use of Publicity, Premiums, and Events

In this part, I explain the difference between publicity and public relations, help you write a good press release, and show you how to get it published (hey, it's free advertising). I also walk you through the unique nature of advertising specialties and premiums while showing you how to increase their effectiveness, and I reveal how to become involved in sponsored promotions and events. I even show you how to invent successful promotions of your own.

Part VI: The Part of Tens

What, you may be asking, is a Part of Tens? It's the part of every *For Dummies* book that cuts right to the chase. If you don't have time to read anything else in this book, read these short lists of do's and don'ts. In these lists of ten I instruct you on writing effective, creative, clear copy for all media; offer you some tricks of the trade for money-saving media negotiations; and help you decide whether or not your business could use the services of an advertising agency. (If you're too busy to even read that chapter, hire an agency right away.)

Icons Used in This Book

Icons are those little pictures you'll find in the margins of this book. I use them to grab your attention and steer you toward key bits of information. Here's a list of the icons I use in this book and what they mean:

Some of the points I make in this book are so important that you'll want to commit them to memory. If you file these tidbits in your memory bank, you will have gathered some very important details about the advertising business.

This icon marks insider tips I've gathered over the years. They will help you avoid some of the mistakes I've learned about the hard way and give you a leg up as you navigate the various elements leading to effective advertising.

As I lead you through the hidden back streets of advertising, I don't want you to stumble and fall. So I've marked some of the larger potholes and cracks in the sidewalk with this Warning icon.

Insider information is a wonderful thing. Secret, obscure advertising stuff that took me decades to absorb is yours for the taking whenever you see this icon. Having discovered these ambiguous tidbits, you will be in a position to confuse and dismay even the best media reps.

Whenever I wax nostalgic and feel the need to share stories of my questionable past experiences in the ad biz, you'll see this icon.

The advertising trade brings with it a ton of technical stuff, and I've marked these areas with this icon. The good news is that you can safely skip over any paragraph marked with this icon. But if you read it, you'll discover information that you can use to wow (if not confuse and dismay) the sales reps and other ad people you deal with, not to mention your neighbors down the street.

Where to Go from Here

You are holding this book because you felt a need to discover the ins and outs of the ad game. Think of this as a traveler's guide that contains the charts and maps you need in order to find your way through the weird and wonderful world of advertising. You can begin your journey in the beginning, or you can dive right into the middle — whichever works best for you.

Part I
Advertising 101

In this part . . .

Advertising: It's here, it's there, it's everywhere! Everyone is assailed with advertising messages every waking moment. The obvious media, like television, radio, newspapers, magazines, billboards, and direct mail, are just the tip of the advertising iceberg. Your cereal boxes, milk cartons, clothing, bedding, fashion accessories, and even your automobiles are covered in advertising. Into this cauldron of advertising vehicles has been thrown the Internet, grocery carts, the reverse side of cash register tapes, ATM screens, even displays in some public restrooms — and all of this contributes to advertising clutter.

If you want to advertise your business (and you most certainly should), you have to enter this world, jumping in with both feet. Daunting? You bet. Impossible? No way. In this part, I share the fundamentals of advertising, explain the advantages and pitfalls of hiring an agency, help you define and position your message, and aid you in deciphering the mysteries of a sometimes complex business as you begin the process of creating your own unique advertising message.

Chapter 1

An Introduction to Advertising

Many a small thing has been made large by the right kind of advertising.

— Mark Twain

Someone once defined good advertising as something that "tells people lies to get them to buy things they don't need anyway." Funny? Perhaps. Cynical? Definitely. Untrue? Absolutely. Abraham Lincoln was more accurate when he said, "You can fool all the people some of the time, and some of the people all the time, but you can not fool all the people all of the time." What Lincoln's quote means in the advertising world is that if your product doesn't live up to your advertising hype, not only will you reduce your chances of success, but you could actually be made to fail faster.

If your advertising makes bold promises about your product, you may convince a lot of people to try it. But if those people buy your product and give it a try, and the product turns out to be less than you advertised it to be, you will most certainly never see those consumers again. Think about it: How many times have you responded to an advertising message for a new, improved, astounding product, only to be disappointed with the item after you tried it? You probably even felt like you'd been ripped off. If your advertising message leaves consumers with the same feeling, you simply won't get anywhere.

In this chapter, I fill you in on the basics of advertising — what's effective and what isn't. Then I give you a short course on the two main types of advertising — image and retail — and explain how you can put them to work for you. Finally, I end with stories from two of the all-time best in the business, because if you focus on the best and figure out what they've done well, you can try to incorporate some of their genius into your own advertising — and come out ahead of the competition.

What Makes Advertising Work

Only 1 in 1,000 new products makes it permanently into the marketplace. Those odds are tough. But keep in mind that most of those 1,000 products that try to find a way in are also bad (or totally irrelevant) products in the first place. If your product fills a need for your customers, and if your advertising is effective, your odds improve dramatically.

So what makes advertising effective? Effective advertising is:

- **Creative:** It delivers the advertising message in a fresh, new way.

- **Hard-hitting:** Its headline, copy, or graphic element stops readers or listeners dead in their tracks.

- **Memorable:** It assures that the audience will remember *your* business when they think about the products and services you are selling.

- **Clear:** The message is presented in a concise, uncomplicated, easy-to-grasp manner.

- **Informative:** It enlightens the audience about your business and products, while giving them important reasons to buy from you.

Effective advertising sells a product that fulfills all the promises made about it. On the other hand, effective advertising will also sell inferior products, but only once!

The well-established brands that most people use every day — brands like Coca-Cola and Pepsi, McDonald's and Burger King, Budweiser and Miller, Bayer and Advil, Ford and Chevy, Tide and Cheer — live up to the promises made in their advertising. In fact, the products live up to the promise in such a dramatic fashion that those products have become a part of the everyday lives of millions of people. These products have been *branded,* which simply means that when you think of soft drinks, fast food, beer, pain relievers, cars, or laundry detergents, these brands come to mind. As surely as the cowboys of the Old West branded the haunches of their cattle, these products have been branded into your psyche — and the psyches of millions of other consumers.

When you begin to create advertising for your product or service, keep these suggestions in mind:

- **Don't make promises you can't live up to.** Although your ad may draw more people to your product initially, you won't retain these people as loyal customers in the long run if you make promises you can't keep.

- ✔ **Identify the best features of whatever it is you're selling, and develop your advertising around these features.** Think about how your product stands out from the competition, what sets it apart, and then focus on those attributes.

- ✔ **Try to create a memorable advertising message for your product.** You want people to think of your store, or your widget, or your professional service whenever they're in the market for such a thing.

If your message is creative, clear, and concise, if your product or service is something that will truly benefit people and live up to its hype, then you're on the road to producing effective advertising.

The Main Forms Advertising Takes

Advertising takes two main forms as it tries to attract the attention of an audience. One form is the big-time, national (or international) *image advertising* (also known as *brand advertising*), which is produced by large companies with even larger advertising budgets. The other form is known as *retail advertising* (or sometimes *direct response advertising*), and it is made up of everything else — in a nutshell, it is all the advertising produced by any business that does *not* have unlimited funds.

Image advertising is what the *manufacturer* of whatever product you are selling will use; retail advertising is what *you* will use. Image advertising creates the interest; retail advertising generates the sale. Image advertising tells you *why* to buy it; retail advertising tells you *where* to buy it. Image advertising presents the sizzle; retail advertising sells the steak.

Image advertising

Image advertising, as created by the advertising agency that handles the manufacturer's account, is the flashy commercial you're likely to see on prime time television during your favorite show. It may be a beautifully filmed spot showing a $75,000 car driving down a country lane on a crisp fall afternoon with leaves blowing across the road, while a full symphony orchestra plays in the background. In the car sit two of the most beautiful people you have ever seen, smiling at each other with the smugness that comes from knowing that they can afford this luxury automobile and their neighbors cannot. They turn into the circular driveway of their million-dollar mansion and pull to a stop. Their two perfect children run to greet them. The symphony builds to a crescendo as a mellow voice-over says something like, "Now that you've arrived, arrive in style."

In this ad, no one is beating you over the head to buy this car *today*. No one is mentioning the car's price or the terms of sale or the interest rates. Instead, the sponsor is showing you its product in the most glamorous setting possible and giving you something to aspire to. (This advertisement should include the disclaimer, "Perfect children not included.")

Another form of the image advertising genre is an advertisement in which the car's performance, rather than its comfort and elegance, is featured. This *spot* (ad-speak for a TV or radio advertisement) opens with a very long shot of the car screaming across the desert at 100 miles per hour. The music background is big, with a frantic, driving beat that matches the breathtaking pace of the commercial. Heat waves shimmer in the foreground and voluminous dust clouds rise from the tires into the crisp, blue sky as the camera, fitted with a telescopic lens, tracks this high-performance automobile across the course. As the camera zooms in for a closer look, the car makes a sharp turn and goes into a slow-motion, four-wheel drift and then comes to a sudden stop. As the dust settles on the scene and the car reappears (as if by magic, it's been washed and polished), the voice-over says, "Of course you wouldn't. But it's nice to know you could."

These examples are image advertising in its purest form — advertising fashioned by major advertising agencies with nearly limitless production budgets, inexhaustible media funds, and the best creative talent money can buy. You see it on your television during the prime time lineup, throughout major sporting events, and during the network national newscasts — all very costly times to run ads. In the print media, image ads are the full-color, full-page ads you see in national magazines and in your local newspaper. As direct mail, image advertising may take the form of a free sample of a new product placed in the plastic bag that contains your morning newspaper.

Image advertising has one purpose in mind: *branding* (getting the name and the attributes of the product and the company that manufactures it embedded as deeply into your brain as possible). This is not advertising that screams at you to "hurry in today!" This is advertising that gently, entertainingly, obnoxiously, or even deviously nudges you to remember the product the next time you're in the market for such an item. You can call it image advertising, or national advertising, or brand advertising, but the bottom line is that this is big-time advertising created by big-time agencies for big-time clients who have big-time ad bucks to spend. And some of it is spectacularly good.

Like it or not, advertising at this level actually shapes your life. You're bombarded with it each and every waking moment. You may not even be aware of it, but it slowly, surely, and insidiously sinks into your mind. Most people have favorite commercials and probably have even used some of the phrases from the most popular ones in their everyday lives. Lines like, "Where's the beef?", "I can't believe I ate the whole thing!", "Got milk?", and "Whassup?" are just a few of the many ad slogans that have been copied, parodied, remembered, and repeated on the lips of millions.

And one important thing to remember about this highfalutin form of advertising is what ad man Morris Hite said long ago: "There is no such thing as national [read, *image* or *brand*] advertising. All advertising is local and personal. It's one man or woman reading one newspaper in the kitchen or watching TV in the den." Hite makes a very good point, but it doesn't negate the simple truth that this type of advertising is very expensive.

Even though image advertising requires a lot of cash, I strongly encourage you to examine the best of it and put certain facets of it to work for you.

Retail advertising

Where image advertising sells you on a specific make or model of car, retail advertising is done by the local car dealer, trying to get you to buy the car from him (as opposed to the dealer down the street). You may not see this spot during prime time. Instead, the dealer may buy time on local stations or cable channels during late-night or weekend shows, or in *fringe* time (during the early local newscast, the afternoon talk shows, and so on). The local car dealer probably can't afford the *production values* (the costly location shooting and high-priced creative help) of the factory ads for this car, nor is he the least bit interested in entertaining you with perfect scenery, beautiful actors, or high-speed driving. His one and only goal is to sell you a car. The factory-produced image advertising (covered in the preceding section) has gotten your attention. Now the local dealer wants to motivate you to come to *his* showrooms and take a test-drive — and he does this by advertising his prices and terms of sale.

For his television spots, a local car dealer will often use *factory footage,* which is simply the beautiful video prepared by the national ad agency that created the car company's image ad. The car company lets all dealers use that footage — in which the car is shown in lovely settings, like winding mountain roads, tree-lined streets, or tight curves — in their local advertising. Over this footage, your local dealer will superimpose bold, colorful, and maybe even flashing words showing his low prices, easy terms, and hard-to-resist interest rates available only from him. Way down at the bottom of the frame, in type so small it looks like a smudge on your screen, is the disclaimer in which all the legal mumbo-jumbo and caveats are revealed. The voice-over person shouts at you to "hurry in today for best selection," or to "call right now to arrange a test-drive."

The bottom line is that if the national agency has captured your attention with the image ad showing the beautiful couple driving the car on a crisp, fall day, then your local dealer wants you to buy or lease this car from *him.* And he'll beat you over the head with advertising to encourage you to come in and buy *now.*

A spectacularly ineffective advertising vehicle

One of the other tenants in our office building — a small insurance company specializing in assigned-risk auto coverage (for customers whose driving records aren't exactly stellar) — recently unveiled its latest, breakthrough, advertising vehicle. And I do mean vehicle.

I came to work one morning and there it was, parked out on the curb in all its glory. They had pounded out the dents on a 1960s Volkswagen bus, spent $50 to have it freshly painted a sparkling bathtub white, and bolted a 4-x-8-foot double-faced billboard to the roof to advertise their business. Because the old wreck needed brakes, they quit driving it around town and parked the thing conspicuously in the parking

lot in front of our building, much to the chagrin of the other tenants. The sign that sat atop this moveable beast, purportedly to tell the world about their insurance business, included no less than 32 words (including *sure thing* and *no driver refused*) and an 11-digit phone number, all arranged helter-skelter in 6 different fonts and painted in 3 different colors.

The bus was a gigantic waste of advertising dollars. But the business owner probably thought, as so many small to mid-sized retailers and service businesses do, that he couldn't afford "real" advertising. So he tried the VW bus routine instead. I don't think I have to tell you to avoid this kind of mistake at all costs.

Whether you own an automobile dealership that spends a million bucks a year on advertising, or an automobile repair shop that spends a few thousand a month, you will design and produce advertising with one purpose: to bring customers through your door, to your toll-free number, or to your Web site. To accomplish this goal, your advertising must be eye-catching, memorable, filled with *sell* (motivational copy that will bring customers to your business, such as an irresistible price they can't get elsewhere), and placed on media that will maximize your chances of reaching your target market in large numbers.

Where your advertising appears is every bit as important as what message it contains — maybe even more so. Advertising is a numbers game: You want to spend as little money as possible, as effectively as possible, to reach as many people as possible, in order to make your phone and your cash register ring.

Consider your many media options very carefully. You can waste your advertising dollars very easily by using the wrong media for your advertising goals. Mass media advertising *is* affordable (turn to the chapters in Part IV for more information on costs). But so-called "affordable" advertising in the wrong media is a gigantic waste of your dollars and your time. No matter how affordable the media is, if it doesn't bring customers through your door, you aren't really saving money. On the contrary, you're draining your limited budget without being the least bit effective.

The Best in the Business

In early 2000, the editors of *Adweek Magazine,* an advertising industry journal, picked a memorable group (listed in alphabetical order in Table 1-1) as the best image advertising done over the past two decades.

Table 1-1	The Top 20 Advertising Campaigns, 1980–2000
Product Name	*Advertising Agency*
Absolut Vodka	TBWA
American Express	Ogilvy & Mather
Apple Computers	Chiat/Day
Bartles & Jaymes	Hal Riney & Partners
BMW	Ammirati & Puris
Coca-Cola	McCann-Erickson
Energizer Batteries	Chiat/Day
ESPN SportsCenter	Wieden & Kennedy
Federal Express	Ally & Gargano
John Hancock	Hill, Holliday
Levi's	Foote, Cone & Belding
Little Caesars	Cliff Freeman and Partners
Milk Board	Goodby, Silverstein & Partners
Miller Lite	Backer & Spielvogel
Nike	Wieden & Kennedy
NYNEX Yellow Pages	Chiat/Day
Pepsi-Cola	BBDO
Rolling Stone	Fallon, McElligot, Rice
Saturn	Hal Riney & Partners
Wendy's	Dancer Fitzgerald Sample

The advertising agencies on this list are some of the biggest names in the business. They have become leaders in the advertising industry because of the outstanding creativity and the fresh approaches they bring to much of their advertising in order to get consumers' attention. You may not agree with all the selections on the list, but I bet that you recall at least *some* of each of the winning sponsors' advertising campaigns.

Although your retail advertising won't come close to the ads created by these agencies (after all, that's not your intent in the first place), you can still learn from the best. The creative legends of the advertising business have a perceptive understanding of consumers (and how to motivate them). Because they understood consumers, they were able to produce advertising that was so effective that it remained memorable decades after the campaign's end.

In the following sections, I cover two gurus of advertising whose work has taught me much of what I know — and can do the same for you.

One of the most inventive campaigns ever produced

One of my favorites on the list of top ad campaigns is the advertising for Bartles & Jaymes, created in 1985 by Hal Riney & Partners of San Francisco. That campaign has been off the air for well over a decade, but most people can still picture those two old geezers sitting on their front porch talking about their wine coolers and thanking you for "your support."

Frank Bartles and Ed Jaymes were the two salt-of-the-earth types who sat on the porch of their farmhouse and sold wine coolers. They were the product of the wonderful imagination of Hal Riney, the creative talent and copywriter responsible for the entire campaign, and the founder of Hal Riney & Partners. (Riney even picked the names at random from a San Francisco phone book.) The down-home tagline,

"We thank you for your support," was repeated in 160 ads over the 3½ years of the campaign.

Each ad ran for only about two weeks, but they were all very inexpensive to produce. With the two recurring characters and the ongoing joke about starting their own wine cooler company, the campaign was part sitcom, part ad spoof. Jaymes never spoke, rocking in the background while Bartles gave the very low-key sales pitch.

Gallo Winery was the company behind Bartles & Jaymes, but its name never appeared in the ads — and many consumers believed the guys on the porch actually made the coolers themselves. The Gallo ads brought Riney national recognition, and, even though Riney himself is no longer directly involved in the creative department, his agency still wins awards today.

David Ogilvy

The first book I ever read about the advertising business was *Confessions of an Advertising Man,* by David Ogilvy. Ogilvy was an inspiration to me (and to thousands of other advertising professionals) from my very first day in the business. He was so classy, stylish, and true to himself and his selling philosophy that he made the perfect role model for a young guy just getting his feet wet in the advertising business (yep, that was me).

Ogilvy, who died in 1999 at the age of 88, was famous for succinct statements that came to be known as *Ogilvyisms.* Here are just a few that I try to live by when writing ads for my clients:

- ✔ "On the average, five times as many people read the headline as read the body copy. When you have written your headline, you have spent 80 cents out of your dollar."

- ✔ "Never write an advertisement you wouldn't want your own family to read. You wouldn't tell lies to your own wife. Don't tell lies to mine."

- ✔ "Every word in the copy must count."

- ✔ "We sell or else."

- ✔ "Advertise what is unique."

Born in the Beatrix Potter country of England, David Ogilvy didn't get into the advertising business until he was 39 years old. He had tried everything from selling stoves door to door, to a brief tenure as a chef in Paris. He was even a member of the British Secret Service. Financially broke at the age of 39, he cofounded an advertising agency, Hewitt, Ogilvy, Benson & Mather, in 1948. Ogilvy made a list of five clients he wanted to land: General Foods, Bristol-Myers, Campbell's Soup, Lever Brothers, and Shell Oil. Eleven years later, he had them all.

Ogilvy preached the virtues of sales-driven copy. He also expected advertising copy to be expressed with clarity, relevance, and grace. He knew that the real purpose of advertising is to sell. His ads may have been gorgeous, but they were filled with unique product difference and sell — albeit with an emotional edge. He invented eccentric personalities to capture the reader's attention, and many of these advertising icons are still remembered today: The eye-patch-wearing "Man in the Hathaway Shirt," the bewhiskered Commander Whitehead for Schweppes — memorable faces that helped make memorable brands. His ad for Rolls-Royce, created in 1958, smugly stated, "At 60 miles an hour the loudest noise in this new Rolls-Royce comes from the electric clock." That headline was written way back in the Dark Ages before digital; back when clocks still ticked — but in my estimation it remains one of best car ads of all time.

Dot-coms to dot-bombs in one easy lesson

Whenever I think of Bill Bernbach's very insightful quote, "Dullness won't sell your product, but neither will irrelevant brilliance," I'm reminded of the recent spate of dot-com advertising, particularly on television. The Super Bowl broadcast in January 2000 included commercials from dozens of fledgling dot-coms, most of which had never bothered to read Bill Bernbach. Their commercials simply reeked of "irrelevant brilliance."

And most of the dot-com spots, purchased for as much as $1.5 million per 30 seconds, were so contrived, so devoid of a selling message (let alone a call to action), and so downright confusing that most, if not all, of their millions of ad bucks were wasted. The majority of these companies didn't survive more than six months after their spots appeared — other than Pets.com, whose adorable sock-puppet spokesman

starred in several Super Bowl commercials (before the company eventually went kaput).

Why weren't these flashy ads successful? Because they not only forgot Bernbach's rule, they also ignored one of Ogilvy's — namely, "We sell or else." Their spots were so clever that they forgot to include a selling message that may actually motivate someone to buy. Sadly, many even forgot to mention what service or product it was that they were selling. And, most importantly, they forgot to tell us why we should buy it.

These companies and their agencies got so lost in having a creative good time on unlimited production budgets that they forgot why they were buying the incredibly expensive time on the most-watched show on television in the first place — they simply forgot to sell us something.

Ogilvy also said, when talking about creative types who worked for (or wanted to work for) his agency, "Every copywriter should start his career by spending two years in direct response." (Here, *direct response* is another name for retail advertising, which is exactly what you're doing and what this book focuses on.) What he meant is that the primary purpose of advertising is to sell. And that is what retail advertising is all about.

Bill Bernbach

In the 1960s, Doyle, Dane, Bernbach (with Bill Bernbach as its Creative Director and the trail-blazing Helmut Krone as Art Director) invented a new way to project a message to consumers. The norm for those days was hard-sell advertising copy and straightforward, boring production values. Bernbach and Krone added wonderful creativity and a kinder, gentler approach to their advertising. The agency led the way with its fanciful Volkswagen ads that supplied both entertainment and product information. Do you remember "Think small"? It was a huge shift in advertising communication, and it became the industry standard that lives to this day.

So memorable and trend-setting was the original Volkswagen advertising created in the '60s by Bernbach and Krone, that when the New Beetle was introduced just a few years ago, the agency for Volkswagen of America, Arnold Communications of Boston, chose not to create a completely new campaign from the ground up, but rather to emulate the original concept. For example, the current campaign for the New Beetle features lots of *white space* (a Krone innovation that means just what it says — the ad isn't filled with color and copy from edge to edge), a small photo of the VW New Beetle in profile, and brief copy that reads, "Zero to 60? Yes." This kind of advertising is great stuff, and a compliment to the original ads created by Doyle, Dane, Bernbach over 40 years ago. In fact, Arnold Communications, when submitting its work for awards, still lists Krone and Bernbach as creative contributors.

Bill Bernbach, like David Ogilvy, was good for a pithy quote now and then, including the following: "Dullness won't sell your product, but neither will irrelevant brilliance."

ANECDOTE

Imitation: The sincerest form of flattery

Every now and then I see or hear an image advertisement that is so creative, so wonderfully conceived, and so (relatively) inexpensively produced that I wish I had written it myself. It has been said that there are no original ideas, but occasionally a fresh new approach to delivering the same old message comes along. And I file it away in my memory as something that, someday, I may want to imitate. If the ad is especially impressive, I even find out which agency is responsible for it and write them a congratulatory note.

I heard just such an ad on the radio the other day. It was a spot for Berkeley Farms, a major Northern California dairy. Instead of creating a straight consumer-directed ad extolling the virtues of their milk, they created a recruitment ad for "new employees." Instead of just telling their audience what superior milk they will take home when they buy the Berkeley Farms brand, a warm, motherly, female voice opens the spot with the wonderful line, "If you're a cow, I want to tell you about Berkeley Farms — it's a great place to work." She goes on to tell any cows who may be listening that they can expect to be fed only the finest hays and grains, that a full-time vet is always on call in case they get sick,

that their stalls will always be kept clean and tidy, and that they'd be foolish cows indeed if they chose to work anywhere else.

This spot is a memorable one because it uses a creative twist — talking to the cows, not the consumers — to great advantage. Hey, if this dairy is good enough for the cows, then it must be good enough for you! And this spot will undoubtedly inspire me to think of a fresh point of view for some retail commercial I will write in the future.

When you sit down to write advertising for your business, using ideas and techniques from other advertising to help you find your own "creative hook" is perfectly okay. No, I am *not* giving you permission to lift someone else's copy verbatim or to steal a concept out of hand. But good advertising done by others can be a great source of creative inspiration. Even the big boys do it. One advertising agency comes out with a fresh, new look in their ads, something that hasn't been seen before, and everyone else jumps all over it. It happens all the time. Just be sure you know the difference between imitating and plagiarizing, and stick to the former.

Chapter 2

Deciding Whether to Hire an Ad Agency

In This Chapter

▶ Understanding what an ad agency can do for you and who is involved in the process

▶ Knowing how an agency gets compensated for its work

▶ Figuring out when to give your account to an agency — and how to choose one

▶ Communicating with your agency so that your ads — and your business — succeed

Do not compete with your agency in the creative area. Why keep a dog and bark yourself?

— David Ogilvy

*I*n addition to the above quote, advertising icon David Ogilvy also once said, "Most agencies run scared, most of the time. Frightened people are powerless to produce good advertising. If I were a client, I would do everything in my power to emancipate my agency from fear, even to the extent of giving them long-term contracts."

As an ad agency owner, I agree with that position, except for the part about long-term contracts. I don't insist upon binding contracts with my accounts for the simple reason that if either of us feels that things aren't working out, I don't want a bad business relationship to be extended on account of legalities. I have always assumed that as long as I'm creating good advertising and spending the clients' money as though it were my own, that I'll retain the accounts and everyone will be happy. Think twice before signing an Agency/Client Agreement.

What makes an advertising agency "run scared" are clients, or I should say, *some clients* (clients who are usually running scared themselves). When you hire an ad agency you are taking a giant leap of faith that these professionals will do a better job of promoting your business than you can do yourself. One sure way to make this a self-fulfilling prophecy is to give them a loose rein. Let their creative department shine. Allow their media buyers to use their hard-earned experience to spend your media money wisely and effectively. Do not hire an agency and then dictate what they must do or what media they must buy. And don't turn down creative advertising ideas simply because they're not something you would have thought of yourself. An agency can be only as good as its clients, and the best clients are those who recognize that, although advertising professionals will never know as much about your business as you do, they absolutely know more about creating and placing effective advertising. Your account will be important to your agency, and they, if they're truly dedicated to being your marketing partner, will do everything they can to assure your business success and their long-range future with you.

Because you have been kind enough (and astute enough) to purchase this book, I feel that I must come clean with you right here and now: My editors (God bless their erudite souls and little, blue pencil stubs) have cautioned me about being overzealously one-sided when writing about this extremely important subject. I will, therefore, do everything I can to remain unbiased, impartial, and objective as I delve into the industry that pays my bills.

What an Advertising Agency Does and Who the Players Are

Like the many hats their employees have to wear, advertising agencies come in all different sizes: The giants of the advertising industry handle the major national and international accounts; the not-so-giant agencies handle the regional, not-so-giant accounts; and the local ad agencies, for the most part, specialize in retail accounts. In addition, some agencies specialize in the design and development of collateral materials, Web site and Internet advertising design, the production of corporate videos, and on and on. But this chapter will focus on the full-service agencies that can help your business in all facets of the ad game. All full-service agencies perform the same duties; provide the same services; have the same access to research and media opportunities; employ the very best, most talented people they can afford; offer the finest creative product they can possibly conjure up; and earn essentially the same remuneration — with one major difference: the size of their clients and their clients' budgets.

The major agencies handle accounts like General Motors, which spends billions of dollars (yes, that's billions with a *b*) each year on advertising. And because GM spends so much money on advertising every year, one agency couldn't possibly handle all of that business. So different agencies handle each make of car manufactured under the GM umbrella. But even though GM hires multiple ad agencies, each agency handles many millions of dollars a year in advertising business just for that one segment of the overall GM account. And each agency employs hundreds of people who work exclusively on the GM car brand the agency is in charge of (and when an agency loses an account of that size, a lot of people are put out on the street). Advertising is, and always has been, a very insecure business because, as I always say, the moment the ad agency gets a new account is the moment they begin to lose it.

Agencies like mine have billings of several million dollars a year but nothing close to the astronomical billings of the major *shops* (that's advertising slang for agencies). These smaller shops, shops like mine, handle advertising chores for a wide variety of local and regional accounts. My agency has accounts in the wireless, automotive, financial, education, furniture, and occasionally (these days, very occasionally), dot-com industries. The services we perform for our accounts are many and varied, and each account requires different services. But essentially, we, like all agencies, handle for our accounts everything from writing and designing ads, to negotiating with and buying the various media, and all the many details in between.

If it's doing its jobs properly, an agency takes the burden of creating great advertising off your shoulders and frees your time to do something the agency will never be able to do — properly run your business.

Advertising agencies are made up of people performing many different jobs, which I outline in the following sections. My agency doesn't employ people in all these positions, but you may end up working someday with an agency that does. So knowing who the players are and what they do is always a good idea.

Owners and Senior Management

Just about all you need to know about these people is that they're there. Like their job descriptions indicate, they own and manage the agency. If you work with an agency, you will likely see these people only twice:

- When they, along with their entire creative and account service staff, come into your office to make their pitch and to present their dog-and-pony show to secure your business.
- At their annual holiday party, *if* you're spending enough money with their agency to have earned an invitation.

Other than that, these folks aren't usually involved in the day-to-day servicing of individual accounts. They're much too busy being, well, Owners and Senior Managers — steering the ship, so to speak.

Account Supervisor

The Account Supervisor is the person who, as the title implies, supervises the creative and account service team handling your account on a daily basis. (She probably also supervises other accounts in addition to yours.) This is the person who makes sure things are running smoothly in the day-to-day servicing of your business. The Account Supervisor is at the middle-management level in the hierarchy, so you'll probably see this person more than twice. She will usually have the last word when it comes time to make creative, account service, and billing decisions.

Account Executive

The Account Executive is the person who will service your account on a daily basis. He may have been the person who originally called on you and solicited your business in the first place. Depending upon the size of the ad agency, the Account Executive may handle more than one account. The number of accounts the Account Executive handles is usually predicated upon total advertising budgets; the bigger the budget, the more work is involved and, ergo, the fewer accounts handled by one person.

You can easily identify Account Executives by their starry eyes and eager, optimistic dispositions. The Account Executive wants your business to succeed and prosper — and your advertising budget to grow — so that someday he can become an Account Supervisor. And if he does his job correctly, your business *will* succeed and your budget *will* grow, exponentially.

Creative Director

I am a Creative Director. I love this job title because it's so deliciously omnipotent. ("And on the second day, he created . . ." — well, enough of that!) David Ogilvy and Bill Bernbach, two advertising geniuses I cover in Chapter 1, were Creative Directors. The Creative Director typically oversees and shapes all the creative product, for all media, that is developed and designed at the agency — radio, TV, print, whatever . . . this person has a hand in it. The Creative Director supervises the writers, designers, photographers, actors, voice talent, and anyone else who contributes to the final creative product. The Creative Director probably came up through the ranks and was, at one time, a stellar Copywriter or Graphic Designer but now sits in a huge corner office behind a big desk wearing torn tennies, faded blue jeans, possibly a ponytail, and a wrinkled T-shirt on which is printed: "Advertising: 85% confusion, 15% commission."

Copywriter

The role of Copywriter was my first agency job. The Copywriter, as the job title suggests, writes the copy. This is the person who brings up the blank computer screen and fills it with wit, humor, drama, and, above all, *sell.* This person is given a fact sheet encompassing the product and the advertising project and goals at hand, some sort of cursory direction, a pat on the head, and a few words of encouragement by the Creative Director. She is then expected to generate an award-winning ad each and every time so the Creative Director can hang the tacky, gold plaques on his office walls.

Graphic Designer

When I first entered the agency business back in the '60s, Graphic Designers were an unkempt lot. Ponytails, tie-dye shirts, sandals and dirty feet were the uniform of the day. Not so anymore! Nowadays, Graphic Designers occasionally even wear dress shirts and ties and have no fear of ever getting dirty because they do all their designing on computers. No more messy paints, smudgy pencils, and chalk dust for these guys.

Graphic Designers are the bane of the Creative Director's existence. They may or may not show up for work on any given day, and they continually suffer from their own patented brand of writer's block. Good Graphic Artists can work magic with any product you put in front of them. They are the people who make print and collateral advertising sparkle with eye-catching, unusual graphic elements and typefaces. They are among the most talented people I have ever met, and they will often share their capacity for conceptual thinking to aid other agency specialists, like Copywriters.

Media Buyer

If you work with an agency, the Media Buyer will become very important to you. The Media Buyer fields all the phone calls from, and takes all the meetings with, the dozens of media sales reps who want a piece of your business. Then she gently or firmly, as the case requires, says no to them if the offer isn't right (and yes, if it is).

If there is one good reason to hire an ad agency, it is the Media Buyer. A good one will be fair but firm with the media, insisting upon the correct format, impressive ratings or circulation, and the right audience composition and demographic before committing your hard-earned dollars to a station, newspaper, or magazine. She will also do the very important job of *post analysis,* in which she pores over the media invoices to make sure everything bought is accounted for.

Media Buyers love numbers. They can stare at a printed list of *station rankers* (where each station in a given media market is ranked against all others) for hours. The Media Buyer is the person within the ad agency who, if diligent and knowledgeable, will give you the most bang for your buck and stretch your media budget, regardless of its size, as tightly as it can be stretched without breaking.

How Agencies Get Paid

As much as I enjoy creating wonderful advertising, as much as I look forward to writing a new commercial that presents a client's message in a fresh, new way, as much as I appreciate the talents of those who work around me and the faith and trust placed in my agency by our clients, I also really like the getting paid part! Nothing says, "I love you" like a big, fat check at the end of each month.

"Make sure that your agency makes a profit. Your account competes with all the other accounts in your agency. If it is unprofitable, it is unlikely that the management of the agency will assign their best people to work on it. And sooner or later they will cast about for a profitable account to replace yours." Those immortal words were spoken by advertising legend, David Ogilvy, and it's the best advice I could ever direct toward an account. You wouldn't work for free, so why should your ad agency? I have handled a few accounts during my career who begrudged every nickel I earned from them. It put too much strain on the business relationship, and I replaced (or simply resigned) those accounts at my first opportunity.

Advertising professionals, like any professionals, have the right to be paid a professional's wage. But (and here's some news that should allay your fears) advertising agencies don't cost nearly as much as most people assume.

Media commissions

Since the dawn of advertising history, and because of some obscure arrangement made between the early founders of the advertising agency business and the newspapers of the time (a rather one-sided arrangement, the details of which are lost in the mists of time), an agency earns a media commission of 15 percent. This figure has not changed over the ages, even though agencies have been crying about it for eons. Is 15 percent enough? You know I'm going to say no! But that's the way it is, the way it's always been, and the way it shall remain.

The commission is paid to the agency by the media in the form of a discount. If *you* buy a newspaper ad with a space cost of $1,000 directly from the paper, you will be charged $1,000. If your *ad agency* buys the same ad, it will be charged $850, but the agency will bill you for the full $1,000 and keep the rest ($150, or 15 percent) as its commission. So, in effect, having an agency place your media buys doesn't cost you a dime, because you're paying the same amount to buy that ad whether you have an agency handle it for you or you do it yourself — it's just that if you buy it with the help of an agency, some of your money goes to the agency as well as to the newspaper.

Creative and production charges

Agencies also charges their clients for something they call *creative and production,* which is essentially the writing and designing of the ad. How much an agency charges varies from agency to agency. So before you commit to having an agency design an ad or produce a radio or TV spot for you, ask them how much they'll charge for creative and production. Some agencies have truly astounding creative charges (especially those which do not earn additional monies from media commissions); other agencies have fairly modest charges. The bottom line is that the media commission is *not* enough to cover the cost of running an agency, and the addition of creative and production charges to the clients' invoices is a necessary one, so be prepared to pay for it.

Markups

An agency will also add a markup to all the buyouts they make on your behalf. *Buyouts* are charges incurred by the agency for voice talent, recording studios, photographers, models, actors, props, photography, printing, and so on — basically, everything that outside vendors contribute to the cost of producing your advertising. These charges, because the agency went on the hook to order them and will ultimately be responsible for payment, will be added to your monthly invoice along with an agency markup. The markup your agency charges is another item you may want explained to you before approving certain creative and production jobs. You don't want any surprises when it comes time to pay your bill.

Retainers

Sometimes an agency and a client will work out a monthly *retainer,* which is a set monthly fee you pay the agency for its services. The retainer may be in addition to agency commissions, or it may be in place of them — it depends on how much you (as the client) are spending on advertising and on whether all the media options the agency is purchasing for you are commissionable. For instance, if you're buying only newspaper advertising at a retail rate — a reduced rate to make the publication more affordable for local advertisers like you — your agency will usually not earn a commission on that space. Why? Because the retail rate is usually so low that newspapers refuse to subtract a 15 percent commission from it. Instead of having your agency add markups to each newspaper invoice, you and your agency may opt for a monthly retainer figure that comes close to the amount of commissions that the agency would have earned had the newspaper space been invoiced at a higher rate.

Newspapers have very complicated, sometimes arbitrary, rate cards which make agency retainers a necessary evil in some cases. Retail ad space for a furniture store, for example, is *not* commissionable, but automotive advertising for a local car dealer — which is, most certainly, retail — *is* commissionable. If you can figure out why this difference exists, drop me a note, because I never have been able to.

I've also never liked the idea of charging a retainer. Inevitably, either the client or the agency feels they are getting the short end of the stick. But in some cases, retainers are unavoidable, even desirable. However, the monthly dollar amount is something that needs to be carefully worked out between the two parties. Retainer agreements can be beneficial to both clients and agencies. For you, the client, a retainer may guarantee you a certain amount of access to the agency and all of its personnel, regardless of the size of your media budget. For the agency, the retainer helps them plan for the number of people who will be directly employed to handle your account.

When and How to Hire an Agency

Deciding when you need to hire an agency to help with your ads can be difficult. Here are some situations when hiring an agency makes sense:

- ✔ When phone calls from media sales reps are taking up too much of your time
- ✔ When you are simply overwhelmed by the myriad details inherent in producing and placing your advertising
- ✔ When you no longer have the time, or the energy, to write and produce your advertising yourself
- ✔ When creating and placing your advertising on a regular basis has become a job instead of fun
- ✔ When your own creative efforts aren't yielding the results you desire

- ✔ When your advertising budget has grown so much that you're no longer certain you're spending it as wisely as you could be

- ✔ When the bookkeeping process of sorting through multiple media invoices each month has become too complicated and time-consuming

- ✔ When you finally admit that media invoices are written in a secret code that you will never learn to crack, and you want to be assured that you're getting everything you're paying for

- ✔ When you're eager to have creative professionals generate fresh, new ideas for your advertising

- ✔ When you want to put a team of highly-trained specialists to work, with the common goal of growing your business

- ✔ When you would welcome the professional creative, account service, and media buying expertise that an agency can provide

- ✔ When you want someone to buy you lunch, treat you to a round of golf, tell you the latest jokes, and present you with free tickets to area concerts, sports events, and movies

You don't need an advertising budget in the millions to seek out the services of an ad agency. Many local, retail-oriented agencies will provide you with all the services offered by the major agencies, but scaled down to fit within your budget and your advertising requirements. These are the one-man shops and the smaller agencies that handle retail, direct response advertising for all kinds of local and regional accounts.

These shops employ people in all the various job titles I list earlier in this chapter (although, in the case of the very small shops, one person may wear several of those hats). And you get all the important services inherent in those job titles as well. These smaller agencies also know your local market intimately, and may even specialize in a particular business segment such as health care, financial, telecommunications, or automotive. They know where the bodies are buried, they know the local media, they know which radio stations are hot and which ones are not, they know rate cards and demographics and all the important research data relevant to your local market that they can put to good use when handling your business. They're friends with station owners and managers, newspaper editors and retail advertising managers, account executives and creative talent. They are a wealth of local knowledge.

Perhaps the most important reasons to give your account to an advertising agency is to elevate the quality of your creative product, hone your strategy and positioning, and have a professional team working for you that can identify, negotiate with, and get the best possible price when buying the various forms of media that will do the best job for your account.

Advertising is an extremely important part of your overall marketing plan. Hiring a team of professionals to handle it for you is something you should think about. And, in the case of many local ad agencies, it very likely won't cost you as much as you think.

If you do decide that you need to hire an ad agency, you need to spend some time finding a good one. You want to find an agency that lists its specialty as retail, local, or direct response — an agency that operates on a local or regional level. When you're looking for an ad agency, don't just let your fingers do the walking through your local Yellow Pages and expect to find the best one right off the bat. Any of the media reps or sales reps who call on your account can put you in touch with some good ones, possibly agencies that specialize in your business arena. Of course, the agencies they recommend will be the agencies that they work with, but after all, fair is fair.

If you aren't being called upon by media reps or sales reps, you can get creative. Have you seen or heard an ad for a local business that was particularly creative and really caught your attention? Call the newspaper or the station and ask about it. Talk with the paper's Retail Sales Department, or the station's Traffic Department, and ask which agency is responsible for the ad. Then give that agency a call. What could be simpler? Upon receiving your call, the agency will be immediately flattered and will dispatch an Account Executive or Account Supervisor to your business to chat you up and try to get your business.

Nowadays most agencies also have Web sites. You can research the agency's work and its client list before you even call. See what the agency is doing first, and find out if it's compatible with what you're looking for. Figure out who the agency's clients are and whether its client mix appears to match with your specialty. Invite a few agencies to come to your office to make their pitches — this is called an *agency review*. When the word gets out that you're having an agency review (and the speed with which industry gossip spreads never ceases to amaze me), you will get calls from many agencies that you have not personally contacted. That's okay. You may want to give them an appointment. Get to know each one, listen to what they have to say, look at and listen to their creative work, see if it feels right. Be sure to think about which of the agency Account Executives you will be able to get along with over the long haul, check each agency's references, and then make your choice.

Many extremely competent, enormously talented, retail-based advertising agencies are out there. With just a bit of research, you'll find the one you feel most comfortable with. Then your new agency will work hard at bringing lots of customers through your door, you'll get back to working hard at closing them once they've arrived, and you'll all live happily ever after.

How to Work with Your Agency to Get What You Need

You hire an ad agency because you want to put their expertise to work for you. But the advertising gurus know advertising; they don't know your business. So when you hire an agency, keep one thing in mind: You must have a continual dialogue with your agency contact person to be sure you're working toward the same goal. Tell your contact everything you can possibly think of that is relevant to the advertising that will be created for your account — regardless of how minuscule and unimportant this detailed information may seem. Your agency needs to know as much as they can about your products and services in order to sift through the information to find your *unique selling proposition* (what is it that separates you from the herd?) and to develop the *creative hook* (a fresh, new way to tell the world about you and your business) that they will use when creating your ads.

You will expect from your agency the finest possible creative product for your account. But that product will never live up to your expectations if the agency has to guess about what it is you want to convey to the buying public. The more facts you can provide, the easier it will be for the agency writers, designers, and media buyers to make quality decisions when producing your advertising and placing it on the various media.

Tell your agency as much about your product and business as possible, and keep updating this information to them as time passes. Here are some key kinds of information you need to share with your agency:

- ✔ What makes your product so great and why people should buy it
- ✔ Which demographic group is your prime market
- ✔ What is unique about what you're providing (for example, your service, location, convenient hours)
- ✔ Whether you compete with giant, impersonal chain stores
- ✔ Whether you offer free delivery, a lifetime guarantee, or something the consumer won't find elsewhere

These are just a few of the myriad details you will want your agency to know so they can generate first-rate advertising for you on a monthly basis. *Remember:* No detail is too small or irrelevant. Tell them more than they ever wanted to know, and let them sift through it all for the important stuff.

Your agency will likely want to set a regular meeting time with you (weekly or monthly, for example). These regular meetings are a great time for you to impart all your wisdom regarding your business. If anything relevant pops into your mind outside of this meeting, call your Account Executive. The more your agency knows about your business, the better the ads they can create for you.

If your agency seems disinterested in the details you're sharing or doesn't want to hear your ideas, or worse, doesn't ask you tons of questions, start looking for another agency. You want to find an ad agency who views themselves as a marketing partner and you as an integral part of the success of the ad campaigns they will create for you.

One agency contact person eliminates scores of media reps

This may be one of the best reasons to hire an agency. I am not trying to imply that media reps are obnoxious or bothersome — some of my best friends are media reps. But these people have a mission, and that mission is to get as large a share of your advertising budget as they possibly can. They will phone you, drop in on you, and send you faxes and e-mails to "simply stay in touch," and then they will drop in on you again. They are extremely tenacious, and they rarely take *no* for answer. They work on commission, what else can I say? Their Sales Managers give them a quota and, if they know your business is buying local media, they will target you like a mosquito targets a bare leg. And, in the legitimate process of trying to earn a living, they sometimes become a nuisance.

An advertising agency, particularly the media buyer, will remove these pesky (albeit well-meaning) people from your life. Even though some of these media reps may have taken you golfing, given you concert tickets, and sent a lovely bottle of wine to your spouse for his or her birthday (how do they find out about those dates?), after you have hired an agency and the word gets around, you will never hear from these people again. "No budget, no friends," as my former partner and crackerjack media buyer, Marnie Doherty, always says.

Each station has assigned a rep to work with your advertising agency. That rep will now earn *all* commissions generated by your account whether or not he was the rep who called upon you directly. If they are about to lose your account, the reps who call on you directly will moan and groan about this, and some — the misguided ones — will even try to talk you out of hiring this particular agency. But, in my experience, what goes around comes around — a rep may lose your account today but pick up a new one from the agency he has on *his* "list" tomorrow. It all works out.

You need to spend your limited and very important time productively running your business. When you hire an advertising agency you will eliminate a lot of daily phone calls and drop-in visits from various reps so you can do just that. You will also, in all likelihood, receive a more polished creative product from the agency than you have been producing, because a whole gang of professional writers, designers and creative directors will be working on your business.

Chapter 3

Defining and Positioning Your Message

* *

In This Chapter

▶ Knowing what customers are looking for in your business, product, or service — and making sure you provide it

▶ Getting clear on what you want to say

▶ Coming up with a campaign that'll knock their socks off

> *The philosophy behind much advertising is based on the old observation that every man is really two men — the man he is, and the man he wants to be.*
>
> — William Feather, *The Business of Life*

With a limited advertising budget, your product or company name will not be on the tip of the national tongue, nor will people from New York to Los Angeles be whistling your jingle. But you can define your strengths and position your advertising message in such a way that you give yourself the best possible chance for success. And with 50 percent of all new businesses going under within the first two years, you want to do everything you can to improve these rather daunting odds for your business.

When you first opened your business, you probably felt confident in doing so because you were convinced you could provide better service, a more unique line of products, and more creative solutions to consumers' problems than they could find anywhere else. You found an attractive, convenient location; stocked up on really cool merchandise; expanded your business hours for better customer convenience; and have been enjoying at least the first blush of the success that will usually follow a well-thought-out business plan. To paraphrase mass production genius, Henry Kaiser, whose ship-building division, during World War II, built one new Liberty Ship every day, "You found a need and filled it." But now you need to take it one step farther with an advertising campaign that will bring in more customers, add more dollars to your bottom line, and validate all the reasons you went into business in the first place.

In this chapter, I fill you in on a few of the key factors that customers use when they choose one business over another — factors you'll want to keep in mind when you come up with ways to advertise your business's strengths. Then I walk you through the process of positioning your message, where you let your customers know exactly why they should buy from you. Finally, I end the chapter by outlining the basics of coming up with an effective ad campaign, using a real-life example from my own business as a guide.

Understanding Why People Choose One Product over Another

As you devise your positioning strategy and, ultimately, your advertising message, you need to keep in mind why people choose one product over another. That way, you can help to ensure that they choose your product over your competition's. In the following sections, I cover some of the main reasons people choose one product (or company or store) over another.

Image

People will drive or walk long distances past one fast-food restaurant, service station, donut store, or hair salon in order to patronize another because the image of the store they seek out is more in tune with their own tastes and desires. Image, as they say, is everything.

When it comes to image, peer pressure (or what you think the rest of the world is doing) also comes into play. People want to project the right image, and often, they do that by choosing the product or store that they think helps them do so. For example, if dozens of people are working out at one particular gym in town, their friends will also try that gym because "everyone else is doing it." Price, quality, convenience, and many other factors come into play, but if that gym's image is the one that the customers can best identify with, then it will most certainly get the most business.

Your business's good reputation for customer service, fair value, good prices, and after-sale concern and care will also go a long way toward ensuring your success. If you can honestly say that you provide the very best of any of these virtues, broadcast it widely.

Personality

Customers often choose one business over another based on the personality of the business. And that, of course, begins with you and the people who work for you. I have become a regular at a very good Italian restaurant in my hometown for the simple reason that the personality of the place (and of the people who work there) suits me to a tee. It has just the right combination of location, ambience, menu choices, and friendly, caring management and staff to have won my undying loyalty.

A half-dozen outstanding Italian restaurants are all within a six-block walk of the one I frequent, and my wife and I have tried them all. But we visit the same one quite often because, from the moment we walk through the door until we waddle out a few hours later, we are treated like visiting royalty whose continued satisfaction and patronage is a very high priority. From the bartender to the waiter to the busboy, we are made to feel not only welcome, but at home.

If you own a restaurant and want to advertise your establishment's unique personality you can use a headline such as, "Like having dinner at Mama's, but without all the kids." If you are a car dealer and want to tell your customers that they'll find something unusual during their service appointment you could say, "Put your feet up, have a cup of gourmet coffee, catch up on the soaps, and relax in our customer lounge." In other words, if you truly believe that your business has a sparkling personality and offers certain benefits that customers can't find elsewhere, then find a creative way to use these strengths in your advertising. Then be sure you deliver on the promise after the customers arrive. Don't call attention to something that isn't really there, something that you don't, or can't, really offer.

Convenience

The top three factors in getting rich on real estate are: location, location, location. The same may be true of your store or business. Convenience can be a huge incentive to customers. And when I say *convenience* I'm not just talking about location. Convenience could be ample free parking within a few feet of your door, or easy freeway access, or a well-thought-out store design so your customers can get in and out quickly, or a store policy of always helping customers load merchandise into their cars.

If you do have a convenient, available location with great parking and a bright and cheerful ambience, easy access, an easy store layout, or any number of conveniences that customers will find attractive, include this information in your advertising message. Convenience is also a very simple and effective way to differentiate your store from other, less convenient, less attractive stores. For example, when I need hardware items, I patronize a small local store, rather than one of those big discount warehouses, because of the convenience factor. The store is small (it would fit into one corner of one of the large chain stores, and you'd never even know it was there) so I can quickly find what I need and be on my way. It also has a large parking lot right outside its back door. I know I could save a lot of money if I went to the chain stores, but I'm willing to pay for the convenience of the mom-and-pop.

If I were the owner of this small hardware store, I'd advertise with messages such as, "Park within 20 feet of our door. You may pay a few pennies more for nails, but think of the money you'll save on shoe leather!" Or, "Is saving a nickel on nails worth getting hammered in a parking lot?" Or, "Drive for miles, search three acres for a parking place, get lost in a huge labyrinth, save 50 cents. Can we talk?"

Service

Service, in my estimation, is the most overused and under-delivered promise made in advertising today. Just about every business claims to deliver the very best in "service," or "customer service," or "customer care," but in reality, hardly any business actually does. Most market research shows that what customers want *most* from their bank, supermarket, dry cleaner, car dealer, shoe repair shop, accountant, or whatever, is good old-fashioned service. All businesses know this, but most businesses seem totally incapable of delivering it.

My agency handles a local Audi dealer who lives and dies by the results of factory-sponsored telephone surveys done following every new car sale and every service appointment. The results of these "customer satisfaction surveys" go a long way in determining this car dealer's relationship with the factory and with how many cars he is allotted each month. He ranks very highly in his survey results, and we advertise the fact that his dealership is top-rated in customer service. And this advertising focus on service (as well as fair pricing and a wide choice of inventory) is obviously working — this dealer, located in San Jose, California, sells so many new Audi cars that he's now number two in the nation.

If you use service as a reason for customers to try you out, then you'd better deliver the goods. If you can't service your customers in an efficient, courteous, timely manner, or deliver, replace, or repair what was promised when it was promised, then don't tell customers you will. Don't make any promises you can't keep, because people will soon see through you and your promises like a piece of cellophane.

WARNING!

You can't be all things to all people

As you define and position your advertising message, be careful not to over-promise. Promising a level of service you can't deliver, or a convenient location that isn't, or low prices when yours aren't really all that low, can be a deadly mistake. Be honest with yourself about what is really unique and desirable about your store or business, and then be honest when you start making claims about it.

On the other hand, don't panic because you can't deliver the very best of *everything*. Maybe your prices really aren't any cheaper than those of your competition, but your store is located so conveniently, or has such a great ambience and personality, or carries such a unique inventory, that you are confident people will only have to try you once in order to become loyal, happy regulars. If that's the case, then when you're designing your ads don't make up false benefits based on price — position your message to exploit your strengths, namely that perfect location with all that free parking, and all the friendly, cheerful faces waiting inside. *Remember:* One good promise on which you can truly deliver is better than trying to be all things to all people.

Uniqueness

There is no more certain way to attract customers than to offer something they can't get anywhere else. If you have stocked your store with creative, hard-to-find items that other stores simply do not carry, then you are way ahead of the game. If your doughnut store can state for certain that your doughnut holes are smaller (and, therefore, your doughnuts are more substantial) than a doughnut junkie can hope to find elsewhere, then *that* is your message. If you carry truly unique greeting cards in your stationery store, cards that are not available anywhere except at your location, then people looking for such an item are sure to respond.

Of course, if you're selling the idea that your store is unique, you'll need to work overtime to assure that it remains so. Do you remember when Starbucks was the only place where you could get gourmet coffees? It didn't take long for hundreds of imitators to come along and make the same claim. If you are successful in positioning yourself as totally unique, you can be sure that others will copy you — and you'll have to continually reinvent yourself to stay ahead of the competition.

Price

In some (but not all) cases, advertising the manufacturer's suggested retail price (that's the MSRP you hear about on car commercials all the time) is helpful. In the automobile example, where a dealer will typically sell cars for *less* than the MSRP, the dealer looks very good. But in the case of a Snickers candy bar, for example, where the MSRP is 50 cents, but the big chain stores sell it for 40 cents and the airport gift shop sells it for a dollar, customers are left scratching their heads and wondering what the heck the "real" price is on this candy.

Be very careful when using price or terms as reasons for customers to visit your store. When you advertise price, you run the risk of getting caught in what I call the *price trap.* If you're only selling price, you'll have to continue to lower that price — or come up with even better terms — on an ongoing basis in order to continue to attract new customers.

The cellular phone business has fallen into the price trap. When you look in the paper, you may have a tough time choosing a wireless phone company or deciphering the best available bargain because you have to sift through the various stores' offers of free minutes, free phones, free long-distance, free mobile-to-mobile calling, and any number of price and terms offers. And all of these stores have to continually create new and better offers in order to compete.

Identifying What Sets Your Product Apart from the Rest

Creating an ad campaign is a big step that will cost you some serious money, so it deserves some very careful planning. Before you get into the actual process of designing your advertising campaign, however, you need to give some significant thought to what it is you want to tell the world about you and your business; what makes your company, products, or service the best that customers can ever hope to find anywhere; why your company will provide the perfect solution to each customer's needs; and why the world would be foolish indeed not to beat a path to your door. In other words, you need to identify and promote the things that make your product unique, known in the ad world as your *unique selling proposition* (USP).

Your advertising should never speak in generalities. Including just your store name, location, and all the wonderful things you're selling isn't enough. You need to give the consumer a very good reason — or better yet *several* good reasons — to visit you. You do this by first identifying your distinctive strengths and then calling attention to those strengths in your ads. This process is called *positioning your message.*

Determining the key reasons that consumers should drive (or surf, if you're online) right on past other stores that may sell the same merchandise as you do, in order to seek out *your* store, is the first step in identifying your USP and positioning your message. You need to convince consumers that your store is the smartest, best, most logical place that they could ever hope to buy that merchandise. After you identify these keys, focus in on them as the basis for your creative advertising message — in other words, promote and publicize your strengths.

A good way to start this process is to let your mind wander backward to recapture all the reasons you were convinced that your business would succeed in first place. Ask yourself the following questions:

✔ What makes your company special?

✔ What is unique about your inventory?

✔ What service do you provide that clients cannot find elsewhere?

✔ Are your business hours more expanded than the competition?

✔ Is your location easier to find? More convenient? With better parking?

If you can remember what it was that got you here originally, you're halfway home in identifying what will motivate customers to seek you out. The same reasons you were enthusiastic enough about your business plan to take the entrepreneurial plunge should translate nicely into a creative concept and motivational copy that will drive business to your location (turn to Chapter 4 for more information).

A unique selling proposition successfully exploited

One of my agency's clients owns a chain of furniture stores. These are not your everyday, garden-variety furniture stores featuring living room, bedroom, and family room items. These are some of the only stores in the entire San Francisco Bay Area that carry a huge inventory of hard-to-find dinette sets and bar stools. Although most furniture stores carry *some* of these items (usually hidden way back in the corner of the showroom), this guy has hundreds of styles of dinettes and a huge inventory of hard-to-find bar stools and home bars. His showrooms are cavernous, and when he has a floor sample clearance sale (which he runs twice yearly), customers beat down his doors.

His repeat business percentage is astounding, thanks to his complete dedication to customer service.

His advertising hits hard at what he calls *casual dining furniture,* which he has available in more styles than a customer could possibly find at any other store, and in price ranges to suit any budget. In fact, casual dining furniture is all he does. And he originally opened his stores with this limited, but unique inventory in mind. So he uses this unique selling proposition in his advertising with great success. This guy truly does have something unique to sell, which makes writing his ads all the easier.

Don't confuse your potential customers with too much information — inform them with a well-conceived, creatively executed, and carefully positioned message. Don't try to sell everything you have in the store in a single ad. It will only cause sensory overload. Zero in on one or two important, relevant items so your customers have a prayer of understanding your message.

You want to position your message keeping in mind not only your business's strengths, but also your primary market (the people who will be buying your product). When you take both of these important factors into consideration, the resulting message will not only be positioned, it will also be targeted — targeted as in a bull's-eye, so you can then take your best shot.

Designing Your Advertising Campaign

After you've identified the many good reasons people would be foolish *not* to shop at your store, or to utilize the unique services you provide, and assuming you know your market and to whom you want to sell, you're ready to move forward with planning your ad campaign. You know why you're selling what you're selling, you know whom you're selling to, and you are now armed with the information you need to create wonderful and memorable ads. This is the fun part.

Being able to run a sustained radio and TV campaign; buy flashy, full-page print ads; slap your message up on dozens of billboards and buses; and do a major-league mailing to every zip code within a mile of your store all at the same time would be fantastic. But that kind of ad campaign — one that covers all the bases — is very costly. Assuming you *don't* have unlimited advertising funds, you need to get a bit more creative with your message and your spending. And that process begins with two questions: "What can you afford?" and "What media will best target your primary market segment?"

Regardless of how much you spend or where you spend it, you need to make sure *your* ads cut through the clutter of advertising messages that bombard your customers every day. Focus your message in a clear and creative way so that your ads will attract the attention of, and motivate the largest possible number of, your primary market.

For example, if you're targeting women between the ages of 25 and 54, you'll want to write and design your ads using words, phrases, and graphics that will most appeal to them; words like *savings, sale,* and *free;* phrases like *New fall colors and styles, Free gift with every purchase, Buy one get one free,* and *Hurry in today for best selection;* and for print or mailers, graphics elements that illustrate in a clean, uncluttered fashion what it is you are selling. You will also want to place your ads with media that give you the best chance at reaching these women in quantity. If you're buying radio, select those stations that can prove to you that its audience composition is heavy on your primary demo (women between the ages of 25 and 54). Running your spots on a teeny-bopper station that plays only *NSYNC and Britney Spears wouldn't be wise (regardless of what the radio time salesperson tells you about the station's audience composition). For print, place your ads in the Main News, Local News, Entertainment, Gardening, and Society sections. You may not want to place your print ads for this market in the Sports section of the paper. (Yes, women read the Sports pages, but not in the numbers that men do). Above all, no matter who your audience is, you want to include in your ads enough creativity and content so your ads will be not only heard and seen, but also understood and remembered. And where you place your ads is every bit as important as what you say in them.

Using this target demo (women in the 25 to 54 age bracket) as an example, here's how I went about designing and executing an ad campaign for a northern California chain of women's stores. My client's product was "plus-size" clothing, which, of course, is very visual — a customer needs to see it in order to get interested in it. And stylish, attractive clothing in plus-sizes is often hard to find. So I leaned toward TV as the primary media to buy right away. I also figured that, when the stores had specific sales, I would add newspaper ads, but primarily to advertise price. The television ads would establish the store name in the minds of the store's target audience, and the newspaper ads — when they had really great markdowns and discounts to advertise — would serve them well in augmenting the TV spots.

Although this client did have a dozen stores throughout the area, he didn't have a budget substantial enough to be on the air or in the paper every day. So, when designing the campaign, I had to consider that each of the spots would need to include all the relevant information a customer needs about the stores. In other words, he couldn't do what the major clothing chains do — namely, use a spot showing all the hot new fashions and end the spot with just a logo and company slogan, assuming that everyone already knows his stores and where they are. I had to pretty much start from scratch and do the whole sales pitch within each commercial. Each commercial needed to stand on its own.

For this campaign, I wrote several TV spots with an eye toward relatively inexpensive production, hired some professional models, employed the services of a truly remarkable film company in Sacramento, California, scouted some locations, and headed to the state capitol to shoot some spots.

My agency produced three 30-second spots for under $20,000 (although this figure may sound expensive, the client ran these same three spots for several years, so they ended up being rather cheap). Then we put them on various TV stations in *flights*. (*Flighting* is an ad biz term that means, for instance, buying advertising for two weeks at a time, then going off the air for two weeks, then back on the air, and so forth.) The spots showed the models wearing various dresses and separates and wandering around beautiful locations such as the mall, the zoo, and the park. Everything was shot outside on location (as opposed to in a studio) with 35-millimeter film, and the footage was simply gorgeous. The clothing this chain sold was very stylish and very unique, and the commercials showed the merchandise beautifully. Because this is hard-to-find clothing, and because the commercials did such an excellent job of simply showing a wide variety of styles, the campaign was a very successful one that we brought back, as though it were brand-new, about twice a year. And I enjoyed a good relationship with the store owner until he finally decided to retire just a few years ago.

What my agency did to sell women's specialty fashions on a budget is what you need to do — we sat down and planned our work, and then we worked our plan. It's a step-by-step process that, when done right, will usually produce excellent results. I cover the steps of this approach in the following sections.

Identify the unique selling proposition

We began with the product (women's specialty clothing) and the primary target market (plus-size women between the ages of 25 and 54). This type of clothing is sometimes difficult to find in the latest colors, patterns and styles, but our client's stores offered an enormous inventory of flattering, complimentary, up-to-date fashions in all varieties and in special sizes. The market for these fashions is substantial; it was really just a matter of reaching the primary audience in sizeable numbers with a message that was relevant, informative, and creatively presented. These stores truly had what plus-size women were looking for; our job was simply to get the news out there.

Consider the budget

After we had identified the unique selling proposition, we added into the equation the advertising budget, which, when compared to major clothing chains, was extremely limited. However, knowing that these fashions did not necessarily change with every season, we came up with some very visual, relatively inexpensive, TV spots that we could then run in flights over a period of several years. Our *production costs* (the actual cost of filming and editing the commercials) were modest in comparison to the quality of the final product, because we were willing to travel a few hundred miles in order to employ the services of a not-so-big-time, but extremely talented, film company. And we also hired a wonderful group of plus-size models who worked on a *buy-out basis* (with no residual payments, just a one-time fee). It was a successful example of what you can do with just a bit of planning and a dab of creativity.

Come up with a creative strategy

The strategy for our television commercials was pretty straightforward — no need to get too clever or cute, just show a variety of the clothing in the most attractive of settings. Again, these fashions, in up-to-date, attractive styles, can be hard to find, so our creative goal was to pack as many different styles as possible into each of the three 30-second spots. I recently reviewed one of the spots and it contained 15 different outfits worn by 3 different models in 4 different location settings. And regardless of whether any of those 15 individual fashion items appealed to members of the TV audience, the spots clearly demonstrated the remarkable variety of plus-size fashions available at these stores. The spots also clearly demonstrated that we were right in our assumption that we only needed to "get the news out." The stores felt a positive business impact almost immediately.

Select the media

We had created some wonderful television commercials showing our beautiful fashions, and now we needed to place those spots into TV programming that would not only reach our primary demographic, but also would be affordable within a limited media budget. Notice I said, *TV programming,* not *stations.*

How many times do you grab the remote and click to other stations while you're watching TV? You bounce all over the dial looking for programming that appeals to you, don't you? You don't stay with one station all day and night out of loyalty (as you may do with radio). With that in mind, remember this: When you are buying television advertising time, don't buy the station, buy the programming.

We placed our ads on programs — affordable programs — that attracted women in large numbers: soaps, afternoon talk shows, early-morning and afternoon news, game shows, and so on. Local and regional advertisers can usually afford to buy advertising on these shows, while the prime time stuff is often out of reach (although some highly successful and well-watched game shows, like *Jeopardy!,* are affordable when combined with a broader schedule that includes less desirable programming).

These same rules apply to any and all products. So, whether you're selling hardware or fast food, cars or doughnuts, ceiling fans or fashions, follow these guidelines as you begin to design your advertising. Look hard at what it is you're selling and to whom you're trying to sell it. Identify and hammer home what it is that makes your product or service unique, different from all the competition. Then, in the most creative, hard-hitting way you can devise, create your ads to focus attention on your unique product difference. Then you only need to place those ads in media that will bring you the greatest return on your investment, media that will reach large numbers of your primary target demographic. It sounds simple, right? And it is. This ain't rocket science . . . it's advertising, and you can do it just like anybody else.

Chapter 4

Creating Effective Ads

> *Advertising may be described as the science of arresting the human intelligence long enough to get money from it.*
>
> — Stephen Butler Leacock, English-born economist and humorist

*W*hether your advertising budget is a million a month or a thousand a year, that money will be wasted if your ads aren't effective. And what makes ads effective is a combination of content and creativity. Your ads need to give the consumer a good reason to act (that's the content), and they have to be unique enough in their design and copy to attract the consumer's attention in the first place (which comes from creativity). Consumers are exposed to so much advertising on a daily basis — some of it so subtle they don't even know they're absorbing it — that generating advertising for your business that will cut through all that clutter is a real challenge. Creating good advertising is a challenge, but it's not impossible — it just takes some serious thought.

Consumers see advertising every day that doesn't instruct them, or sell them, or entertain them — it only annoys them. They also see and hear advertising that is unclear in its message, confusing in its content, and just plain aggravating in its production. On the other hand, they're also exposed to some truly great advertising that sells in a highly creative and memorable way. They remember the good advertising for years — and they immediately forget the bad. Sadly, in many cases, the people doing the bad advertising are spending more money than the people doing the good.

Truly superior advertising, on the other hand, is created every day — and much of it is done on a budget. Effective advertising has certain key elements, including memorable graphics, killer copy delivered in a clear, concise manner and a fresh, new creative hook. The good news is that you don't need a huge ad budget in order to create effective ads. On the contrary, much advertising done with million-dollar production budgets is absolutely forgettable, and just as much advertising, done on a shoestring, is remembered long after the campaigns have gone off the air.

No matter what your budget, you can do good advertising, and in this chapter, I show you how. I want you to use a bit more creativity than the other guy, feature interesting information and good reasons to buy, put a spin on your message so that it's presented in an exciting new way, and enjoy the fruits of all the hard labor you expended in finding the unique creative hook that will separate your advertising from all the other, not-so-effective stuff that's out there.

Finding a Creative Hook to Snag Your Audience With

Because you want your ads to stand head and shoulders above your competition, you need to work hard at finding — or, if you prefer, inventing — a *creative hook,* something that will grab your potential customers (but not necessarily by the neck) and drag them into your store. A creative hook is an emotional trigger that attracts buyers, something that appeals to the self-image of buyers, an affirmation that you provide what the buyers are looking for. It may be a slogan, a phrase, a jingle, a single line of copy, or a unique look that appears in all your ads. But whatever it is, it must be yours and yours alone, because you will use it, across all media, to differentiate your business from all the others. The bottom line: You need to put a new spin on the same old message by coming up with a memorable creative hook.

The Taco Bell Chihuahua, for instance, was a creative hook (although I never could understand why I should want to eat something that was so mouthwateringly attractive to a dog). The talking dog appeared in all TV, print, and in-store ads for Taco Bell, and it worked. McDonald's creative hook, at one time, was its jingle, "You deserve a break today," which became permanently burned into everyone's memory. The minute you heard this jingle, you instantly knew what the product was. And, if you're in the market for a new pickup truck, Chevy wants you to think of them with their creative hook, a tagline in which actor James Coburn tells us that Chevy trucks are, "Like a rock." (Personally, I'd like my truck to be more like a truck than a rock, but whatever . . . the ad campaign is a success.) The AAMCO Transmission horn used in its radio and TV spots is a creative hook, and they've even gotten you to remember how to spell their unusual name ("Double A, honk-honk, M-C-O").

A creative hook can be a sentence within your advertising, such as, "I can't believe I ate the whole thing!" or a headline, "Got milk?" It can be a character that appears in all ads, such as Commander Whitehead for Schweppes Tonic, the talking lizards who sold Budweiser, or Ronald McDonald for you-know-who. It can, on the local advertising level, be an eccentric owner and an ongoing inside joke, like Cal Worthington, a California car dealer, who appears in all his TV spots with a different animal (elephants, hippos, camels, and so on), all of which he refers to as "My dog, Spot."

A creative hook is what every good ad needs in order to cut through the advertising clutter. ***Remember:*** You can always find a more creative, memorable, unique way with which to get your message across. It doesn't need to be earth-shattering in its creativity — just different, clever, and memorable enough to grab the eye or ear and motivate the consumer to at least give you a shot. The trick, of course, is to find what that hook is for your business or product.

So, how do you get creative? What secrets can you uncover that will transform you magically from businessperson to creative genius? Unfortunately, it's not that easy. But you can jump-start your creativity by gathering a few friends, family, or employees around and doing what the professionals do: Hold a creative session.

Advertising agencies, when designing new campaigns (or redesigning old ones), often hold what is called a *creative session* or a *brainstorming session.* These meetings are, in my mind, the most fun an ad person can have (at least while at work). In a creative session, all the people who will be working on a particular account — owners, creative directors, copywriters, artists, even the account service people — gather together in one room. They trade as much information as possible about the account and the product, and then they're encouraged to toss out ideas. These ideas then beget more and more ideas, which will, eventually, result in the perfect creative answer to the problem at hand. The only rule of these meetings is that no idea will be laughed at or discarded out of hand. It's sort of a stream-of-consciousness type of gathering, and no idea is far-fetched or stupid. Everything gets tossed onto the table.

In creative sessions, when someone throws out an idea, it is written with marker along with other ideas onto large sheets of paper. As the sheets of paper are filled, they're taped to the walls. And, before long, the room is festooned with ideas — whether good or bad — from wall to wall. The ideas are studied by the entire group, and then refined, changed, and resubmitted. Eventually the creative hook, the new advertising message, begins to take shape. And when everyone agrees that a certain concept is the best answer to the problem, the group focuses on that one superlative idea and begins to massage it into the final product.

Creativity is hard work. Ideas don't just jump up and bite you. You need to search for them very diligently. But they *will* happen. I have gone into creative sessions with no clue as to what we could come up with for a particular account, and I've walked out armed with a great, new idea that we could then ride for months to come. The ad agency creative session is the two-heads-are-better-than-one approach — a tried-and-true method of generating tons of fresh, new ideas.

How a creative hook became a marketing phenomenon

When I first came up with the idea for the Pet Rock, I envisioned it as a spoof of a dog-training manual. But in researching book publishers, then distributors, and then retailers, I soon realized that trying to sell this highly unusual concept as a book would be an uphill climb. Plus, according to my research, the average shelf life of the average book (at least one not written by a big-name author) is just a matter of weeks — if you can get the thing printed and onto the shelves in the first place. That was unacceptable as far as I was concerned. Maybe, I thought, Andre Gide was right when he said, "If a young writer can refrain from writing, he shouldn't hesitate to do so."

So, back to the old drawing board. I knew that what I needed to find was the creative hook. And the answer was that, instead of simply writing a book, I'd create a product. I'd devised a way to package *The Official Pet Rock Training Manual,* along with an actual rock lying on a bed of excelsior inside a miniature pet carrying case, complete with air holes. That way, I could skip the bookstores entirely and put the whole enchilada into department stores and gift and stationery stores. It was simply a better, more creative way, to sell the book.

When this innovation came to me and the packaging was designed, the Pet Rock — the novelty gift product that quickly became an instant sensation — was born. And the creative hook that took the Pet Rock from paperback book to upscale gift item was so subtle that it seems to have gone over the heads of many marketing experts, who still think I had a lot of nerve selling rocks for five bucks. I wasn't selling *rocks* for five bucks apiece (who in his right mind would pay to buy a rock?); I was selling *books*.

Before you begin the creative process of finding your inimitable message, ask yourself a few simple questions:

- ✔ What are you selling, and what makes it so unique?
- ✔ To whom do you want to sell it?
- ✔ Why should people buy it from you?

You don't have to create the next "Fly the Friendly Skies of United" advertising slogan to get people into your store. You just have to use a bit more creativity than the other guys in devising a compelling message — so people will choose your store over the competition.

Creativity can take the form of copy content, the actors you use in your commercials, the graphics you choose for your print ads, an unusual music background for radio spots, humor, or any number of things. Even though being creative is often a strenuous task, finding a new twist that you can inject into your ads is worth the extra effort.

My agency handles student recruitment advertising for two Bay Area community colleges. In order to devise a fresh, new creative approach for this account, we first went back through all their previous advertising to see if we could identify any glaring flaws and found it to be . . . well . . . kind of boring. The ads just listed a bunch of facts and figures (like which classes were being offered during certain enrollment periods and how much those classes would cost). They were throwing those statistics out there in the form of print and broadcast advertising, and hoping for the best. Unfortunately, the ads weren't differentiating their colleges from the many other junior colleges doing equally boring advertising in the market — and their advertising wasn't getting very dramatic results. Needless to say, they came to us looking for something that would actually work.

By applying the list of questions earlier in this section to this particular creative problem, I can walk you through the various steps we took to produce some new ads that have been increasing student enrollment each and every time they run.

First question: What are you selling and what makes it so unique?

Answer: We are selling quality education delivered by highly-qualified instructors in a beautiful campus environment.

Next question: To whom do you want to sell it?

Answer: To kids fresh out of high school, and to adults who want either to upgrade their current job skills or to return to the job market after an absence.

Final question: Why should people buy it from you?

Final answer: Because, unlike so-called trade schools and private technology schools (which can be quite expensive) or four-year colleges (which can be downright unaffordable), these community colleges deliver a first-rate education, in either day, night, weekend, or Internet classes, for just $7 per credit hour to California residents.

After answering those questions, what did we come up with? A radio soap opera with the authentic sound and feel of the old-time radio soap operas that were all the rage before television came along. We used this creative hook to challenge the listeners into bettering themselves by becoming more educated, and we did it in a fun, nonthreatening way. But wait, you say, what do teenagers know about old-time soap operas? Well, nothing, but they do respond to what they call *retro,* and what is more retro that old-time soap operas?

For our college soap opera spots we created imaginary people with imaginary problems and, using really corny organ music in the background (just like the good old days) and a completely over-the-top actor to read the copy, we introduced each character, his or her problem, and a solution as provided by a quality education from our colleges. Here's one of our scripts directed at young adults:

Background: Soap opera music.

Emily awoke to the big day. She had spent a year as mustard squirter *(squirt),* then ketchup squirter *(squirt, squirt),* then pickle placer *(one, two, three).* But today, at the pinnacle of fast-food success, she would occupy the drive-through window *(. . . and did you want fries with that?).* This was big, she thought, *really* big. But after a day spent watching other young women cruising through in BMWs, gabbing away on their cell phones, Emily knew that what *she* needed was a *career,* not a job. Especially not *this* job. No education, no career. No career, no BMW. Simple, huh? She called Silicon Valley's winning education combo — Foothill and De Anza Colleges *(music change, upbeat, jazzy).* With day, evening, and weekend classes, as well as Internet and telecourses available, Emily could get top-quality instruction for just seven bucks a unit. Foothill and De Anza offer an affordable way to earn a college degree, or to update job skills for today's competitive job market. Do what Emily did. Get back to school. Enroll now for fall classes at Foothill and De Anza Colleges. Call 555-1212. That's 555-1212.

In addition to creating a series of spots directed at teenagers fresh out of high school, we also invented other characters and wrote spots that were directed at adults who were stuck in go-nowhere, low-paying jobs, or who were eager to return to the job market after a long absence and were in need of an upgrade in skills. We then placed these commercials on radio stations specifically programmed to attract our prime demos — whether it was adults between the ages of 18 and 24, women between the ages of 25 and 54, or just adults in general. The results have been more than gratifying. Our clients have even entered these new radio commercials into various community college creative advertising contests and have taken several first prizes. More importantly, enrollments at both colleges are up and our clients are happy. What more could you want from an ad campaign?

We want to buy your friendship

One of the other partners in an agency of which I was a part-owner made a presentation to introduce our agency to a small, regional bank — a bank that was having a terrible time competing with the monolithic California financial institutions like Wells Fargo and Bank of America. As creative director, I was invited to attend a get-acquainted session with the bank's very flamboyant president. This guy was way ahead of his time. He sported a closely cropped beard and always wore his signature bright red suspenders (which he proudly showed off by strolling around the bank without his jacket). He was, to say the least, unlike any bank officer I had ever met.

Located in a small regional strip mall in a Bay Area suburb, the bank had come up with a very generous interest rate on savings accounts as a way to attract a few new deposits. The trick was to tell potential customers about the bank's rate and other good reasons to move money there — and to do so within the parameters of a somewhat limited ad budget. Because the president was such an unusual character, a guy who truly humanized the banking experience, my best idea was to feature him in all the ads.

Now, coming up with a great, new idea is one thing. In the ad agency biz, getting clients to agree to the more far-fetched of them is quite another. In this case the bank president was just egotistical (and creative) enough to see the logic in, and go along with, the new headline I invented for his bank, which was (and I change his and the bank's names here), "John Smith, President of Regional Bank, wants to buy your friendship!"

Instead of droning on about the bank and its higher interest rate on Money Market savings accounts, then adding in all the caveats and details about minimum balances, and so on, I thought we should go straight to the heart of the matter. We would tell potential customers that, although John Smith was being a bit mercenary in attracting deposits with a promise of a higher interest rate, he didn't take himself too seriously, and it may actually be a fun place to bank.

We did a photo shoot of John wearing his suspenders and used it in all print ads and in-lobby display materials. We even designed and silk-screened T-shirts with red suspenders front and back, and the slogan, "John Smith Bought My Friendship" and the bank's logo on the back. We also did a series of radio spots (which we ran on economically-priced regional stations) in which we went way over the top to explain that this bank was totally different from any other.

Here is one of the scripts that was read by a very deep voice in a over-acted, highly dramatic delivery, with "The Battle Hymn of the Republic" playing in the background:

Who is this Bay Area banker, and why does he wear red suspenders? Well, his name is John Smith. He's the president of Regional Bank. He's a bit unusual as financial types go, and he wants to buy your friendshp. Bring a minimum of $5,000 to Regional Bank, open a money market savings account, and John will pay you an extremely generous interest rate. Regional intends to pay the highest money market savings rate in this area . . . period! And, as if high interest weren't enough, you'll also receive your very own official "John Smith Bought My Friendship" T-shirt, complete with red suspenders. Visit Regional Bank today at 100 Main Street. John is saving a T-shirt in your size; he has room in his vault for a few money market savings accounts; and, don't forget, he wants to buy your friendship.

Off the wall, you say? Exactly. And it worked. The bank took in savings account deposits at a very satisfying clip. It also proves that, even if your business is less than exciting, you can still write and produce eye-catching (and ear-catching) ads with just a little creativity. This bank campaign would have worked even if we'd used the concept only on radio, or print, or point-of-sale materials, rather than across all media. It was strong enough to stand alone in whatever form it took.

An added bonus is the fact that these spots were very cheap to produce. The most expensive element of the whole campaign was the cost of the actor, who did a superb job of reading (or, I should say, emoting) the copy. All in all, we devised a good creative campaign, which still left most of the client's money available to spend where it would do the most good — on radio stations with strong audiences of prospective students (buyers).

Incorporating Your Message into an Ad Campaign

When your great new idea hits you right between the eyes, when the light bulb of creativity suddenly shines brightly, it's time to begin incorporating this message into a full-blown ad campaign (or at least as full-blown an ad campaign as you can afford). After you've identified all the ways your product is unique, and after you've put your finger on a hard-to-resist, eminently-logical reason that people should seek you out in order to buy it, you then need to find ways to make this idea fit into various forms of advertising.

Often, your creative hook will dictate what media you should use — the hook will literally drive your campaign. If your hook (whatever it may be) is visual, then you'll use print, *collateral* (such as mailers, brochures, and so on), and/or television. If your concept is audio-driven (a skit between two people, or a hook using your own voice or a unique music background, for example), radio may be your best bet. If your clever new idea is a catchy slogan or a headline, you can consider using any variety of media including billboards and bus cards.

You can't buy a 50-pound ad campaign with a 10-pound budget. So you need to pick and choose your media and adjust your message accordingly.

The good thing is that you don't need to buy every media in town in order to get your message across. You can accomplish your goals not only with a creative message, but also with a creative media buy. So, before you start designing your campaign, you need to come to grips with how your message will translate into various media, and how much of this media you can afford.

Whatever your unique message turns out to be — whether it's a headline, sentence, slogan, graphic, or other creative hook — be sure to use that message consistently in all media. You need to apply the same message in all the forms of media you use, in order to establish it as yours and yours alone and in order to give the consumer a better chance of remembering it.

Don't say one thing in your radio advertising, and another in print. Don't advertise one item in the newspaper and another on TV. Retailers (and a surprising number of national advertisers) make this mistake over and over again, and it only serves to confuse the consumer and to water down your overall advertising impact (and budget). If your radio commercials are talking about a half-price sale on a specific item, then your newspaper ads should be featuring the same sale terms for the same item. This point is a pretty basic one, really, but it's one many advertisers fail to remember.

The good thing about consistency from one medium to the next is that translating your message is even easier. If you've spent hours and hours writing a 60-second radio script for an ad, and you decide to augment your radio advertising with some small newspaper ads, your time isn't lost. In fact, your job is all but finished, because you can easily edit the same copy you wrote for radio so that it works for print, thereby creating a cohesive advertising message across both media. One good piece of advertising copy will always lead to another as a campaign is being designed and begins to take shape. One radio spot becomes two, three, or more — all with the same message, but with each spot presenting that message in a different way. When I write one good radio spot, for instance, I can easily spin that first spot into a half dozen more within minutes. When the creative hook is established, the campaign easily takes shape. And one good creative concept, written for one media, will always lend itself to many other forms of advertising. A good creative idea takes on a life of its own and actually drives the design of the campaign in a certain direction.

The real challenge of creating your advertising (the challenge of creating any advertising, for that matter) is to devise something that will cut through the clutter of advertising that consumers are exposed to each and every day. A really clever, creative two-column newspaper ad with a headline that reaches out and grabs your attention can stand head and shoulders above a full-page, four-color ad that completely misses the mark. A radio spot that takes a fresh, new approach will enjoy much more listener recall than a spot that just drones on and on without giving the listener a clear reason to actually hear it. Each ad must contain all the information the consumer needs in order to make a thoughtful decision as to whether he will act. But each ad must also contain some element of creativity that will give the consumer a good reason to read it or listen to it in the first place. The search for creativity can be daunting, but it's definitely worth the extra effort.

In the following sections, I give you a few simple guidelines for creating effective ads. Turn to the chapters in Part II for more in-depth information on each of the different kinds of media.

Keeping it simple

The best rule you can use as you work toward creating memorable advertising for today's marketplace is summarized in an acronym you won't forget: KISS, which stands for "Keep it simple, stupid."

Why is keeping it simple so important? Because today, more than ever before, consumers are deluged with information. Many people are connected to the outside world every minute of the day. Computers, cellular phones, global positioning systems, personal digital assistants (PDAs), radios, television sets, the Internet, pagers, and many other electronic devices keep people within reach of information 24 hours a day, 7 days a week. The amount of data available is overwhelming, and into this cauldron of information is thrown advertising. At the very least, you hope your ads will be noticed; in a perfect world, consumers will remember them and act upon what they've heard. And one way of ensuring that your customers will remember what you're saying is to keep it simple.

David Ogilvy (covered in more detail in Chapter 1) was famous for writing thousands of words of informative copy — copy that, if actually read, would be of true value in helping the consumer make an educated, thoughtful decision. But I don't believe that approach works anymore. No one has time to read a lot of words. Actually, no one *wants* to read a lot of words, especially in ads. People need to get their information quickly, make a decision, and move on to the next problem. (Sort of why you bought this book, right?)

What makes people respond to one advertisement over another? Why do they choose to shop at a particular store when dozens of stores out there carry essentially the same products? It's likely because they were captured by an ad that gave them a clear, concise reason to buy — an idea presented in an eye-catching, creative way. At the very least, they read or heard a message that filled some need they had at the time, and so they made a point of traveling to that particular store for that specific piece of merchandise. Perhaps it was a great low price, or a special that included the addition of a free gift, a discount on future purchases, or any number of things. Whatever it was, it grabbed their attention and they responded. And, whatever it was, I'm willing to bet that it was presented in a very simple, easy-to-understand manner.

Using words that sell

Certain words and phrases, when used in retail advertising, have a better-than-even chance of attracting consumers' attention. You see these words over and over again in ads, but they're used (maybe even overused) because they continue to *work*. Here are some examples of words that sell:

- ✔ Clearance
- ✔ Discount
- ✔ Everything must go
- ✔ Final closeout
- ✔ Free
- ✔ Going out of business
- ✔ Grand opening

- ✔ Improved
- ✔ Markdown
- ✔ New
- ✔ Overstocked
- ✔ Sale

Go through your newspaper and look at the ads. The use of certain words and phrases by most advertisers will quickly become apparent to you. Look at the words and phrases that appear in ad after ad and you'll discover what I mean when I say that these words sell. They form a similar thread that runs through much retail advertising. If you can use any of these same words and phrases in your advertising, by all means include them. If they're good enough for all the other advertisers in your area, they will most certainly be good enough for you.

Just as some words really sell, there are others that you should be sure to avoid. Don't use swear words, most slang or vernacular (Budweiser's use of *Whassup* is certainly the exception), and words with more than three syllables. You can use *some* four-syllable words (words like *incredible* and *absolutely,* as in "absolutely incredible savings!" for instance), but be careful. Keep in mind that most people haven't expanded their vocabularies since early high school (most newspapers are written to the sixth-grade reading level for this reason). So, if you're tempted to use the word *ubiquitous,* you may consider saying "all over the place" instead. (I'm not trying to underestimate the intelligence of the general public, although few people have gone broke doing so. I'm only trying to make it easy for them to grasp your message.)

If ever you needed to use the KISS rule in full-force, it is in the vocabulary you use in your ads. But you need to walk a fine line between using simple, easy-to-grasp words and phrases, and writing the way people think (in the vernacular). Bottom line: Make your ads simple in their language, but creative in their content and presentation.

Delivering your message with clarity

Whether you're designing advertising for print, radio, television, direct mail, or any of the myriad forms of media, be sure to explain your message in very clear, easy-to-understand terms so that the consumer can see at a glance what it is you're selling and then make a snap decision as to whether or not he wants to read or listen further. Place your most powerful *selling* message at the beginning of the radio spot, or in the form of a headline for your printed advertising. So, for example, if you're having a two-for-one sale, you'll want to get that information out there right away. Don't drone on for half a radio spot without giving the listener a reason to actually hear it. Get down to the nitty-gritty as soon as possible and then, and only then, explain the various details.

Here are two examples of how to write the opening copy for a radio spot to advertise a two-for-one sale. See if you can tell which spot is better.

> Smith's Hardware, conveniently located in the Neighborhood Shopping Center, a family owned and operated business for over 50 years, and a store where you've come to expect the very best in top-quality merchandise and friendly, helpful service, is proud to announce its annual two-for-one sale.

> Announcing the annual two-for-one sale at Smith's Hardware — the sale you've been waiting for since last year. Buy one gallon of paint, get another gallon absolutely free.

Both examples include the same information. The difference is that the second example gets the most important point across immediately (that Smith's Hardware is having a sale) and the rest of the 60 seconds can then be filled with the specifics about its convenient location, store history, and other good reasons to visit there. The first example may put listeners to sleep within the first couple of lines. Nothing in the spot makes them want to listen, because getting to the point takes too long.

Following the same rule in a print ad (whether newspaper, direct mail, flyers, or any other form of printed advertising) simply means that the words *two-for-one sale* become the headline, with all the other information the consumer needs to know placed beneath it (as briefly and succinctly as possible). And, in this case, the two-for-one sale *is* the creative hook, because it is the single element of the ad that separates it from other ads for similar stores.

Adding graphics to enhance your message

Graphics can go a long way toward explaining a concept or creating a hook that will attract the eye of the consumer. An eye-catching graphic element, even in a small space newspaper ad, can boost readership in a very dramatic way. A graphic element for the two-for-one sale print ad may be a photo of two cans of paint, one that has a label reading "Buy me" and the other with a label reading "And I'm free." Then, directly above or beneath the graphic element, you can place the headline: Smith's Hardware Annual Two-for-One Sale.

Graphic elements can be photos, illustrations, borders, ink colors, paper textures, or unusual type styles. In newspaper advertising, especially if you're buying small space ads, I recommend using line drawings instead of photos.

Newspapers have a talent for making some photos look like they've been smeared with mud prior to publication. It has to do with something called *line screen,* which, in the case of newspaper printing, is rather coarse, so the printed photo is lacking in detail and clarity. (For more information on line screen, turn to Chapter 7.)

A good-quality, relevant photo can add a lot to a print ad, attracting the reader's eyes to your ad — and giving the ad a fighting chance to be read. By *relevant,* I mean a photo of something that pertains to what you are selling, as opposed to the gratuitous use of a babe in a bikini to sell garage doors.

Some of the best newspaper ads I've ever seen are the ones that have lots of *white space* (blank newsprint with no words or graphics squeezed into every square inch) along with a very attractive, eye-catching graphic element like a photo or drawing. These ads also excel because they make it easy on the reader by delivering the message instantly. Some advertisers make the mistake of thinking that, because they're buying the ad space at a very hefty rate, they owe it to themselves to fill it up. But what they end up doing is cluttering up their own ads — and clutter, especially in advertising, is never effective.

Part II
Writing Great Ads for Every Medium

The 5th Wave   By Rich Tennant

"I SENSE YOU'RE IN A HURRY, SO I'LL BE BRIEF."

In this part . . .

From radio and television to newspapers and magazines, from bus cards and billboards to direct mail and the Internet — the variety of media available to accept your advertising, and evaporate your budget, is mind-boggling. Whether you can afford a full-blown ad campaign across all media, or you're just looking to find out as much as you can about one particular media choice, you'll find answers, suggestions, advice, and the inside scoop in this part.

Chapter 5

Radio: Effective, Affordable, and Fun

··

In This Chapter

▶ Making sure you tell your listeners what they need to know

▶ Using sound effects and music tracks to spice things up

▶ Finding the right person to read your spot

▶ Getting the spot aired on the station

··

My father hated radio and could not wait for television to be invented so he could hate that, too.

— Paul de Vries

Sitting before a blank piece of paper or an empty computer screen and attempting to write a 60-second radio commercial that will effectively and memorably motivate listeners to buy *your* product or service can be an intimidating task. How do you separate yourself from the herd? What magic words can you use to describe all the wonderful reasons why consumers should buy from you instead of buying from the dozens of other businesses out there trying to convince them of the same thing? How can you turn hard facts into clever copy that will cut through the clutter and stop listeners dead in their tracks?

Radio ads are there to get the attention of your listeners — people you hope will become customers if they aren't already. In order for your radio ads to be effective, you need to do the following, all within the span of one minute (or between 180 and 200 words):

Good grief!: Debunking the myth of writer's block

The late Charles Schultz, creator of the fabulously successful *Peanuts* comic strip, drew fresh and funny strips each and every day for several decades. He was once asked by an interviewer how, day after day, year after year, he was able to bring new ideas and creativity to his work. I will never forget his answer and have, when asked the same question, blatantly plagiarized his reply as though it were my own. Schultz simply said, "Writer's block is for amateurs."

I think what Charles Schultz was saying is that there is always a fresh approach to be found when it comes to doing something creative. Regardless of how mundane a product may be, there is always an angle that can make it sound original, exciting, and desirable. And even if you're writing new copy each and every week in order to sell the same product or service, you can always find a new way to present the same old thing. The trick is to find this fresh, new hook, however elusive, and incorporate it into your radio advertising with every new spot you write.

- ✔ Grab the listeners' attention.
- ✔ Tell them something they want to hear.
- ✔ Sell them something they may not need.
- ✔ Mention the name of your business several times.
- ✔ Get your phone number or Web address indelibly written into their brains.
- ✔ Motivate them with a *call to action* (something that tells your reader what to do, such as "Hurry in today!" or "Call right now!").

Writing radio ads is a process, like anything else, and it gets easier the more you do it. In this chapter, I lead you through the process one step at a time and, with any luck whatsoever, by the end of this chapter you'll be writing spots like a pro. To pack a thousand seconds of information into a 60-second bag isn't as hard at it appears if you follow these guidelines.

Step 1: Summarizing Your Business in 60 Seconds

You may think it a daunting prospect to tell your customers everything they need to know about your business within the limited time frame of one minute. But a minute is quite a long time, actually. Look at your watch and let a full minute go by. Tapping your fingers or fidgeting in your seat is not allowed. Concentrate on the second hand (or the seconds ticking off on your digital watch). See what I mean? A minute is a long while. Sixty excruciatingly slow clicks. Just think of all the wonderful information you can squeeze into a spot within that *huge* amount of time.

The trick here is to concentrate on the relevant information you want to impart and to discard everything else. You simply cannot summarize an encyclopedia's worth of information in 60 seconds, but you can tell the world quite a lot about yourself in that length of time. Writing radio 60s, as they're called, will be good practice for you because, if you're ever interested in writing ads for television, you'll need to do this in 30 seconds. Whew!

So what information do you need to convey? Okay, here it comes, folks, a professional copywriter's secret, a revelation so incredible, so astute, so amazing that you'll likely say to yourself, "Humph! I knew that!" It's the same basic informational formula used by journalists — namely: who, what, when, where, and why (otherwise known as the five *W*s).

When they're arranged in a radio spot, the five Ws don't always fall in that particular order, of course. Including them all is a good idea, but you can arrange them any way you like — within reason.

Who

The first thing you want your listener to know is *who* you are, so you need to mention the name of your business within the first line or two. I hear commercials all the time that drone on and on and never seem to think that the sponsor's name is important enough to mention until somewhere around the last five seconds. This is a big, fat, money-wasting mistake because by then it's too late. The listener will *never* hear every word of your commercial. It doesn't matter if he hears it 20 times, or even 100 times, he will not listen carefully to each and every word. Instead, he will hear bits and pieces of it. He will recall some elements of it. He will know he's heard "something" that appeals to him. He will even respond to it (at least you hope he will). But he will never be able to recite it word for word. So telling him who you are *immediately* is very important.

What

The next thing you'll want the listener to know is *what* you are selling. Which of your products or services are you featuring in this spot? Don't try to sell your entire inventory in one 60-second spot. It just won't work — you'll confuse the listener even more than he's already confused. Instead, target your message to one or two important elements. Give the listener a fighting chance to remember what the heck you're talking about.

If you have too much information to squeeze into one spot, write two different spots and rotate them 50/50 on the air.

The consumer is being deluged with advertising information, both audio and visual, each and every waking moment of his life. The first thing he sees in the morning is advertising on his toothpaste tube, then on his cereal box and milk carton, then on his coffee can, then on the labels of his clothes, and only then, after subliminally absorbing dozens of advertising messages, does he pick up the newspaper, or turn on the radio or TV, all of which literally bury him in advertising. All you're trying to do — all you can *hope* to do — is get your foot into his door with one juicy tidbit of information so he will recall at least *something* of what you're saying. Target your message very carefully and succinctly. Narrow your message to simple, hard-hitting, important facts that the listener can remember and act upon.

When

When do you want the listener to act? When does your special sale price take effect? When does this offer go away? When is your store open? This is a great area into which you can insert your calls to action, like the following:

- ✔ "This offer absolutely ends midnight Saturday."
- ✔ "Hurry in today!"
- ✔ "We're staying open until 10:00 every night to keep up with customer demand."
- ✔ "Sale ends Thursday."

If you can insert an element of urgency into your commercial you'll give the listener just that much more to think about and a good reason to act.

Where

You definitely want to tell your listeners *where* you are and how they can find you. Although this sounds rather basic, you'd be amazed at how many spots wait until the end of the spot to mention it, or forget this all-important information altogether. If you have multiple locations, you'll want to include your toll-free number so customers can call for directions to your nearest store. If you have just one location, give the address and phone number, but be careful here: The listener cannot be expected to remember too many numbers or complicated directions. Chances are he'll hear your spot while driving and won't be inclined to jot down any information. When was the last time you were so blown away by an advertising message that you pulled the car off the road and wrote down the advertiser's name and address? Probably never.

Putting the five Ws to use

If your head is spinning from the thought of incorporating the five Ws into one radio spot, here's how you can even incorporate them into one sentence that will open a 60-second radio commercial:

> CALIFORNIA DINETTES *(Who)*, PURVEYORS OF FINE CASUAL DINING FURNITURE *(What)*, IS HAVING THEIR ANNUAL SPRING DECORATING SALE *(Why)* BEGINNING FRIDAY *(When)* AT THEIR BEAUTIFUL SHOWROOMS IN SAN JOSE, SAN CARLOS, AND PLEASANT HILL *(Where)*.

This would be a good opening sentence to a 60-second spot because it tells the listener nearly everything he needs to know right off the bat. It also leaves 50 seconds in which to get more specific (a broad description of the furniture items on sale, what the prices and terms are, the telephone number, the sale deadline, and so on). But if the listener only hears the first few words of this spot, the first sentence gives him all the truly important information about this furniture sale.

This spot is also a completed 10-second spot, which stations sometimes call *billboards* or *I.D.s* or *promos.* If your media buy includes 10-second spots (which are often included at no charge), then this spot is what you want to air. Listeners may not even hear your 60-second spot, but they may hear one of your billboards. Try to include everything they need to know within those first ten seconds.

You can expand this spot into the complete 60-second version as well. Add more specific information and dress it up with adjectives and a call to action. See if you can identify the five Ws in this spot. They're all there — and more than once.

CALIFORNIA DINETTES, PURVEYORS OF FINE CASUAL DINING FURNITURE, IS HAVING THEIR ANNUAL SPRING DECORATING SALE BEGINNING FRIDAY AT THEIR BEAUTIFUL SHOWROOMS IN SAN JOSE, SAN CARLOS, AND PLEASANT HILL. WE'VE BEEN BUSY GRABBING UP FABULOUS DEALS ON CASUAL DINING FURNITURE FROM THE NATION'S BEST MANUFACTURERS. RIGHT NOW THE CALIFORNIA DINETTES SHOWROOMS AND WAREHOUSE ARE BULGING. WE NEED TO GET THIS FINE FURNITURE OFF OUR FLOORS AND ONTO YOUR FLOORS RIGHT AWAY, SO WE'VE SLASHED PRICES. CHOOSE FROM THE LATEST DINETTES IN IRON AND GLASS, NATURAL WOODS, AND LAMINATES — WITH ELEGANT TABLETOPS OF GRANITE, CORIAN, AND WOOD INLAYS — ALL AT 15 TO 50 PERCENT OFF! NEED BARSTOOLS? ALL BARSTOOLS REDUCED AN EXTRA 30 PERCENT. SO FOR SUPER DEALS, COME AND GET 'EM DURING SPRING SAVINGS DAYS AT THE CASUAL DINING SPECIALISTS — CALIFORNIA DINETTES, CONVENIENTLY LOCATED IN SAN CARLOS, PLEASANT HILL, AND SAN JOSE. HURRY IN TODAY FOR BEST SELECTION!

Notice that the complete 60-second spot mentions the name of the store three times and their locations twice. It describes what furniture is on sale, lists the many whys, and inserts two calls to action ("Come and get 'em" and "Hurry in today for best selection!"). If the listener hears only the first sentence or the final sentence, that listener has heard enough to know that something interesting is going on at California Dinettes.

The simpler the better. Include a phone number rather than an address. Don't include the area code unless you live somewhere with multiple area codes within your business sphere of influence. Be sure to repeat the phone number a minimum of two times. If you absolutely must include an address, write something like, "Located on Main Street near First," rather than expecting anyone to recall "36452 East Main Street."

If you have a Web site address, use it in your spot *instead of* the phone number. Don't mention them both — remembering that many numbers and letters is just too much to ask of your listener.

Why

And now the most important of all the elements of a commercial, the *why*. Why should the customer buy from you rather than from some other merchant? Why is your deal the very best deal this guy is ever going to find? Why should anyone go out of his way to seek out your product or service when buying it somewhere else may be much more convenient? Sell your expertise; a great price and terms; a friendly, family-like atmosphere; a closeout price that is irresistible; or any number of other points. The why part of your ad is very likely why you're advertising in the first place. It's your hook, your reason for being, your unique product difference. This is the area that separates the grownups from the kids and the successful merchants from the also-rans.

You must always find the magic *why* in order to have any hope of listener response to your commercials. Your listener can buy a car anywhere, from any dealership. But your dealership, and your car, and your price, and your terms, and your convenient location, and your incredible service department, and your friendly salespeople, and your free gourmet coffee and plush, posh, golly-gosh waiting room are so much better than any other car dealer's that he'd be a fool not to rush right in and give you his business. That's the *why*. And, to the ultimate success of your spot, the why is everything.

Step 2: Deciding on the Format for Your Ad

Knowing what to include in your ad is one thing, but an equally important part of creating your ad is knowing how exactly to communicate that message. In the following sections, I cover some common formats for radio spots. Within these different formats, of course, there is endless room for creativity. So flex those creative muscles!

Dialogue

Dialogue is a common form of radio spots, but like fingernails on a blackboard, it makes me cringe. The problem with dialogue radio spots is that they're usually poorly written. Can there be any more ridiculous radio commercial than a poorly written, poorly acted dialogue spot? You know the ones I mean — they're the spots in which two people are engaged in doing, or are talking about, something totally unrelated to the product being sold, and then awkwardly bring the product *sell* (or message) into the dialogue. For instance, the spot opens with the sound of a golf ball being hit and the following dialogue takes place:

Jim: "Wow, great drive Bill. I've never seen you hit the ball *that* far before."

Bill: "Thanks, Jim. I'm seeing the ball a lot better since I went to Dr. Fishburn's Laser Eye Center where I had both eyes done for just $2,495."

Jim: "Gee, Bill, do you mean that if I undergo major eye surgery at Dr. Fishburn's Laser Eye Center, and spend only $2,495, I can hit the ball farther, too?"

Bill: "No doubt about it, Jim. You'll improve your game and improve your life at Dr. Fishburn's Laser Eye Center. Just call 1-800-555-1212 and make an appointment."

Jim: "What was that number again, Bill? Did you say 1-800-555-1212?"

Bill: "Yep, 1-800-555-1212. Call them today."

The reason I hate these kinds of radio spots is that nobody talks like that in real life! These spots just cry out to be ignored, if not laughed at, because they are completely unbelievable. Even the major advertising agencies do this stuff, especially for pharmaceutical clients — and they should know better.

I stay as far away from dialogue spots as I can, and I think you should, too. In my opinion, nothing is more effective on radio than a single-voice read of good, believable copy. Don't offend or insult your listener with a premise and copy that is unbelievable, contrived, confusing, and just plain dumb. If you do, you'll have no one to blame but yourself when that listener reaches over, punches the radio button, and makes you instantly disappear.

While consumers are listening to your spot on the station you just spent a bunch of money to buy, you owe it to yourself and to your listeners to capture their limited attention spans with some good, clear copy — copy that gives them a reason to listen and a reason to buy your product. If you confuse the issue with an unrealistic concept and improbable copy, you'll lose them.

Sound effects and music tracks

Want to jazz up your spot? This may be a good time to touch upon the wonderful world of effects. Sound effects (SFX) and music tracks (MX) are the magic that makes radio "the theater of the mind." The sound effects and music tracks of the old-time radio shows put listeners right in the middle of the action. And that's what it can still do for your listeners today. Do you want 500 wild horses to gallop through your commercial? Go for it. Do you want your announcer to read your spot while standing on the starting line of a noisy racetrack? No problem. Do you want your entire spot to take place in a driving thunderstorm or in the middle of a battlefield? Be my guest.

Most radio stations and all production houses have huge collections of stock sound effects and music for use in commercial backgrounds. Pick a sound, almost *any* sound, and they are sure to have it — and it can be woven seamlessly into your spot. Then choose some appropriate music and mix it into the backdrop of your spot. With these production tricks, even if you're only producing a straight read, you can enhance it with effects and background music to help it cut through the clutter.

Comedy

When it comes to good comedy writing, you've either got it, or you don't. I don't think that you can be taught to write good comedy. Personally, I've had good success with comedy writing (the *Pet Rock Training Manual* comes quickly to mind) and I've used it in many radio spots, but very few products and services lend themselves to this genre. And, like dialogue spots, a poorly conceived premise and badly written copy will do a lot more harm than good — so tread lightly. Setting up an amusing idea, including some copy that actually sells your product in an amusing manner, and then delivering a good punch line in the span of 60 seconds is difficult. The sad number of unfunny spots on the air that are trying to be comical is a testament to the difficultly inherent in comedy writing.

Including some tongue-in-cheek styling to your copy, maybe poking a little fun at yourself, or at least not taking yourself too seriously is okay. But, unless you're very proficient at it, leave the comedy writing to the pros because comedy is very serious business.

Just the facts

A single voice reading 60 seconds of clear, concise, fact-filled copy that motivates and sells the listener is always a good bet. No frills. No jokes. No unrealistic dialogue. Just the offer — the selling proposition — read by a good, strong, male or female voice. You may want to toss in some background music or even some sound effects (see the nearby sidebar for more information), but this is the format I prefer when writing and producing direct-response broadcast advertising. To me, a straight read is the most effective copywriting method you can use to convey a selling message. And it's the easiest, which, if you're new to the game, may be the best reason of all to employ it.

You sit down and write a wonderful 60-second spot with a clear message and a compelling call-to-action. Then you hand this script to the voice talent who records it, the engineer adds some appropriate music or sound effects, and the station puts it on the air. Voilà! Your ad campaign is out there beating on the ears of your potential customers. It's not a cute spot. It's not even a fancy spot. But it's on the radio getting your message in front of listeners who, if you've followed the writing instructions I outline in this chapter, should be banging on your door any minute now.

Step 3: Putting It in a Form the Station Will Recognize

In case you're wondering why the commercial scripts you see in this chapter are written in all capital letters, it's for two reasons:

✔ Professional voice talent and studio announcers are used to seeing copy in all caps.

✔ By typing in all caps, you reduce the number of words to a page and, therefore, 60 seconds of copy will fit perfectly onto a 60-second copy form.

There isn't one right form to use when submitting broadcast copy. But If you follow these guidelines, you'll have success every time:

✔ At the top, put your company logo, company name, all contact information (phone number, address, e-mail, fax, and so on), the media and spot length, the date, and the title of spot.

✔ Set the margin width so that the copy area is 5 inches wide.

✔ Set the line spacing to 1½ lines.

✔ Use 12-point type, all caps, for the copy.

✔ Limit the copy to 20 to 22 lines for a 60-second spot or 10 to 11 lines for a 30-second spot.

✔ Use SFX to indicate sound effects and MX to indicate music tracks.

✔ Insert 10-point italics between lines of copy for any special audio directions.

Here's what an actual broadcast copy form would look like:

Your Company Logo

Your Company, 1235 South Main Street, Anytown, CA 95000, Phone: 800-555-1212, Fax: 888-555-1212, e-mail: jsmith@email.com

MEDIA: Radio :60 **DATE:** 9-00 **SPOT TITLE:** "Annual Fall Clearance Sale"

SFX: Thunderstorm, heavy rain, wind

NEITHER RAIN, NOR SNOW, NOR SLEET WILL KEEP ACME DOOHICKEY COMPANY FROM HOLDING THEIR ANNUAL FALL CLEARANCE SALE.

SFX: Cars drive by on wet roads, tires screech

AND IT LOOKS LIKE A LITTLE RAIN CAN'T STOP SMART BARGAIN HUNTERS FROM TAKING ADVANTAGE OF THESE ONCE-A-YEAR PRICE REDUCTIONS. DRIVE CAREFULLY, BUT HURRY IN RIGHT AWAY FOR BEST SELECTION.

If you write your ad in a format like this, the radio station and the person reading the spot will understand exactly what you want read and where. You can't go wrong if you follow these instructions.

Step 4: Figuring Out Who Should Read the Script

After you have your radio spot written, you need to find someone to read it. And the possibilities are numerous. You can read the spot yourself, have a studio announcer (someone who works for the station) read it for you, or hire a professional voiceover talent. I cover each of these options in the following sections.

Doing it yourself

I have generally been against clients voicing their own spots on radio, or getting in front of the cameras on TV. Everyone wants to be in show business; everyone wants to hear their friends say, "Hey, I heard you on the radio today!" But, generally speaking, reading your own radio spots is not a very good idea. When you read your own spots, it usually comes off as amateur night. Generally, you're much better off using a professionally trained voice talent who can give a spot the believability and sincerity it needs, rather than standing as an inexperienced rookie in front of a microphone and hoping for the best. Of course, two of the best known exceptions to this very flexible rule are Frank Perdue of Perdue Chickens and Dave Thomas of Wendy's, both of whom bring a unique, charming talent to their commercials and are completely believable.

Even the most gregarious, enthusiastic, vivacious person can be reduced to a blubbering bowl of jelly when you put them into a sound-proofed booth and flip the switch on a mike. The same person who is the life of the party and the best joke-teller in the world, the one who has more personality than five people, is suddenly reduced to a monotone robot. Nothing is worse than a spot that sounds like it's being *read*.

On the other hand, you may have exactly what it takes to come across as believable and memorable on the air (see the nearby sidebar on my client Matt Fidiam for more information). If you're a natural voice talent, by all means go for it. No one could possibly sell your products and services better than you. But be objective when you critique your final commercial. Don't just play it for people who are only going to tell you what you want to hear, such as friends and family. Instead, play it for vendors and customers and watch them, especially their eyes, carefully while they listen to your spot. They may be able to lie to you, flatter you, but their eyes (and their body language) cannot. Of course, in the final analysis, you must make the final decision.

Listen to your finished spot very objectively and try to hear it through the ears of John or Jane Doe driving down the road being bombarded by commercial message after commercial message. Does your copy give the listener a reason to act? Do your voice and delivery motivate the listener? Is your finished commercial memorable? Do you sound excited, sincere, and believable? Ask yourself, honestly: If I heard this spot would I be motivated to respond to it? If not, you should probably admit that you're not the next Ed McMahon and move on to the following section.

Using a studio announcer

Another option when you're looking for the right voice for your radio spot is to rely on the station-employed studio announcers (disk jockeys or on-air personalities). The advantage to this route is that it's the cheapest way to go. The service is usually free of charge as part of your media buy. You'll only have to pay a talent fee if you use a studio announcer who works for a station other than the one the spots will air on. By and large, studio announcers do a good, if not always enthusiastic, job on most commercial copy they read.

On the other hand, just handing your script to each station you want to advertise on and having the spots read by various station-employed studio announcers immediately negates one of the most important elements of a successful broadcast campaign: continuity. Listeners tend to bounce around from station to station and, if you're lucky, they will hear your spots on more that one. So you need to be sure they hear the same message regardless of the station they happen to be listening to at the time. Plus, if you use a studio announcer, your commercial may wind up sounding just like all the other spots on that station. After all, your ad isn't the *only* one those announcers are reading.

ANECDOTE

The exception to the rule

Having issued all my warnings about reading your own radio spots, I want to share with you the story of one client I have who is the exception to the rule. His name is Matt Fidiam, and he's the General Manager of Parrot Cellular, a major Northern California wireless retailer.

My agency had been trying unsuccessfully to get the Parrot Cellular account for so long that I finally just admitted to myself that it wasn't going to happen and had just about given up. Happily, my business associate, Marnie Doherty, did *not* give up. She simply wouldn't take no for an answer and kept after the account like a pit bull. In a final attempt to attract the client's attention and, hopefully, to secure the business, she and I went to a micro-brewery and whipped up a batch of our very own beer. Then we bottled it, complete with custom-labeling Marnie had designed. Knowing that Mr. Fidiam has a fondness for the occasional exotic beer and a well-developed sense of humor, we packaged several bottles into a lovely wooden gift box with an outside label reading: "You may be shocked to learn we are *not* above using bribery!" We then placed the gift box of custom-brew on the doorstep of Matt's corporate offices early one morning before anyone arrived for work. Hey, we had nothing to lose.

It worked. He called us that very morning and said, "If you guys are as good at advertising as you are at sales, I've got to give you my account." That was five years ago and we've been handling his broadcast advertising throughout Northern and Central California ever since.

After having had a few meetings with Matt (even before we secured the account), it was immediately apparent to me that he would be his own best on-air talent. He's a very animated, articulate, enthusiastic guy with a great sense of humor and a very unique voice. It was obvious that with properly written copy he would be the best person to project the personal enthusiasm he had about his own products. And, in the process, we would have a one-of-a-kind voice on the air in the Bay Area selling Parrot Cellular stores. It was that revelation that made me sure we could do a great job on the account in the first place. And it was that revelation that kept Marnie Doherty tenaciously pitching the business long after I had given up. We knew that, given a chance, our idea of putting him on the air would work for him. And we were right.

After finally landing the account, we didn't have to talk too hard to get him to agree to do a few spots as a test. I wrote several spots in the first person ("Hi, this is Matt Fidiam for Parrot Cellular . . ."). We then went into a recording studio, put him in front of a mike, and he was, as I had hoped, a natural. Oh, he'd stumble a bit here and there, but even the pros do that. And, because the recording process is digital these days, we were able to cut and paste the spots so he didn't have to go back to the beginning each time he flubbed a line. He wasn't a pro (not yet, anyway), but the final commercials were great.

Now, five years and hundreds of commercials later, Matt Fidiam's voice is one of the most recognizable on Bay Area radio, which is precisely what I was after in the first place. Recently, he and I attended a hockey game and while we were chatting in the concession area a stranger walked up to him and asked, "Hey, aren't you that guy who sells cell phones on the radio?"

I have written so many commercials for Parrot Cellular that I have begun to think like my client. I know the words he likes to use and the ones he stumbles over. I know the phrasing that he prefers, and how to insert just the right amount of sarcasm and "edge" that have become his trademark. And now, when we go into a recording studio, Matt is there for no more than ten minutes. He reads the spots, usually straight through on the first take, and then he leaves. He

has become the consummate professional voice talent.

So successful has Matt been with radio advertising that he has moved nearly 80 percent of his advertising funds into broadcast and has grown, since I first started working for him, from 11 local stores to 70 stores throughout Northern California. Parrot Cellular now accounts for nearly 25 percent of the total new telephone activations of Northern California Cingular Wireless. And, today, Parrot Cellular *owns* Bay Area radio. No other wireless telephone dealer has even tried to compete with Parrot through the use of broadcast advertising.

Hiring a professional voice talent

If you're willing to pay a little more to make your radio spots top notch, you can hire a pro to read them for you. Your station sales rep, the production manager at most stations, or even your Yellow Pages (look under "Talent Agencies") can steer you toward professional voices in your area. These men and women don't work for any particular station; instead, they're freelance talents or voice actors who make their living doing commercial voiceovers, radio and TV spots, corporate sales videos, and anything else that requires the talents and abilities of someone who is better than most of us are at simply reading.

Depending on the size of the area where you live, you may have a harder time finding a good voiceover talent, but they're out there. Your local radio or TV station's creative and production personnel can put you in touch with talent agents or voice talent outside your area, all of whom can do a great job for you from a distance and either send you the finished copy on compact disc (CD) or digital audio tape (DAT), or even send the spots electronically directly to the stations. My ad agency uses the same six or eight male and female voice talents for a variety of accounts, because these people have the ability to bring something fresh and new to everything they do. Even if their spots for different clients run back-to-back on a station, the listener will never know he's hearing the same person, because the content of each spot sounds so different. If you're going to do a lot of broadcast advertising, hook up with some professional voice talents. Then pay them promptly so they're always available when you call.

A pro will usually charge a flat fee to voice one 60-second radio spot, and a different fee to voice a 30-second television spot. You want to hire a voiceover talent on a *buy-out basis,* which is simply a fee for service, with no strings attached. The talent does the spot for a previously agreed upon price, you give him a check, and he gives you full and unlimited rights to the finished spot for as long as you want to air it. In other words, you own it and you can do with it as you please.

Be clear about the terms of your agreement with voice talent from the beginning so there is no confusion.

Some professional voice talents (usually the very best of them) are members of the Screen Actors Guild (SAG) or the American Federation of Television and Radio Artists (AFTRA). In other words, they're union. What this means is that they get paid a union minimum fee to record the spot and grant you the use of it on the air for 13 weeks — plus they will earn residuals if the spot stays on the air longer than that or is brought back on a later flight of commercials. And the really high-powered talent can ask for, and get, far more than the union minimum. You may not want this. Working with union voice talent gets very expensive, but by employing union talent you are making the trade-off of a higher fee in exchange for a better finished product. And the whole point may be moot anyway because you, as a client, must be what's called a SAG or AFTRA *signatory* in order to employ these union members in the first place (although, and I'm not trying to get anyone into trouble here, I have worked with union talent who waived their residual rights in exchange for a flat fee just to get the extra work). If you have employed an ad agency don't sweat these details; they will handle this stuff for you.

Professional voice talent in my neck of the woods usually charge less than $500 per 60-second radio spot on a buy-out basis for the area. Shop around, though, because costs may vary significantly from one market to the next. Ask your station rep what the going rate is in your area. Get an upfront quote from the talent and go from there.

Step 5: Setting It All in Motion

You've written your spot. It's perfect. It's interesting. It sells. And it even includes some clever effects. You've had it recorded and produced by a top-quality voice talent (or, in the interest of frugality, you've done it yourself) and you're ready to put it on the air. You've bought advertising schedules on several radio stations. And you're ready to go. Now what?

First you'll need a few *dubs,* which are copies of the *master* (the original), which will likely remain in the custody of the station that produced it. I always take a dub for my agency's archives and leave the master on file with the station. (Who needs the extra responsibility of archiving a master tape?)

Dubs come in the form of the more archaic reel-to-reel format, or the compact and infinitely more high-tech DATs or CDs. DATs are small cassettes that have perfect sound clarity and are inexpensive — get DATs for dubs when possible. Or you can ask for CDs, although they're a bit more expensive than DATs.

You'll need one dub for yourself, and one for each station on your media schedule. Only the most mercenary of stations will charge you extra for a few dubs.

Label the dubs (or the box they come in) with your company name, the spot title, the spot length, and the date the spot was produced. If you want to get really fancy, order some custom audio labels. But your standard company mailing labels will work just as well.

Don't send out anything to the stations on your buy that isn't carefully labeled. Radio station traffic or continuity departments have enough problems without trying to find unlabeled dubs in a sea of commercials. The traffic or continuity department schedules and runs the correct spots at the correct times for each and every advertiser the station has on the air. That's hundreds of commercials every day — which can make for a very hectic and high-stress environment in which mistakes can, and do, happen. So make your instructions to the traffic department very clear, to eliminate confusion.

Here is a sample of a good traffic instructions form:

> **Your Company Name, address, phone, fax, e-mail, and any other contact information**
>
> **Date:** August 15, 2002
>
> **Traffic Instructions to:** [LIST STATION CALL LETTERS HERE]
>
> **ATTN:** TRAFFIC DEPARTMENT
>
> **For:** Your Company Name
>
> **Flight date:** September 1 through October 15, 2002
>
> RUN "FALL CLEARANCE SALE :60," @ 100% OF SPOTS SCHEDULED (PER YOUR STATION'S CONTRACT) BEGINNING SEPTEMBER 1 AND THROUGH OCTOBER 15, 2001
>
> Put any special billing instructions here.
>
> Put your name, title, and phone number here so the traffic department can contact you with any questions.

Note: A radio schedule is called a *flight*. Notice on the Traffic Instructions that I call out the flight date. This alerts the Traffic Department that, at the end of this flight this particular spot will no longer run and new copy and instructions will be forthcoming (or your radio schedule will have concluded).

Help is available

The process of getting your spot on the radio can seem very technical, complicated, and even overwhelming. But your station sales reps can help lead you through the actual process one step at a time. Believe me, if the station rep has gotten a foot in your door and you've placed a buy with him, the station wants everything to go smoothly for you. They want your spots to be successful so that you will continue to place buys on their station. So they will help in anyway they can to assure that your advertising works.

Don't be afraid to ask questions and to request your station rep's expert assistance in giving your advertising flight the best possible chance to succeed. *Remember:* Your station rep, the person who is actually calling on your business, is especially interested in your success. He is paid on commission. He wants your spots to work, your business to prosper, and customers to beat down your door, so you will stay with him month after month, year after year. He will help you get copy written, spots produced, traffic instructions submitted, dubs sent to other stations, whatever it takes to make you happy (at least he will if he's any good).

Chapter 6

Television: Demystifying the Black Box

Television is a device that permits people who haven't anything to do to watch people who can't do anything.

— Fred Allen

Television commercials are nothing more than radio commercials to which you add pictures. Well, maybe they're a bit more than that, but that's the basic idea. As a matter of fact, I have often written television commercials in just that way: first writing a 60-second radio spot for the campaign and then editing the radio spot into a 30-second audio script for a TV spot, and, finally, adding the visuals. Removing a full 30 seconds of copy from a radio spot (a radio spot that you may think is about as tight as it can get) to end up with a clear and concise 30-second TV spot is difficult, but it can be done. The main idea is to have all your copy — radio, TV, print, and so on — saying basically the same thing and delivering the same message (this is called *continuity*).

Continuity is the key when designing an ad campaign. You don't want to water down your budget by advertising different messages on various media. And the foremost element you want to keep in mind as you write your TV spot are your visuals — think visually and consider your production budget as you create your spot. TV isn't like radio, where you can add the sound effects of a herd of wild horses for free. On TV you must *show* the herd of wild horses and that will cost serious money, even with the remarkable digital capabilities that are available today.

In this chapter, I walk you through the process of actually writing your own TV commercial — from the audio to the visual to the computer graphics. I also help you find ways to cut costs to stay within your budget. And I let you know what to expect when your commercial is actually shot and edited. Producing a TV commercial can be a daunting task, but in this chapter, I demystify it for you so that you can put TV to work for you.

Designing Your TV Commercial in Layers

When you set out to create an effective TV commercial, you can easily become overwhelmed by the various aspects of the job. But keep in mind that there are three basic elements to a retail TV spot: audio, video, and computer graphics. If you divide your commercial up into these three elements, the job is much easier to accomplish.

Every television spot will not necessarily include all three elements, but most good retail spots do, so you should consider designing your spot to include all of them.

Audio

Audio is the sound track that augments and enhances the visuals, the sell copy, the description, and the story that you want to tell. The audio can be a voiceover (a voice — maybe even yours — doing a sales pitch from off-camera) or an on-camera actor. The audio track may also include any music or sound effects you select.

The best place to start when you're creating a TV commercial is with the audio. Sit down and write the script first, but while you're writing your script, think visually. Consider the visual elements as you create your copy, and keep in mind your budget as you create your visuals.

Video

The video is obviously the visual component of the commercial. These are the pictures that the viewers will see — they're what should capture the eyes and the attention of the viewers. The video can be anything from you doing an on-camera sales pitch to product footage provided to you by your supplier, to video you shoot in your store, to anything else you can think of.

Don't get too carried away with elaborate visual elements that will add dramatically to the look of your spot, but will also add greatly to the cost of it. You can create visuals that are effective but cheap — particularly with the help of computers — it just takes a bit of thought. Instead of you standing on-camera pitching your business as a herd of wild horses gallops through the scene, the sound effects of a herd of wild horses galloping by "off-camera" (and someone off-camera kicking up copious amounts of dust) will do quite nicely. Viewers will swear they saw a herd of horses go by as you stood there selling them your products.

Computer graphics

The final element of a TV commercial is the computer graphics (CG for short). CG is the lettering (or possibly price numbers) that will appear on the screen to drive home certain points you want to make. It can be made to flash on and off, wipe or crawl across the screen, spin into the frame, explode into the frame, or do any number of eye-catching effects.

You can also use computer-generated effects, which can be entire scenes made to fly into the frame, spin, explode, appear out of infinity, and perform other interesting tricks. The computers that are available to television editors do amazing things these days. When you get into the actual production process, you can enhance your commercial greatly with these wonderful effects.

While you are writing and planning your commercial, meet with the art director or creative director of the production facility you are using so you can see the computer graphics and effects that are available to you. If you're going to spend some serious money on a schedule with a station, you should get a tour of its production facility and a demonstration of all the state-of-the-art tricks that you can insert into your spots. Don't be satisfied to just do another mundane spot if you can use the latest in computer technology to enhance and improve your spots and make them into something interesting and memorable.

Computer graphics by themselves will not rescue a poorly conceived and badly written spot. (Garbage in, garbage out.) Start with well-written copy and a sound creative premise and go from there.

All this computer technology brings with it another less obvious benefit: It will cut your production costs dramatically. Nowadays, the computers make the entire editing process so fast and painless that you can get in and out of the editing suite quickly and, therefore, cheaply.

Professional help is available to you

You are the best person to write the preliminary draft of the script for your TV spot, because you know your merchandise better than anyone. At the very least, you should be the one to write the *fact sheet* (the list of relevant facts and features that should be included in your spot). You are also the best person to decide *where* you want to shoot the commercial — in studio, in store, outdoors on location, or wherever — and what merchandise you want to feature in it.

But the TV station from which you are buying the airtime has all sorts of professional creative help available to walk you through the process. The station has copywriters, art directors, producers, directors, and editors who are there to make sure your commercial is as professionally done as possible. They all want your spot to generate business for you so you'll stay with

their station. They want their viewers to respond positively to your spot, not to tune it out. Because they don't want an amateur production going onto the air, they'll assist you in many ways to make sure your commercial looks professional. They'll also throw in their two cents when it comes to creative content, so be sure to listen to them. They've done this thousands of time before.

If you are looking for higher quality (and can afford it), you may want to employ an independent production company and professional director to do all this stuff for you. Most TV station production departments are certainly capable of doing good work, but independent houses, in an effort to build their own résumés, will often bring a higher level of creativity and production skills to the job.

Bringing the Audio and Visual Together

When you're writing a TV commercial, you need to think visually. Try to picture in your mind's eye what will appear on the screen as the words you write are spoken. If you're selling furniture, for instance, and your copy opens with a description of a cherry wood bedroom set, will your opening scene be the bedroom set, a wide shot of your entire store, or a beautiful cherry tree in full bloom? Or will you use all three of these shots in quick succession? Personally, I would choose the image of the cherry tree, opening the spot with a shot of the tree and all its pink blossoms, then cutting to the bedroom set you are featuring, and then zooming out to show the size of your showroom, or cutting to a shot of the showroom. Or you may even get really ambitious and place the bedroom set in front of the cherry tree for a lovely outdoor opening shot.

Your opening scene is all-important because it is the first thing that greets the viewers, the first thing that will either grab the viewers or cause them to leave the room to grab a soft drink. When you're working with a limited budget, you won't be able to show a supermodel sitting on the edge of the Grand Canyon as your opening scene grabber. But you can, with a little thought, come up with some elements that are creative and eye-catching enough to at least give your spot a fighting chance at capturing the attention of some prospective customers.

Keep the budget, which I cover in more detail later in this chapter, uppermost in your mind. All sorts of creative thoughts will come to you as you begin to write a commercial to sell your product or service, but you will likely discard many of these as being too unrealistic and expensive to actually include in your spot. Wild horses cost a lot of money, but the *sound* of wild horses does not.

Finish the script before going back and adding the visual elements. Squeezing everything you want to say into 30 seconds of clear copy is hard enough without also worrying about what's appearing on the screen. Do one thing at a time. Write the copy, then go back and fit the pictures and graphics to the soundtrack.

To help you write your TV spot, here's a sample first draft script showing the *audio* (the spoken words) in all caps, the *video keys* (TV production–speak for lettering that will appear on the screen either over the footage or as its own element), and the *video* (the camera and staging directions; how you visualize what will happen on the screen as the voiceover talks in the background) squeezed in between. (*V/o* stands for *voiceover,* which is just a voice speaking from somewhere off-camera.)

Video: *Automatic donut machine shot through store window*

V/o: MAN HAS BEEN BUYING AND EATING DONUTS FOR CENTURIES. YUM, YUM.

Video: *Close up of donuts being flipped in oil bath*

V/o: BUT, UNTIL NOW, IT NEVER OCCURRED TO DONUT MUNCHERS THAT THEY WERE BEING CHEATED.

Video: *Wide shot of donuts being sprinkled with cinnamon and sugar*

V/o: YES, CHEATED. BECAUSE THE DONUTS THEY WERE BUYING HAD GREAT BIG HOLES IN THE CENTER!

Video: *Close up of variety of decorated donuts*

Video Key: *Fresh *Delicious (actual printed words appearing on screen)

V/o: WELL, NOT AT SMITH'S DONUTS. SMITH'S DONUTS ARE ALWAYS DELICIOUS, ALWAYS FRESH. AND, IN A BOLD INNOVATION THAT IS SURELY AS EARTH-SHATTERING AS PAVED ROADS OR SLICED BREAD, SMITH'S DONUTS HAVE SMALLER HOLES.

Video Key: Smith's Donuts (logo)

1234 Main Street (in the Acme Shopping Center)

V/o: DON'T ACCEPT BEING CHEATED BY BIG DONUT HOLES. ALWAYS GET YOUR DONUTS AT SMITH'S DONUT SHOP IN THE ACME SHOPPING CENTER.

Video Key: *Tiny little holes *Tiny little prices

V/o: TINY LITTLE HOLES. TINY LITTLE PRICES.

Keeping in mind your budget

Before you go crazy with creative opening shots, or any shots for that matter, consider your budget and try to calculate what it will cost you if, for instance, you must pay for a video crew, their equipment, their truck, and a location shoot in order to show that cherry wood bedroom set sitting outdoors in front of a tree. If you can afford it, go for it. But an infinite variety of other shots may work just as well and cost you far less in production charges.

Discuss production charges with your TV station sales rep, and haul out the old calculator as you create your script. I have done location shoots that cost very little in comparison to the final result, so going outdoors to shoot footage shouldn't intimidate you. You can't expect to create a TV spot as inexpensively as a radio spot, but with some advance planning, you can keep the costs within reason.

Shooting the entire spot in the station's studio will cost far less than having to go out on location. And not having to shoot any footage at all is cheaper still. If, like automakers, your vendors have footage or still photos available to you, take advantage of it. Then, by adding a few hundred dollars per hour to pay for an editor and the

rental of an editing suite, your TV commercial can be ready to go.

All but the tiniest TV stations have editing suites where you can cut and paste factory footage (vendor-supplied footage) or still photos into a finished spot, but all TV stations do not have studios or remote capabilities (with trucks filled with equipment for on-location shoots). Check with the station you are dealing with to see what production facilities they offer, and, of course, how much those facilities cost.

Video editors can be your best friends when it comes time to make a TV spot. These people are well acquainted with working with rookies and, with a combination of professional talent and patience, they will guide you through the various complicated steps required to produce a finished spot. I've gone into an editing suite with some very definite ideas in mind, and tossed them out when an editor pointed out a better, more creative, way to do what I wanted to accomplish. They know how to make the best product possible within the budget guidelines set before them. Listen to them, watch them, and learn.

This is a sample of a first draft script, the initial pass through the various elements that will ultimately become a finished spot. At this point in the writing process, the video keys and the video camera directions that you call out are really only suggestions — they often change in the editing suite as better ideas are considered.

Deciding What to Feature in Your Commercial

Are you a good enough actor to star in your own commercial? Do you even *want* to? Is your store interesting and unusual enough to feature in your commercial? Or would it be a better idea to just put a camera on the products you're selling and let it go at that? The choices are endless — but I cover the basics in the following sections.

I want to put you in the movies . . .

You've probably seen many spots in which a store owner steps in front of the camera and does her own commercial. These kinds of commercials can, more often than not, be a very uncomfortable, even embarrassing, experience for all concerned — the store owner as well as the viewers. Nothing is more excruciating than watching someone make a fool of herself for a full 30 seconds, but that is what some store owners choose to do every time they star in their own commercials.

As you write your commercial, if you're thinking about doing your own spots, be objective enough to admit that, perhaps, you aren't anywhere close to winning an acting award and may be better off paying a few bucks to a pro. Starring in your own spot can be self-defeating if all the audience sees is someone who is obviously uncomfortable and, therefore, unbelievable. The viewers will quickly tune out and never give you, or your commercial, another thought.

On the other hand, you may be a natural and, if you are, then by all means go for it. No one else could possibly bring the enthusiasm and expertise that you can to this endeavor. No one else will ever be as good as you at selling your business. If you have a strong desire to be your own spokesperson, practice, practice, practice. Have someone shoot some home video of you doing your script, and do an objective critique of the finished product. Are you believable? Do you look comfortable? Does your presentation make your audience want to visit your store and buy something? Or do you look ill at ease and sound as though you're reading a script? Above all, be honest. Only you can decide whether you're a good enough actor to pull it off.

If you choose to stand in front of the camera and deliver the pitch yourself, keep in mind that the best opening scene for your spot is probably *not* a close-up of you. This will only make you yet another *talking head*, something that viewers get far too much of on the various news and entertainment shows. Instead, find an opening scene that may be a bit more creative than a headshot of you (even if you do have a million-dollar smile).

ANECDOTE

An in-studio car commercial gone awry

A former partner of mine had a car account back in the '50s and '60s that wanted new TV spots on a weekly basis. This account insisted that his spots be done in the studio of the station with which he spent his entire budget. There was a very simple reason for this — the production was free, a value-added part of the media buy.

My partner always did the spots the same way; driving that week's featured car into the studio, lighting the car so it looked much better than it actually was, putting a show card on the windshield that had big, bold letters showing the price, and standing next to the car and reading his copy from cue cards.

One evening, after a few cocktails at the local watering hole, he ventured down to the TV station to cut that week's new spot. The car of the week was parked in the studio, the lighting was set, the camera was focused, the showcard, in large red letters, read $2,995 (hey, I said it was the '50s). He stepped into the scene, leaned against the car's front fender, and, reading his cue cards, did the entire spot in one take, which was a good thing because this was before the days of digital editing.

He was very pleased with the fact that, even though he was slightly tipsy, he had aced the spot in one smooth take. There was just one little problem. Throughout his whole read, and perhaps because he had spent a bit too much time at the bar, he had repeated over and over that the price of the car was $2,895 instead of $2,995. When he had finished the copy, the director pointed out to him that he had voiced the car's cost at $2,895 while the showcard on the car's windshield clearly stated it was priced at $2,995. Certainly a dilemma. But not to my partner. He walked off the set to return to the local pub and yelled back over his shoulder, "Hell, no one pays attention to these spots anyway."

Maybe he was right. The spot went on the air as is, ran a full week, and no one ever called to complain about the discrepency — including the client.

Shooting at your store

Another option is to hire a remote crew to come to your store and shoot the spot. If the store looks really good, if it's nicely decorated and inviting to prospective customers (and, as a matter of good business, it should be), why not? Plus, shooting footage inside your showroom may be a lot easier than hauling a bunch of your products down to a TV station studio — especially if you're selling large, heavy merchandise like the cherry wood bedroom set I mentioned earlier in this chapter.

Focusing the camera on your product

Another option is to cut to the chase and immediately show the products you want to sell with this TV spot. Instead of getting too fancy with long shots of your store or close-ups of yourself, you may be better served by getting right down to business and featuring the items that are going to make you some money.

You can never go wrong by showing an item and price in a retail TV spot. If you're selling power tools, line them up in an attractive display, lay in some computer graphics to show the prices (video keys), and use a voiceover to explain why your store is the only store to sell these power tools so cheap. Nothing too complicated. Just a good, hard-sell spot that will generate some business for you.

If you opt to focus on your product, you can still use voiceover talent to read a script highlighting the important features.

Figuring Out Where to Shoot

When you've purchased a fairly hefty schedule on one of your local TV stations, and you've written a script and outlined the visual elements you want to include, you're ready to go into production. You have two basic options: a location shoot or an in-studio shoot. In the following sections, I outline what you can expect from both options.

On location

If you're going to shoot on location, the first thing you need to do, of course, is to find the location. It could be the interior of your store, or it may be a scenic park or point of interest in your area. I've done location shoots all over Northern California including the local zoo, shopping centers, restaurants, parks, and upscale neighborhoods. The location you choose depends on what you're selling and what kind of place will add something to your commercial.

Shooting at many locations isn't always free and you may have to go through a bit of bureaucratic nonsense in order to shoot there. You will quite likely need signed permission to use certain locations such as public parks and some shopping centers. Many public facilities also charge you a rental fee to use their locations in a commercial. Don't just show up at your local zoo with a video crew and start shooting. This could get you into trouble and end up costing you a lot more money than you would have spent by going through the proper channels. If you're using an independent production company, they will usually take care of these details for you. But don't expect a television station crew to care one way or another.

Where to find great ideas

Some of the best creative talent in the business is handing you their most advanced video production ideas on a silver platter each and every day. Creative ideas on staging, backgrounds, editing, computer graphics, and computer-generated effects are offered up 24-hours a day and you can learn a lot by simply tuning in. Where? How? I'm talking about music videos. Several cable TV channels show nothing but music videos, and if you spend a little time watching them, you will see the cutting edge in video production techniques — techniques and tricks that you can emulate and incorporate into your own video productions.

Some of the industry's best directors, producers, camera people, lighting specialists, sound technicians, and editors are working on music videos. And if you want to add a bit of panache to your commercials, you can watch and learn from the best. Especially observe their editing techniques, how they use different effects when they cut or dissolve from scene to scene, and how they sometimes go from color footage to black and white with wonderful effectiveness. You can make your own retail commercial a thing of beauty if you use some of these state-of-the-art effects in your production. Computers make it not only possible, but also very inexpensive.

Another great place to find new ideas is in the commercials produced for national advertisers — the commercials you see every time you turn on the TV. If you see something that really attracts your attention, some effect or editing trick that jumps out at you, by all means talk to your station creative people about it. Chances are they can help you to incorporate the idea into your spot. Imitation, as they say, is the sincerest form of flattery.

Scout the location for camera positions and backgrounds before your video crew shows up. They'll be charging you by the day, the half-day, or the hour. So don't waste their time (and your money) scouting the location after they arrive — have this all planned in advance. Drive or walk around the park, or whatever locale you've selected, and choose scenes that are attractive and that allow access for the video crew and their van. Keep in mind that the crew comes complete with a van that holds all the electronics, a generator, video monitors, sound equipment, and so on. The van is a self-contained, traveling production facility, and during the shoot it must be very close to the camera, so you'll need to take this into consideration when scouting your location.

The video crew for a location shoot will usually consist of a director, a director of photography (DP) or *shooter* (the cameraperson), a sound technician, and perhaps a couple of grips. *Grips* are responsible for setting up and moving equipment and for holding reflectors to aid the cameraperson in lighting. Interns or some other entry-level people may also be along on the shoot as gophers (as in "go-pher this, and go-pher that"). The crew will arrive in a van at the location you have chosen and spend the first half-hour or so wandering around sipping their coffees or soft drinks. The director (who may be doubling as the shooter) will wander around with you to see where you want to shoot the various scenes. He'll make some mental notes about camera angles and lighting. Whether the star of the commercial is you, or a professional talent you have hired, the talent will be wired with a miniature microphone, a battery pack, and a transmitter, or the sound may be recorded from a distance on a directional mike held by a sound technician. The sound technician in the van will, through his earphones, test all of this gear for clarity. If the shoot has a really big budget, the crew may also include a makeup artist and a hairstylist to make the talent look as good as possible.

The talent will be asked to stand in the first selected scene and the grips will be directed to set up the lights or *reflectors* (aluminum foil–covered panels that are used to direct available sunlight onto the talent). The shooter will set up the camera on a tripod and the grips will anchor it with canvas bags filled with lead shot. The camera will be focused. And you and the director, on the monitors inside the van, can study the view through the lens. The talent's voice level will be given a final test and, when all things are ready, the first scene will be laid down on videotape or film.

If you have selected more than one scene, the entire process will be repeated until the whole spot, scene by scene, has been shot and is, in the vernacular, in the can. Each scene is not necessarily shot in order. You may begin with the final scene and work your way to the beginning — this is the director's call and often depends on the layout of the location you have selected. Each scene will be *slated* — the grip holds a board on which is written the spot name and scene number in front of the camera lens for a moment (that's the black board with a *clapper* you've seen in movies when the director calls, "Action!"). Alternatively, an engineer in the van writes a brief description of each scene and its position on the recorded tape on a sheet of paper. Either way, this is to help the director and video editor identify each scene when it comes time to do the final editing back at the studio.

In the studio

Shooting your commercials in a studio is much less expensive than shooting on location, and it may make a lot of sense if you need to shoot multiple commercials or rotate new spots in on a regular basis. The studio most television stations use for shooting commercials is a very large space with a very high ceiling from which hang rack upon rack of lights. You probably won't see any sharp corners where the walls meet the floor. Instead, this space is gently coved and is called a *cyclorama* (or a *cyc* for short). This smooth edge where the walls meet the floors creates the illusion of infinity, a space with no beginning, no end. The floor is cement and is usually polished. The studio may also contain the news program set — the set you see each time you tune into the station's local news programs.

The production crew consists of the director (a station employee), a cameraman (called the *shooter*), a sound technician, and two grips to handle props, move background scenery, set up camera dollies, and so on. In the studio you have much more latitude with camera setups than you do on location. For instance, the camera can be set on a *dolly,* which is a platform on wheels that runs on tracks. The grips pull the dolly slowly along the tracks as the shooter rides on top of the dolly. The effect is a smooth lateral movement that adds interest to an otherwise static, boring camera setup.

Prior to the shoot, the entire script is transcribed to the teleprompter. The *teleprompter* is a screen that sits just slightly above the camera lens. The talent can then read the copy while appearing to look directly into the camera. Your favorite newscasters, while dramatically shuffling through stacks of paper placed before them on a desk, are actually reading the news stories off of a teleprompter.

Props that will be used in the spot are placed into the scene, the talent takes her place, and a piece of tape is stuck to the floor where the talent will stand. This place is called the *mark.* The teleprompter is manned by one of the grips who rolls the copy up or down in synchronization to the talent's reading speed, the camera is brought to the correct speed, and everyone is ready for the first take.

If you have a well-rehearsed professional doing the read, one take may be all you need, but I've always done five or six takes just for insurance. When you take the tape into the editing suite, you may see something you missed while doing the actual shoot, so it's good to have several backup takes just in case, especially if the talent has gone home and you don't have a chance to shoot another take.

The makeup artist, with her box of magic brushes and powders, usually stands by in the studio ready to touch up any blemishes and to dry off perspiration on the talent caused by the banks of hot lights.

This process is repeated as often as necessary until the director, the producer (that's you — or the producer you've hired), the shooter, and everyone involved are satisfied that the spot is complete, that it's as good as it's going to get, and that it's ready for final editing. The process is very creative every step along the way, and you will have fun doing it — I know *I* do. I've shot hundreds, if not thousands, of retail TV spots and it's a kick each and every time I do it. The people you will work with are experts in their fields and are there to help you. They're a very creative bunch, so listen to their suggestions and follow their directions. Your final product will be that much better because you did.

Producing Your Commercial

When you produce a TV commercial, you can either use the TV station's production department, or you can hire an independent production house to do it for you. I cover both options in the following sections.

Using the TV station's production department

Chances are the TV station from which you are buying a schedule will have a fairly good production department. If for some reason the station does not, you may want to buy your schedule from a different station. You're going to produce a commercial and you may not want to incur the expense of using an independent production house. Even if the station you select doesn't have all the latest electronics bells and whistles, they are probably capable of putting together a good local retail commercial.

How to get free production

The Media Director for my agency has been able to get free production for our retail clients so often that they almost expect it every time. How is this done? Simple. It's called *negotiation*. When we make a substantial buy on a station, we always grind the sales rep and sales manager a bit in order to get the best deal possible. We rarely buy a schedule as it's initially presented. We always look for something extra, whether it be more spots for the same dollars or our spots running in better *dayparts* (time periods) than were initially offered. And the one area where we always try to get something extra is in production. If we buy a hefty airtime schedule, we always ask for a *production credit* so we will be able to cut the cost of producing our commercials. The production credit is money that may or may not cover all the expense of producing commercials, but it will usually make a huge dent in the cost. Most stations cave in to this request if it's the difference between getting the airtime schedule or not.

Quite frankly, production charges from local TV stations aren't that high. As a matter of fact, they're usually quite reasonable and, in the case of my clients, are hardly noticed when added to our monthly invoices. I've never had a client complain that these charges were out of line. But if you can save the cost of production, which we do, and then pass along the savings to our clients, why not ask?

Often, in the case of cable TV stations and some small independent broadcast TV stations, free production of one commercial is offered as part of the schedule — you don't even need to ask. The station can hardly sell you a spot schedule if you don't have a commercial to put on the air, so they'll throw a production session into the deal. They won't bring a lot of enthusiasm or creativity to the event, however, so be sure to stay on top of them when it comes time to actually do the shoot and the editing.

When you sign the contract to buy an airtime schedule, arrange to get a tour of their production facility and make sure you get to meet the two most important players, the two creative-types who will be helping you produce your commercial:

- ✔ **The Retail Production Manager** is the person who oversees all the commercials produced for the retail clients of the station. It is this person's job to arrange studio and editing times; assign and schedule shooting crews for studio and location sessions; arrange for props, studio backdrops, makeup artists, and hairstylists; and assemble all the many pieces that go into a production session. Everyone who works in the production department answers to this person — you want to be very nice to the Retail Production Manager.

- ✔ **The Video Editor** is the person with whom you will ultimately share the dark and claustrophobic confines of the editing suite. It is this person's job to stitch together all the pieces of your commercial — videotape, soundtrack, computer graphics, special effects — into a coherent and concise 30 seconds of brilliance that viewers will actually notice and remember. This person knows which buttons to push to make commercials look wonderful. She overflows with wonderful ideas to make commercials better. This person hasn't seen daylight for years — and she likes it that way.

Hiring an independent production house

For several years, my agency handled the advertising for a chain of women's clothing stores. When it came time to write and produce a series of new TV commercials for this client I immediately decided to employ the talents of an independent production group that had earned a great reputation in the area for shooting commercials on 35-millimeter film and doing so at relatively low prices. No television station's production department would be capable of shooting film (unless they went out and rented the equipment) and, because we were advertising female fashions and were going to shoot a number of models showing the clothes in a variety of locations, I wanted the crispness, clarity, and color quality you can only get by using 35-millimeter film.

By employing an independent production house, we paid a much higher price to produce our commercials, but the final product was so beautifully filmed and professionally edited that it was worth every nickel. This company didn't just send a cameraman to a location and shoot a bunch of film. They handled the permissions required to secure several locations; they interviewed and hired the models; they arranged for the motor home that was used on location as a changing room; they set up catering for lunches on location; they handled the final film-to-video transfer and editing; and they delivered three complete 30-second commercials to us right on schedule and right on budget. All I did as creative director was write the spots . . . and take all the credit.

Tape or film: Hey, it's only money!

Most local retail production is now done on Beta format tape, which is so superior to the VHS variety that your VCR uses that it actually approaches the quality of film. However, 35-millimeter film offers such depth of color, such crispness and clarity, and such precision in its response to lighting that you may consider using it if your product warrants the added expense. If you're going to advertise food, fashions, fine art, or anything else where the color of the product and its presentation are critically important, you may want to opt for film.

Using film adds considerably to the production costs, however, because the film, which is loaded into the camera in large spools and then exposed in take after take, must first be developed (just like your 35-millimeter snapshots), then transferred to videotape for editing. So why would anyone shoot a commercial on film if you're just going to transfer it to tape? Because film images, even though you transfer the images to tape for editing, retain their unique color quality and make the subject matter look true to life.

Be sure you hire a production company that has experience with film (many of them do not). And don't take the company's word for it. Have them show you samples of past work, also called their *reel*.

If you need something extra in the way of production capabilities, something that simply cannot be offered by the production department of your local TV station, find an independent production company. The Retail Production Manager of your local station may be able to point you in the right direction. Or you may find a few possibilities in your local Yellow Pages under "Video Production Services." Avoid the ones that list themselves as wedding specialists or specialists in some other field, because they won't be equipped to handle commercial jobs. Interview them, tell them what you're after, and have them show you their *sample reel* (an example of their work), so you can judge whether they have the skills to create television commercials from initial camerawork through the final editing process. Also, be sure to get a quote in advance. If you're like me, you hate surprises.

Editing Your Commercial

The editing suite is grandly named but it's actually just a small, dark room into which tons of electronic equipment has been jammed. Somewhere behind the video editor, there will be a chair for you, the producer. You will have a good view of all the monitors and be able to control (or at least participate in) all the action.

The video editor, who has edited commercials thousands of times before, will have a copy of your script and will, with nonchalance, assemble all the pieces into a finished 30-second commercial that you can be very proud of. Most importantly, the video editor is there to make you look good (as are the director, the shooter, and all the other people involved with your project). Listen to your editor's suggestions. Watch and learn. Nothing drives an editor crazier than clients who think they know more about the process than the editor does. Video editing is a very technical and precise talent — a talent that takes years to perfect, years of sitting in that claustrophobic, little, dark room pushing buttons and winding tape. So do yourself a favor — give the editor free rein and enjoy the final result.

First, the sound track (the audio) will be inserted into the master file (which will become your final commercial). Then, all the videotape you shot, either on location or in the studio, will, after having been digitized, be brought up on one of the monitors in front of the editor. The editor will roll through the footage and you both will select the takes that will comprise the final commercial. Each selected take is timed and inserted into the master file piece-by-piece until a full 30 seconds have been stitched together into a finished spot. If you want any of the scenes to fly or spin into the commercial, these computer effects will be selected, designed, and inserted. Any computer graphics — prices, product features, important copy points — are then typed by the editor and inserted into the spot, as is a music background (if any) and your logo, which will appear at the end of the commercial along with your phone number, address, directions, or whatever you'd like. If the spot requires a disclaimer of any kind, this too will be typed by the editor and inserted into the spot in the appropriate place. You may help select the fonts, sizes, and colors of the graphics, or at least put in your two cents worth.

When you add up the writing time, the shooting time, and the editing time, even though most of the process is done using the most powerful computers, the entire procedure of producing a 30-second TV commercial can actually take days. But, at the end of the editing session, you will walk out of the editing suite with a finished commercial in the can, ready for air — and ready to entice customers into your business where they will, you hope, spend lots of money. Have fun with it — producing TV commercials can be very exciting!

Chapter 7

Print: Using a Small Space to Catch Your Readers' Eyes

> *It is far easier to write ten passable effective sonnets, good enough to take in the not too inquiring critic, than one effective advertisement that will take in a few thousand of the uncritical buying public.*
>
> — Aldous Huxley

As television becomes more fragmented by the numerous cable channels now available, as radio formats and magazines become more tightly targeted to very narrow audiences, and as consumers have increasingly more media choices, advertisers have a difficult time reaching their entire target audience with a single medium. For this reason, you also need to consider advertising in newspapers, locally published magazines, and the magazine sections of your local newspaper. Print is a tried-and-true vehicle for advertising, and if you use it well, it can work for you, too.

Despite the fact that newspaper readership has been declining steadily for years, papers still have a lot going for them. They cover the entire demographic spectrum, and their flexibility allows you to stretch your advertising budget. You don't need to buy a full-page ad — newspapers will sell you ads in an infinite variety of sizes. By designing small-space ads, you can buy more frequency and more audience, and, in many cases, you can get great position on the page. Nor do you need to run four-color ads (even the large, national advertisers and their ad agencies rarely spend their money for that luxury), because newspapers are, essentially, still a black-and-white medium. 20 years after *USA Today* forever changed the face of newspapers, costly four-color ads are still very rare in most dailies even though four-color process is used in editorial content and news photos all the time.

Another advantage to advertising in newspapers is the fact that they are printed in sections, each one targeted to a particular interest — from Sports to Entertainment to Business. Buying space in the section that has been formatted to reach the greatest number of persons in your primary target audience demographic gives your ads a better chance of being read by your prospective customers, which, in turn, helps you spend your budget more effectively. Newspapers are the pickup trucks of advertising — solid, sturdy, no-nonsense, and unglamorous — but they get the job done.

Print advertising isn't limited to newspapers, though. Your local newspaper may also include a locally focused magazine section. If you live in a large metropolitan area, several locally published special-interest magazines will be happy to sell you ads. You can also buy ad space in regional editions of major magazines, such as *Sports Illustrated, U.S. News and World Report,* and *Time,* which, although still a bit pricey, are often affordable (and always prestigious) to the local advertiser. Finally, the community papers, college papers, entertainment guides, classified advertising papers, auto-seller papers, and countless other advertising media are options you may want to consider (although some of these publications make better fish wrap than advertising vehicles, so be careful).

Your print-buying options are many and varied, but in this chapter, I focus primarily on newspaper advertising. The good news is that the formula for designing and writing an effective print ad remain the same across the board, so if you decide to use your print ad in a medium other than newspaper, you'll be able to use this information just as well.

Knowing What Makes a Print Ad Successful

Advertising legend David Ogilvy was famous for writing print ads that contained literally thousands of words. He assumed a certain intelligence and curiosity in his readers, and he gave them an incredible volume of facts about the various products he was selling. But that was in a different, less hectic time. Ogilvy's approach probably won't work in this day and age, when the average adult encounters more than 3,000 ad messages every day. In my opinion, today, brevity is the soul of print.

In addition to copious amounts of *white space* (white background without any graphics or type, like the margins on this page), an effective print ad must include three main elements: a strong headline, brief sell copy, and an arresting graphic. Anything else, other than your logo, is clutter, and the average person just doesn't have the time to sift through it.

Some advertisers design *reverse ads* (a black background with white letters) in their effort to attract the readers' attention. But I don't think this technique works any better than a nicely designed, clean ad with lots of white background.

Most print ads are so muddled with copy, headlines, subheads, banners, graphics, prices, and logos that the reader's eye moves right past the ads because deciphering what the heck the ad is trying to sell is nearly impossible. The ads are such a blur that they appear to be in motion! It's as if the advertisers, who spend a lot of money for the ads, want to squeeze as much information as possible into the space to get their money's worth. Unfortunately, a page filled with confusing, poorly designed ads is a page to quickly turn, and that's exactly what the readers do.

The ads that grab your audience's attention, the ones that make an impact and have a chance of being read, are the ones that are attractively designed and invite your audience to stop for a moment. Good ads are uncluttered and have clever headlines and interesting graphic elements — they're reader-friendly.

On the other hand, *some* cluttered ads can still be attractively designed to make them easy to read and simple to grasp. If your business has multiple locations, extensive inventory, or numerous products for example, you may *need* to include a lot of information in your ad. My wireless client uses newspaper to advertise certain cellular offers. These offers can be very complicated, requiring extensive explanation and disclaimers. He also has dozens of store locations that must be included in his print ads. But his ads (which are designed by Pulse Media, a very talented local graphic design firm) never appear cluttered, even though they are rarely larger than 4 columns wide by 12 inches high. Even with all the elements he has to include in his ads, his ads still have ample room for white space. This is a testament to thoughtful, clean design — something you, too, should strive for.

Figure 7-1 gives you a look at a cluttered print ad that works. It could be surrounded with other ads and *still* jump off the page. The ad was produced to offer a free roadside emergency kit with every new wireless service activation, hence the headline "Road Show." It could easily have been a hodgepodge of clutter, because the ad contains so much information. But instead, it's clean and easy to understand, even though it contains the following elements:

Figure 7-1:
A sample
print ad that
successfully
gives the
reader a
great deal of
information.

- Three photos
- The offer of a free wireless phone
- A better wireless phone for $99.95
- A deal on a pager for $49.95
- A free roadside emergency kit
- A headline
- A subhead
- The retailer's logo
- The airtime provider's logo
- 16 separate store locations
- A 60-word disclaimer

So what keeps this ad from appearing cluttered? The ad uses bold graphic elements and typography and, most importantly, the generous use of white space. The first things the eye sees are the pictures of the free phone and emergency kit, then the headline ("Road Show"). Those elements are the foundation of the ad and the primary hooks to attract new customers.

If you must include multiple products and numerous complicated elements in your print ads, you can still create a crisp, uncluttered look by paying careful attention to the design and layout. Leave ample white space in your ad — it will pay off with increased readership. Don't fill every square inch.

Writing and Designing an Eye-Catching Print Ad

Newspaper and magazine readers (your prospective customers) don't care nearly as much about your business as you do. As a matter of fact, they don't care about your business at all. So for this reason, your ads must be clear, succinct, informative, and inviting. Your ads need to give readers a reason to be interested in your business. They cannot be pompous and assume, through complicated copy or confusing graphics, that the readers understand everything there is to know about your business and the products or services you are selling. In fact, your print ad will have just a split second to attract attention and quickly explain why your product or service will have some lasting benefit to those who read about it.

Getting the help you need

The artists who work in the retail design and layout department of your local paper are probably overworked, underpaid, and not always diligent in their efforts. But they *are* capable of doing good work if you insist upon it (if they didn't have talent they wouldn't have been hired by the publication in the first place). Ask for their help, and don't accept an ad that you feel could have been done much better.

Remember: Don't be adversarial in your dealings with the newspaper staff, but do let them know that you have definite ideas on what a good ad layout is. These artists, like anyone else, would rather do work they can be proud of.

When you sit down to write a print ad, keep in mind that those who read it aren't going to spend a lot of time doing so. Plus, your ad, especially a newspaper ad, will very likely share a page with many other ads, each of which is vying for the reader's attention. And you will probably have no control over the page on which your ad is inserted or the position of your ad on that page. Brevity of copy and cleanliness of design are the soul of print, and to achieve the best possible retail ad you must give careful attention to the basic elements of a good print ad. In the following sections, I cover each of these elements so you can use them effectively.

The headline

In nearly all cases, the headline is the single most important element of a print ad. The headline has no more than a split second to grab the reader's attention. It is often the largest element on an ad, is generally placed at the top of the ad, and is the first thing — sometimes the only thing — a reader sees. Research tells us that 90 percent of body copy goes unread, so your headline had better be good. If the headline is clever, informative, and inviting, it can stop the reader dead in his tracks. If the headline is long, drawn out, and boring (or if it doesn't even exist), the reader will skip right past your ad without giving a moment's thought to all the money you spent putting it there.

The headline is worth some extra work on your part because it may be the only element of your ad that anyone reads. When I write a print ad, I probably spend 90 percent of my time devising the headline. When the light bulb finally goes on and I'm satisfied that the headline is as good as it can be, the body copy falls quickly into place. And if the headline is well written and descriptive enough, it can either stand alone, or will pull the reader's eye to the body copy (the copy that sells the product).

Your headline will usually work together with your graphic element, and vice versa — the headline and graphics usually go hand-in-hand. The *head* (that's ad speak for *headline*) and the graphic, whether it is a photo or a drawing, set the tone of the ad and should be able to stand alone, whether or not anyone gets around to reading the body copy. The head and graphic must create the uniqueness of your ad, the extra something that separates you from all your rivals who are advertising in the same print media.

Often, an ad will consist of nothing more than a headline, a subhead, and a logo. An ad for a clothing store may have a headline that reads, "ONE DAY ONLY SALE!" and a subhead that reads, "Hurry! All suits, sports jackets, and slacks reduced 50 percent this Saturday only." Add the store logo, the address, and a phone number, and the ad is complete — it contains all the information the reader needs.

Where the headline is placed within the ad is as important as what the headline says. You need to make sure the headline dominates the ad so it can be quickly understood. Too often, the headline, which includes the most important information within an ad, is lost in a muddle of too many type fonts, graphics, and other elements. The reader's eye isn't drawn to anything, the ad is ignored, and the advertiser's money goes down the drain.

The graphics

Whether it's photography, fine art, line art, cartoon, or typography, the graphic element of your ad is there to attract the reader's eyes and interest her enough to read your body copy. Your graphic, together with your headline, is there to encourage the reader to invest a little time to actually absorb what it is you're trying to sell. The graphic element will usually call attention to, or complement, the headline — the two elements work together to create the overall ambience of the ad.

Make sure your graphic element is relevant to what you're selling. A photo of a girl in a bikini isn't the best way to sell anything except bikinis. Health and fitness spas are always using bathing suit babes as their central graphic. (Are some men really dumb enough to believe that those women are actually members?)

If your ad is for a straightforward, no-holds-barred, clearance sale, your graphic element may be nothing more than a very large headline spelled out in a bold, readable typeface that says, "Get In Here!" If, on the other hand, your ad is meant to announce a new product, then a quality photo or drawing of that product, along with a subtle headline, should do nicely.

Newspapers can sometimes mangle a good photograph in the printing process — and unless you're paying big bucks, the graphics will probably be black and white. To reproduce black-and-white photos, most newspapers use a 65-line screen in their printing process. This means that, if you look very closely, you will see 65 tiny dots to an inch within the photo. Conversely, magazines may use a 300-line screen (or finer). The difference in quality between 65– and 300-line screens is astounding. When a 65-line screen photo is reproduced in a newspaper, it always runs the risk of appearing too dark, too light, or too cloudy (especially if one of the pressmen has neglected to re-ink the rollers). Newspapers do strive for good quality in their printing process, but to avoid frustration and irate clients I usually avoid using photos in newspaper ads. A black-and-white line drawing will usually reproduce much better.

Lines, shapes, borders, symbols, and clip art are available to you inside your computer right alongside a zillion different type fonts. You shouldn't have any trouble creating a good print ad complete with a clever headline and an arresting graphic by using nothing more than your word processing program. Of course, if you aren't all that comfortable with a computer (hey, I still use Wite-Out on the screen), employing the services of a good graphic designer may be a better way to go. Hiring a professional to do a professional's job, regardless of what the job is, always pays in the long run. But whether you're able to hire a pro depends on your budget. The newspaper in which you are advertising can also provide you with design help. If you feel comfortable with their abilities, you may want to just let the newspaper's design department handle the whole enterprise of producing your ad. This is called *pub set* (which means the *pub*lication *set*s the ad), and it's usually free. Keep in mind that, as with anything in life, you get what you pay for.

The subheads

A subhead is used to impart secondary information. The headline should grab them, but the subhead can explain the deal further. Keep your headline brief and clever, and use the subhead to be a bit more expansive with your information. If you're selling a product, the headline may read, "The Deal of the Century!" The subhead could then read, "We're having a store-wide clearance sale." If you're selling a service, the headline could read, "Don't Pay Your Taxes!" The subhead could read, "Until you talk with Smith Accountancy."

Not all ads require a subhead, but this element, generally set in smaller type, is there to give the reader additional information without cluttering up your ad.

The body copy

The body copy, also known as the *sell copy,* is where you can explain your offer in detail. But, as with everything else in a good print ad, you need to keep the body copy brief — and possibly not include it at all. A good ad can get by without body copy, using just a well-written headline and a solid subhead.

Don't expect rapt attention and deep involvement from the reader. (***Remember:*** 90 percent of the time, body copy goes unread.) The reader doesn't have time to sift through mounds of information in order to find a reason to respond. Squeezing 50 pounds of copy into a 1-pound ad is a mistake. When writing body copy for a print ad, regardless of the size of the ad, invoking the KISS Rule — Keep it simple, stupid — is a good idea.

The layout

The design and layout of an ad is everything. Print ads are often very poorly designed. These ads are easily ignored because they don't attract the eye to any particular feature or element, and they certainly don't sell anybody anything. Figure 7-2 illustrates a sample layout for a print ad. If you stick to this kind of layout, you can't go wrong.

It's an ad, not an encyclopedia

The primary mistake made in many retail print ads is verbosity. The philosophy seems to be, why use 5 words when 500 words will do? Readers aren't interested in how to *make* a fine Swiss watch. They're only interested in how much money they can save if they buy the watch from you.

A brief headline is particularly important. A headline reading, "50 PERCENT SAVINGS" is better than one reading, "Everything storewide has been marked down 50 percent." Making your headline brief, intriguing, and easy to grasp will, most certainly, enhance your ad's effectiveness. Trying to fit too much information into the headline will be self-defeating. Use the subhead or the body copy for the nuts and bolts of your sales pitch.

Keep your body copy brief and your graphic elements relevant and bold. That way, you'll make it easy for your readers to grasp what you're trying to say and what you're striving to sell. Just because you've spent a fair amount of money to buy the ad space doesn't mean you have to fill it wall-to-wall. An ad that's easy for the reader to understand may be rewarded with the reader dropping into your store, credit card poised and at the ready!

Do what I do: Write your ad, then go back and see how many superfluous words you can eliminate until your copy is as tight as it can possibly be. In print copy, less is more!

A good print ad will include:

A CLEVER HEADLINE

(an interesting graphic)

POSSIBLY A SUBHEAD WHICH WILL EXPLAIN THE DEAL IN MORE DETAIL

A brief amount of body copy (a.k.a. sell copy) which will quickly give readers all the information they need to know about your store and what you are selling. Do not assume too much reader involvement here, you won't get it — be clear, concise and succinct.

Your logo here

Address, phone, web site, etc.
All major credit cards accepted
Whatever

Figure 7-2:
Layout is an all-important part of your print ad's success.

Image is everything

A clean, well-designed, and orderly print ad can go a long way in telling readers that your business is also clean, well-designed, and orderly. By making your point in clear, concise terms, you're doing the readers a favor. They can see at a glance whether you're selling something they need. You haven't taken much of their time, and they'll appreciate that.

Whether you're buying a full-page ad or a one-column two-inch, your ad must focus the reader's eyes on the most relevant information as quickly as possible. Every other ad in the publication is competing for the reader's attention. Your ad may even be stacked atop the ad of your direct competitor (if it is, get the newspaper to give you a *make good,* in which you get another ad free of charge). Give yourself a chance by designing and writing a superior ad that cuts through all the clutter and gives the reader a reason to stop for a moment.

You can do good print advertisement designs using various computer art programs. But if you're not sure whether you're the best person to handle the layout of your ad, hire a professional to do it for you. The extra money spent will come back to you in the form of increased readership and customer response. If you are using the publication's design department, stay on top of them until they bring you an ad layout that adheres to all the perquisites in this chapter. Don't hesitate to insist on good design, even though you're getting it for free. To find freelance professional designers you can look in your local Yellow Pages under "Graphic Designers" or "Graphic Services." Another possibility would be to ask some of your local printers for references. Printers and graphic designers go hand-in-hand (but not while anyone's looking).

Chapter 8

Collateral: Creating Brochures, Direct Mailers, and More

In This Chapter

▶ Keeping your design and copy simple and clear

▶ Taking into account your budget

▶ Designing your ad on your own or with the help of a pro

▶ Working with a printer

▶ Using a direct-mail house with top-notch mailing lists

Your manuscript is both good and original; but the part that is good is not original, and the part that is original is not good.

— Samuel Johnson

*W*hoever wrote the old adage "You never get a second chance to make a good first impression" could easily have been thinking about the writing and designing of business collateral materials. *Collateral materials* are the brochures, mailers, flyers, and newsletters you produce for your business, all of which make an impression upon your customers. Whether the impression is a good one resulting in increased business, or a bad or ambivalent one that ends up being a gigantic waste of your money, is entirely up to you. As with all advertising materials, the creative ideas and production values you put to use in your collateral materials will make the difference between success and failure. Do it right and you'll reap the rewards. Do it wrong, as so many businesses do, and you'll wish you'd saved your money.

A sizeable portion of the 3,000 advertising messages each of us is exposed to on a daily basis comes in the form of collateral materials. You open your mailbox every day and find a fresh pile of brochures, catalogs, newsletters, direct mail pieces, flyers, and all sorts of fish wrap. Why do you read some of it and throw the rest away? If you're like most people, you're more likely to pay attention to the materials that are provocative, with a clean design. And if the piece is easy to read and simple to navigate, all the better. But the run-of-the-mill stuff, the direct mailers and postcards that don't display the slightest creativity, that don't instantly give you a reason to open and read them, go out with yesterday's newspaper.

Just as with broadcast commercials or print ads, the collateral material you use as part of your overall advertising strategy must make an instant impression upon the recipient — a positive impact that will compel the consumer to open, read, and respond. Writing and designing these materials isn't any big mystery. The same elements you strive for in other media are ones you should strive for in this media as well: an interesting design; clear, concise copy; the promise of something to benefit the consumer; and a call to action. What your brochure says is as important as how it looks. And how it looks — what it does through headline, color, design, and layout to quickly interest the recipient — is where you have to start. A brochure, direct mailer, or flyer is no different than any other advertising effort — it must do its job instantly, because the consumer really doesn't care. Throwing out collateral advertising is a lot easier than reading it, so you need to hit those people right between the eyes, so to speak, and grab their attention.

Striving for a Simple Design and Clear Copy

You have a message you want to communicate. The consumer is bombarded by thousands of advertising messages everyday. So how do you accomplish the former in spite of the latter? Through the simple, interesting design and clear message that are essential to a good collateral piece.

When you're designing a collateral piece, include only those elements that are essential to your message, and avoid the temptation to incorporate too much information. Think about whether a particular graphic element focuses your readers' attention, or whether it only confuses them. If you've included something in your collateral advertising that is pure ornamentation and is, in fact, a distraction, toss it out and start again.

You can't expect much involvement from the reader of your brochure — actually, you can't expect *any* involvement, only a cursory glance at best. So the simpler your message, the better.

Paying attention to what *you* read

A good place to start when deciding on a collateral ad design for your business is to ask yourself, "Why do I read some of the collateral advertising I receive, and why do I toss the rest?" What is it about the design and layout, or the written promise, of some pieces that grabs your attention, even compels you to respond? If you can answer this question, you're on your way to designing your own successful piece, because the design and copy elements that work on you may also work on your customers.

If you find a brochure that you really like, save it. As a matter of fact, collect all the ones you like and make a file. I'm not suggesting you plagiarize these collateral pieces, but they can be a great source of inspiration. I have a client who has saved nearly every direct mail piece, in-store promotional piece, brochure, pamphlet, and flyer he's come in contact with for decades. The guy uses direct mail on a regular basis and always needs new ideas. He keeps huge scrapbooks of this stuff to use as references when he's preparing his own collateral pieces. He doesn't copy them verbatim; he uses them to jumpstart his own imagination.

If you can train yourself to do some subjective analysis of the design and copy of brochures and pamphlets that appeal to you, you can then put this newfound design sense to work in your own advertising.

Jazz man extraordinaire, Count Basie, whose musical style was completely unique, was famous for his minimalist piano playing and, as jazz aficionados have observed, "the notes he *didn't* hit." His band would be wailing on an upbeat jazz tune at full speed and a thousand decibels and, when it was Basie's turn, he would reach over the keyboard and casually hit one note. *Plink!* Count Basie's piano-playing style was *audible white space*. And white space is what you should strive for when designing collateral materials. You don't need to fill every square inch of the page just because the page itself is going to cost you money.

Write an eye-stopping headline and brief, succinct body copy. Don't confuse the reader with a long-winded explanation of how to build a watch; just tell him, in plain English, why he should buy the watch from you. The difference between having your piece read or having it tossed into the garbage is the split second it takes for the recipient to be either intrigued or bored.

Working within Your Budget

If you keep your design simple and your message clear (as I discuss in the preceding section), you'll go a long way toward keeping your collateral advertising affordable. The more elaborate the piece, the costlier it will be. So you need to ask yourself, "What can I afford?" And then stick to that budget. If you get carried away designing something that, in the final analysis, has a printing cost of $5 a unit and you can only afford $1 a unit, you'll probably have to go back to the old drawing board.

Printing is not cheap — never was, never will be. And the number of pages, colors, photos, die-cuts, and clever folds you design into your piece will be in direct proportion to your blood pressure when you get an estimate on the cost of printing.

When cost was no object

My agency once did a direct-mail piece for an Aston-Martin auto dealer. Now, the Aston-Martin automobile is most certainly not for everyone — at $175,000 and up, it's probably not for more than a few people in the entire country. This dealer wanted to pull out all the stops and do a very classy mailing to a list of people earning at least $250,000 per year. As a creative director, it was an irresistible challenge. And the lack of budgetary restrictions was the icing on the cake.

Because James Bond sometimes drives an Aston-Martin (when he's not driving a submersible, torpedo-firing, machine gun-mounted, smoke-screen generating Lotus Europa down the Amazon River), I decided to use a Secret Agent theme in the mailing piece. The printed material included astonishing photos of the cars, which were supplied to us by the factory in England; brief descriptive copy; and the dealer's logo, address, and phone number. The paper I chose had a high-gloss finish and a substantial weight, and the whole thing was printed with a black background and various colors of lettering. It was, if I may say so myself, a gorgeous piece of direct mail.

The kicker of this brochure, however, was the audiocassette inside a clear plastic case glued into each piece. The cassette, produced complete with James Bond–type music and sound

effects, was acted by a man with the deepest, most dramatic voice in the universe, who explained that if the car was good enough for secret agents, then it was certainly good enough for the likes of the recipients of the piece. It had a rich-guy appeal. The copy said things like, "Now that you've arrived, arrive in an Aston-Martin."

The whole package was then inserted into a white cardboard shipper on which the (imaginary) logo of Her Majesty's British Secret Service was printed as a return address. Mail from MI-5? Who could resist opening a thing like that?

The printing and hand assembly of the piece came to a heartstopping $25 per unit. The postage and mailing service brought each piece to $30. We printed and mailed 1,000 units. We sold two cars, the profit on which just barely covered the multi-thousand dollar tab for the production.

The lesson here is that *grander* isn't always *better* when it comes to direct mail collateral pieces. Because we only broke even we may have been better served by printing a more modest direct mail piece and spending the money we saved on a highly targeted radio or TV campaign.

You can get away with producing a very nice and relatively inexpensive piece in just one color: black. If what you're saying is strong, and if what you're showing is interesting, then black ink on a white background may do the job nicely. For example, I receive postcard-size mailers on a weekly basis from local real estate agents showing off their listings. They include a photo of the house, a brief description, the asking price, and a photo of the agent. These pieces of collateral advertising are well-designed with easy-to-understand copy and, if I were in the market for a new home, they would be quite effective in arousing my interest. They're all printed on glossy card stock in black and white. Nothing could be simpler — and the costs are relatively low, too.

If you add just one color to your collateral advertising, you may add a few more zeros to your printing costs. Add two or three more colors and you may be in for a serious dose of sticker shock. Paper costs alone have skyrocketed over the years, and printers have never been embarrassed about charging a lot of money for their work. Be sure you know what you're getting yourself into before you design something so elaborate that you can't afford it.

Surveying Your Collateral Advertising Options

Collateral advertising has numerous purposes — and the different kinds of collateral advertising at your disposal are numerous as well. If you create a brochure, you can leave it behind with prospective clients at the end of a sales presentation; you can keep a stack on the counter at your store; you can send them as direct mail; and you can send them out to people who request more information on your business. You can prepare a one-sheet tri-folded flyer that can be mailed to targeted lists of prospective clients. You can devise a postcard-type piece to be sent to current customers to announce an upcoming sale, perhaps including a perforated coupon or return card good for a preferred-customer discount. Or you can throw caution to the wind and create a full-blown, full-color sales piece that simply oozes your personal confidence in the stylishness and good taste of your customers.

Whatever you're trying to accomplish, a collateral piece, in one or more of its many forms, will do the job. How *well* it does the job is up to you.

Even though collateral advertising should be stand-alone advertising vehicles and must contain selling points and a call to action, they hardly ever make a sale on their own. Instead, they're an integral piece of the overall advertising puzzle. A glossy, well-designed collateral piece can say a lot about your business (for example, that you're a classy place filled with classy products), and, if it's done right, it can play on the emotions of your customers and generate increased sales.

First Things First: Planning Your Collateral Campaign

As with any form of advertising, when it comes to collateral, you need to plan your work and then work your plan. Invest your time and effort into the planning of your collateral advertising — plan it as carefully as you would any important endeavor. The amount of time you put into the planning stage will be the best investment you can make toward the ultimate effectiveness of the piece. Don't just toss together a bunch of words, prices, pictures, and *Hurry on downs*, and hope for the best. It doesn't work that way.

Before you sit down to create a piece of collateral advertising, plan by doing the following:

- ✔ **Define the purpose for the ad.** Are you trying to reach new customers or to inform existing customers?

- ✔ **Determine what you can do within your budget constraints.** Rough out a design and get estimates from printers so you can figure out what you can afford.

- ✔ **Organize your message and crystallize your design.** Don't expect much involvement from the recipient. Make your design and copy clear, informative, and, above all, brief.

- ✔ **Write and rewrite your headline and copy until it's as concise as it can be.** Make sure there are no extraneous words in your headline; make sure it has *sell*.

- ✔ **Toss out any superfluous elements from your ad that will only distract from your message.** Be as objective as possible when tightening your design and copy. Include only those elements that are absolutely necessary to getting your message across.

- ✔ **Do sketches and rearrange the elements until the design is a good as it can be.** Don't just toss your various elements together helter-skelter. Be thoughtful in your design. Make it attractive and easy to grasp.

- ✔ **Make sure your copy and content flow in a logical sequence.** Don't be pompous, ponderous, and boring with too much copy or irrelevant information. Your target audience doesn't have time for it.

- ✔ **Be objective.** Is the piece reader-friendly? Does it quickly communicate a benefit? Would you read it if you found it in your mailbox?

If you write and design your brochure sequentially, if you take it one step at a time and make sure each step is completed with precision, then your finished piece will stand a good chance of success.

Knowing What to Include in Your Ad

Whether you are preparing an elaborate multi-page, multi-color collateral piece such as a company overview or annual report, or a simple black-and-white postcard destined to be mailed to a preferred customer list, the rules are the same:

- ✔ Keep it attractive, relevant, simple, and, above all, reader friendly.

- ✔ Don't expect the recipients to give it much time (they're on the receiving end of tons of this stuff just like you are).

- ✔ Use interesting graphics and a provocative headline to interest them enough to at least give the piece a fighting chance at being opened and read.

In the following sections, I outline the various elements of a good collateral piece and show you how to make each element help to deliver your all-important sales message.

Putting the important copy points at the top

When you're organizing the words (or copy) that will go into your ad, imagine a stepladder. Put your most important copy points on the top step, the next most important points on the next step down, and so forth. Make a list of the various components that you want to include in your brochure, ranking the elements from the most important to the least. Then feature the most significant points more boldly in order to make an instant impact on the reader. If you're creating a piece announcing a sale or other special event, get right to the point and make the line at the very top of your ad say what's most important: "Sale!" Don't get cute and make the first thing the reader sees something like, "Due to continued customer demand. . . ."

Don't be reluctant to throw out unnecessary copy the brochure can live without. Pare down your list of copy points to the bare-bones selling message. Get rid of the superfluous, and concentrate on the important. The less work you create for the recipient the better. Make it easy for consumers to instantly grasp your message.

Choosing the right typeface

Use a typeface that best expresses the tone of your brochure. If the piece is meant to be humorous and whimsical, find a typeface that expresses that. Look at the different fonts in your computer word processing program (like

Microsoft Word), and see what options you have. If your piece is serious, like an announcement of a presale open house for your preferred customers, choose a typeface that's dignified and solid. And if you're sending out a mailer to announce a big sale, use a typeface that is big, bold, and direct.

Don't use more than two or three different typefaces in your collateral advertising. Numerous typefaces tend to confuse and distract the reader's eye rather than focus it. Also, where possible, avoid underlines, boldfaces, italics, outlines, borders, stars, bars, and any other visual distractions. These cutesy elements only add clutter and distract your readers from your message.

Including graphic elements

Your graphic choices are many and varied — everything from photographs to full-color drawings, black-and-white line art to a clever typeface treatment. Choose the graphic element that best conveys the essence of what you're trying to sell, and what you're attempting to accomplish with the printed piece you're creating.

If you're showing a particular product that is now on sale, then a photograph (either one supplied by the manufacturer or shot by a local photographer) may be the way to go. Show the item, give the price or the call to action (for example, "This dress marked down 50 percent this weekend only"), and make sure these elements jump off the page quickly.

Use graphics if they add to the *sell* of the piece. Don't include graphics purely as design elements if they will just distract from the message. Don't clutter your design with multiple graphics images unless each of them has some relevance to the piece. The biggest mistake made by retail advertisers is trying to fit too much information into a single ad. Jamming too much information into a single piece only confuses the reader.

Considering color

Multiple colors increase your printing costs. And, although color does add interest and impact, it's not always necessary. Many effective brochures and mailers are done in black and white. The message and design is what will make or break your sales piece, not the addition of several colors. You can also print one color on a contrasting color paper. Printing papers come in nearly infinite variety and colors. A nice shade of blue ink on a cream colored paper may work as well as four-color process on white paper if your message and design are well-planned and executed.

On the other hand, certain brochures simply cry out for four-color process. If you're selling something — food, clothing, fine art — that must be shown in all its multicolored glory, then you'll want to go the full-color route. A prospective customer would have trouble picturing the beauty of a painting, for instance, if your sales piece were done only in black and white.

Making paper choices

Printing papers come in numerous colors, textures, weights, and finishes. Coated paper (which is usually slick and glossy) will give more depth and brilliance to your piece, and will reproduce photographs much better, even if it's only printed with black ink. Soft-finish, textured papers are perfect for a classy brochure such as an annual report, or for letterheads and cards that require a solid business image. You can also save a tree by using recycled paper (and then tell the world about it in little, tiny type inside your brochure), but keep in mind that some recycled papers cost more.

The different *weights* (thickness and heft) of paper give you multiple choices when you produce collateral. You can use heavy weights for postcards and brochure covers, light weights for mailers stuffed into envelopes, and so on. Paper samples come in small demonstration packets prepared by numerous paper companies. Your printer will trot out paper samples until you're cross-eyed with confusion, and then he'll haul out a bunch more. You may want to find out which papers are available to you before you get too far in your brochure design. Paper is an integral part of the brochure design equation. A paper with a rich appearance and feel will add greatly to the ambience of your finished piece. Your printer can help you make your choice.

Getting Help with the Design

It could safely be said that anyone can design a brochure. You could design one. I could design one. Even your kid — the one who shows great aptitude for drawing lovely pictures or coloring within the lines — could design one. But, why send out a piece that looks amateurish and a bit rough around the edges when you can create something to be proud of with just a little advanced planning and careful thought? A collateral piece, whatever form it takes, is a reflection on you and on the quality of your business. It's worth some time and effort. I have always hired professional talent to do the jobs that I am either incapable of doing or don't have the time to do right, and I think that's good advice for you to heed as well. In the following sections, I cover the various ways you can create a quality collateral piece. The process involves much more than just smearing some ink on paper.

Some cautions on buying art and printing

If you're working with a graphic designer, she will quite likely have a good idea of the look and feel of your finished printed piece, and she will also have some definite thoughts as to which printer she would like you to use. Ask your designer to provide you with an official Request for Estimate form, including all the specifications of your printing job. Important information includes:

✔ **Quantity:** The number of pieces to be printed

✔ **Flat size:** The size before folding

✔ **Finished size:** The size after folding

✔ **Stock:** What quality and color paper the job is to be printed on

✔ **Ink colors:** Which colors will be used

✔ **Screens:** The degrees of color

✔ **Half-tones or color separations:** The number of photos

After your designer gives you this completed form, you can then send it to a few reputable printers via fax or e-mail. With all the job's specs clearly defined on the form, and after determining the number of pieces you will need, you can now ask for printing quotes. Then you can further negotiate with the printers after you receive back all the quotes. Some printers may substitute a particular paper your artist has called for with a house stock (papers they keep on hand) in order to offer you the lowest price possible. Confer with your artist regarding any variances found on the estimate forms.

Using design software you may already own

Some very good collateral material design templates are available to you on various software programs, and you may already have them on your computer. For example, Microsoft Publisher has a huge variety of templates for brochures, mailers, postcards, greeting cards, letterheads, and so on. Software programs also include step-by-step tutorials that are supposed to transform the design klutz into the design pro. Even if you have no experience in design, software can be of enormous value. Think of software as sort of a high-tech paint-by-numbers set. You're given multiple choices at every step along the way (cover art, photos, backgrounds, colors, layouts, type fonts, folds), and you end up with a mailer, brochure, or other item of business collateral. You can also use these design programs for helping you create print advertisements and signage.

One caution here: By using these built-in computer design programs you run the risk of creating something that may have been done by another company, perhaps even one of your competitors. The choices on these programs may look endless, but they have a similar look and feel, and, for the most part, they're not very original.

When you're finished designing the ad, save your final draft to a disk in the specific file program requested by your printer. Then hand the disk to your printer, tell him how many copies you want, and take the rest of the day off.

Hiring a pro to do the design work for you

The best way to get the best possible design is, in most cases, to hire a professional graphic artist to handle these chores for you. A professional designer will help you with the creation of the piece and also assist you in making the many printing decisions required — all in all, a good investment. Graphic designers cost money, but not nearly as much money as a few thousand poorly conceived, badly designed mailing pieces that no one bothers to read.

Your printer can likely recommend talented graphic designers in your area, and you can also look in your good old Yellow Pages under "Graphic Designers." In my local Bay Area phone book this list is seven pages long! Call one or more of them, invite them to your business, and ask each of them to bring their *book* (a collection of the designer's work samples). A quick scan of the designer's work will help you choose the right person for your particular job.

Ask for a copy of the terms and conditions from your designer. Make certain you have a complete understanding of ownership and what is financially expected of you in order to receive your final artwork and your final printed pieces. Some designers will expect to be paid again if their artwork is used to create more than one piece, or if you reuse their artwork to print the piece again at a later date. Negotiating and agreeing upon a flat *buy out* (where you own all rights to the finished artwork) is best. That way, should you choose to reuse the artwork at a later date, you won't incur additional charges.

Finding a Printer

If you live in a large metropolitan area, you're able to choose from many different printers. Quick-print specialists, who are very good at producing small jobs where cost is more important than quality. Large printing firms who have presses that cover a square block — they're capable of doing the most exquisite work if you have the budget for it. Other printers who specialize in small to mid-size jobs such as letterheads, envelopes, and business cards — they're also qualified to do brochures, flyers, mailers, and the like.

I use one local printer for my company newsletters, corporate image items, and one– or two-color mailers. Located in a small strip mall, this printer does great work and charges a very reasonable price for smaller jobs. But for full-color, multi-page extravaganzas, I go to a large firm that has a huge press and the binding capability (collating and stapling the pages together) that is required when producing large brochure jobs.

Digital printers: When you have the need for speed

Digital printing is printing a finished product directly from a computer disk or a CD. The process has evolved over the past decade or so into a viable option to offset printing. Some advantages of digital printing include the following:

✔ **It doesn't require paste-ups (hand assembled, full-size facsimiles containing all the elements of your finished brochure) or film (a picture of your final paste up).**

✔ **There is a quicker turnaround time.** Everything is digital and can be done quickly.

✔ **The printer can afford to be more forgiving in his charges for any last-minute changes because the changes can be made so easily.**

✔ **Short runs (a relatively small number of finished pieces) are more affordable.**

✔ **The ads can be printed on any paper stock.**

✔ **You can merge the ad with a mailing list to print addresses directly onto the pieces.** Your computerized mailing list is fed into the press and each address is imprinted on the individual mailing pieces as they run through the press. This process eliminates the need for later affixing mailing labels to each printed piece and saves money at the mailing house.

Digital printing has become crucial to businesses that may want to test the waters with a particular brochure without printing zillions of copies and spending huge amounts of money. Last-minute digital printing of jobs such as trade show flyers, price lists, and pamphlets has bailed out many a company with the need for speedy, last-minute collateral pieces or multiple copies of a new press release. Turnaround time for the average digital printing job is measured in days, not weeks, and they can sometimes be done in 24 hours.

Quick print jobs usually cost a few cents per copy. The major-league brochure jobs cost a few dollars a copy. And the per-unit cost goes down the more items you print. Printing 5,000 units is often more economical than printing just 1,000.

If you only need 1,000 copies for a particular mailing, you can save money in the long run by printing 5,000 and then, at a later date, imprinting the additional pieces with information relevant to a future sale or announcement. With advance planning, you can save a lot of money on printing costs. I have a client who does regular mailings to his list of current customers — about 2,500 people. We generally print 10,000 pieces, which are designed with space for updated copy that will be printed in one color later. By printing 10,000 units the first time around, then sending the brochure with updated copy and a new sales message in four separate mailings, this client saves a ton of money on printing bills.

Ask your fellow merchants which printers they use, thumb through the Yellow Pages, or let your graphic designer advise you. Although printing services are everywhere, good printers are a little more rare. Plus, the good printers are busy, so allow yourself some lead time. Don't wait until the last minute to hire a printer. They're used to working on tight deadlines (the buck always stops with the printer), but a quality job takes time.

Printing prices will vary widely according to the capabilities and equipment of each printer. Most printers thoroughly explain their pricing and may make some suggestions that can decrease the cost. The single most important factor to any printing project is the final proofing of the artwork before you release it to the printer. Even though you will have the opportunity to see a final proof from the printer prior to the actual press run (usually called a *blue line*), any changes or corrections that were not on the original artwork will be charged back to you at a premium rate.

Choosing a Direct-Mail House

A mailing house will handle all the details for your direct-mail campaign, such as envelope stuffing, folding, sorting, postage, and so on. You simply take your finished printing to them, or have your printer deliver it to them directly, and they will take care of the rest. They will also furnish you with the mailing list you require, print the labels, affix the labels to your mailing pieces, add the postage, sort the pieces by zip code, box them up and deliver them to the post office. Sure beats licking envelopes yourself.

Your graphic artist probably knows of a good mailing house, but just in case she doesn't, you can locate one using the Yellow Pages. The only difference from one mailing house to the next is the quality of their mailing lists. A well-qualified, up-to-date mailing list is the most important part of the direct-mail equation. For this reason, ask the mailing house the following questions:

- ✔ **When was the list last updated?** You don't want to spend your hard-earned money sending out the direct mail only to have them returned by the post office as undeliverable. Look for a house that updates its lists monthly, quarterly at the very outside. On average, most reputable direct-mail houses update their lists every six weeks.

- ✔ **Is the data on the mailing list presorted by carrier routes or 9– or 11-digit zip codes and certified for accuracy of address information?** You'll want your lists to be at least presorted by zip codes so that you receive postage discounts. And the more extensively a mailing list is detailed (zip code digits, carrier routes, carrier route sequence) the larger your postage discounts will be. And certification of accuracy is important so that you're sure you're getting what you paid for.

✔ **Will a summary report that breaks out the counts by zip code and other information be made available to me?** The summary report gives the list buyer (that's you) a snapshot of the list capabilities and detail (income level, gender, education, and so on) before a list purchase decision is made. This report is offered free of charge in most cases.

✔ **Is there a minimum charge?** When you decide to buy a mailing list, the summary report may inform you that there are a total of 2,200 names available on this particular list, and that the cost will be $75 per 1,000 names but with a minimum charge of $250. List companies set a minimum charge on all lists. What you want to look for when buying a list are minimum charges buried in the small print.

✔ **Is the list charge for one-time or multiple usage?** Typically, a multiple-use list will cost you about three times the cost of a one-time-only use. The multiple-use list will *not* be updated prior to each use, so, if you are uncertain about using the list more than once, or if your second or third use of the list will be at a much later date, buy it for one time only.

✔ **What is the charge for output?** Your mailing house will show you a price list for the various forms of mailing labels. In simple terms, a *continuous form* (also referred to as *chesire*) is the typical computer paper with slotted tracks on either side that comes in boxes and is used on dot-matrix printers. A computer program prints multiple addresses on this paper and a machine at the direct-mail house cuts and glues the labels to the mailing pieces. Chesire is the cheapest label form. Sticky labels need to be affixed by hand and may be more expensive. However you choose to get the job done, the list company will either mail a computer disk (floppy or zip) or send the list to you or your direct-mail house electronically (via e-mail).

✔ **What are my label printing options (laser, inkjet, dot matrix, and so on)?** Dot matrix printing is the lowest priced but offers limited versatility in regards to type fonts and readability. Laser and inkjet printing, on the other hand, give you the flexibility of a wide variety of type styles, colors, and graphics. Again, dot matrix is the cheapest way to go.

✔ **Can I select the type font style for my labels?** Keep in mind that the issue of font style is moot when you're using chesire labels and dot matrix printing.

✔ **Can I include a secondary message on my labels (for example, "preferred customer")?** These secondary messages, generally with a double– or triple-spaced separation, will go above the recipient's name and address.

✔ **Will I receive a verification of mailing from either the post office or the mailing house?** This will be either the official United States Postal Service Form USPS 3602 or a form created by the mailing house, which will then be stamped and signed by the USPS to verify that the mailing was delivered as ordered.

You can easily purchase mailing lists online through various Web sites such as www.infousa.com (which has various lists) or www.polk.com (specializing in automotive-oriented lists). These companies provide you, prior to your purchase of a list, excellent, in-depth research capabilities.

I receive direct-mail pieces that are so far off base that I wonder how in the heck my name ever found its way to that particular list. Case in point: I receive mail each month from a singles club inviting me to parties and other social events where I can meet and mingle with other singles and have a high old time. Sounds like a lot of fun to me. Of course, the fact that I've been married for a thousand years would seem to indicate that my address on this list is a gigantic waste of the advertiser's money.

A good result from a direct mailing will be a return of 2 to 3 percent. That's not much. If you send 1,000 mailers, that means you may get *responses* from only 20 or 30 people, and *converted responses* (sales) from even fewer. But if a few of those 20 or 30 people spend a lot of money with you, and if their added business pays for your printing and mailing costs, those 20 or 30 people may be enough — especially if they become return customers. But the fact that a good direct-mail campaign will only bring you a maximum 3 percent return puts that much more meaning into the validity of the list to which you are mailing. You will never be 100 percent certain that the list you are buying is completely current. But you can pressure the direct-mail house to give you assurances that the list is as valid as they can make it.

Your good credit will allow you to be billed for the design work, printing, mailing list, and mailing services, but you'll have to pay for the postage upfront. The cost of postage is the one item for which you will be required to pay in advance or, as we say in the agency business, *CIA* (short for *cash in advance*). The direct-mail house must pay for the postage when they deliver the material to the post office, or they will have had to pay upfront to load postage into their postage meter. One way or another, they will want your check before your mailing moves out of their door.

After going through all the trouble and expense of sending out direct mail, you'll be stunned at the number of direct-mail missives that are returned to you stamped "non-deliverable as addressed." No matter how good the list, some of your mail is destined to make a quick roundtrip. You'll never know how many people actually read your direct mail, but you sure as heck will know how many people never received it in the first place. Direct mail is likely one of the more measurable media, because the returned items just sit there, in an ever-increasing pile, mocking you. For this reason, most direct mail houses use their own return address rather than their clients'. That way, you don't have to see how many items get returned.

Mailing lists: Something for everyone

Mailing houses have mailing lists broken down by demographics (age, race, and so on), geography (zip codes, ethnic neighborhoods), income, buying habits, home value, swimming pool ownership, the works. Name your requirements, and chances are a mailing house has the list you're looking for.

Remember: Any direct-mail house can stuff envelopes. It's the quality and timeliness of their lists that you should be most interested in. Because people move from one place to another, change their marital status, modify their buying habits, increase or decrease their income, and change all sorts of things, mailing lists must be purged and updated often — every six weeks is optimum. If you want to send a mailer to households earning $100,000 and up, there is a list that can get the job done. How up-to-date the list is, however, makes the difference between all your mailers hitting the correct homes and a whole bunch of them being returned.

With the year 2000 census information now available, mailing lists are more sophisticated and informative than ever before. Added to the incredible mix of information is the term *psychographics,* which can pinpoint certain people (for example, "condo-dwelling, SUV driving, techie"). You'll probably find more information in the form of mailing lists than you want or need to know.

Chapter 9

Outdoor Ads: Eat at Joe's and Get Gas

In This Chapter

▶ Putting the different forms of outdoor advertising to work for you

▶ Using the key elements of an effective outdoor ad

▶ Targeting your message to the people who will read it

▶ Keeping your ad brief and to the point

I think that I shall never see
A billboard lovely as a tree.
Indeed, unless the billboards fall
I'll never see a tree at all.

— Ogden Nash

Outdoor advertising is quite likely the earliest form of advertising. Before the billboard became a free-standing structure, advertisers plastered their snake oil logos and slogans on rural barns and on the sides of downtown buildings. And long before that, in an age when most of the population was illiterate, stores and businesses displayed signs that were pictorial (often carved) representations of what they were selling — a mortar and pestle for a drugstore, a tankard of beer for a tavern, a big bloody tooth for a dentist, a hammer and anvil for a blacksmith, the scales of justice for an attorney, and so on.

ANECDOTE

My first real job was in outdoor

The very first job I ever had in the advertising business was as a sketch artist (today that would be graphic designer) for an outdoor sign company. The salesmen for the sign company would take pictures of a prospective customer's building, and it was my job to design an illuminated neon or Plexiglas sign for the customer. Then I used the photographic images of the building as the basis for a full-color rendering of what the building would look like with the gaudy, new signage installed. I taught myself architectural rendering in this way and soon left the sign business to open my first company: Gary Dahl Architectural Arts, a business doing artist's renderings of as-yet-unbuilt subdivision homes, apartment complexes, and commercial buildings.

While still in the sign business (and before sign ordinances with height restrictions prevented such blights), I won a national creative award with a pylon sign monstrosity I designed for an Anaheim hotel near Disneyland. My boss even paid my way to the national sign convention in New Orleans where I (we) accepted my design award. I ran across photos of my winning entry recently and was embarrassed. The design was, to put it simply, tasteless.

Outdoor advertising has, over the years, been an easy target for those who want to beautify America and who launch anti-billboard campaigns. In the 1960s and 1970s, Lady Bird Johnson was very interested in eliminating billboards. But both she and the billboards are still around. Cigarette, beer, and liquor advertisers have been reduced to no other media but outdoor, having been barred from other media forms long ago. Outdoor advertising (also known as *out-of-home advertising*), which includes billboards, bus shelters, subway posters, street furniture (bus benches), stadium displays, mall and airport signs, bus cards, taxi tops, shopping carts, and a multitude of other forms, has been called an "environmental blight" and "pollution on a stick." The billboard has always been the blue-collar grunt of the flashy media universe and, because of its high visibility, it's been easy to pick on. Of the 3,000 advertising messages to which consumers are exposed daily, I'd guess that 2,500 of them are outdoors.

In spite of the bad rap, outdoor advertising vehicles have weathered the storm (pardon the pun), and outdoor is an advertising medium that is here to stay. Outdoor advertising remains fifth on the advertising food chain behind television, radio, newspaper, and magazine advertising. And it can be a highly effective (and affordable) medium when the basic rules of good advertising are applied — namely, an eye-catching design and clear, concise copy.

Recognizing the Advantages of Outdoor Advertising

Outdoor advertising is on display 24 hours a day, 7 days a week, 365 days a year. It isn't surrounded by editorial content and competing advertisements the way newspaper ads are; it doesn't compete with programming and other commercials the way radio and TV ads do; and it can be targeted to reach very specific audiences by board location and neighborhood. Outdoor is exceptionally effective at reaching various ethnic groups, because you can choose which neighborhoods you want to advertise in — if you want to reach a Hispanic audience, you can place your ads on boards in predominantly Hispanic neighborhoods, and so forth.

You can't throw outdoor advertising out with the trash, reach over and turn it off, or use it to line the bottom of a bird cage. It sits up there, big, bold, and impressive, to be read over and over again by passing motorists and everyone who lives in the neighborhood. It gives you continual exposure, like a 30-day-long commercial — and that's just what you want.

Outdoor advertising includes billboards, posters, airport ads, bus signs, mall posters, bus shelters, stadium signs, bench advertising, shopping cart and gas pump advertising, blimps, banners towed by airplanes — the list is endless. And, according to the Outdoor Advertising Association of America (OAAA), outdoor advertising has one big advantage over other media: cost. Outdoor is 80 percent less expensive than TV, 60 percent less expensive than newspaper, and 50 percent less expensive than radio. These statistics from the OAAA confirm that the medium is affordable to advertisers big and small.

Radio stations are among the largest buyers of outdoor ads, because the people viewing the boards are in their cars and are quite likely listening to the radio — and that's a great time to remind them of your station. Fast food outlets use billboards to attract hungry motorists to specific locations at highway exits. Automobile manufacturers and local dealers use outdoor ads to reach consumers who are, when they see the ads, sitting in their cars and trucks.

INSIDE SCOOP

H&R Block hits a nerve

The 2001 tax season marked the introduction of what I consider to be a very effective outdoor campaign from H&R Block, the tax people. Capitalizing on the utter confusion of a tax form, one of their boards read: "Subtract line 64 from line 56 if more than line 56 . . . or call us." Although this board used more words than I think is optimal, the board worked because it was humorous and struck a nerve. It was recalled thanks to its creativity.

INSIDE SCOOP

Altoids' refreshing boards

Altoids, the "curiously strong breath mints" from England, made a big splash on the outdoor scene a few years back with their wonderfully creative copy. One board read: "Mints so strong they come in a metal box." And another winner said: "Refreshes your breath while you scream." Very little copy, but a whole bunch of creativity. It was a billboard campaign that put Altoids on the map in the U.S. without, as far as I know, any other media support.

But what about advertisers with more modest budgets? Small to mid-size retailers can also benefit from outdoor advertising and make their media buy more affordable by selectively choosing board locations that are near their stores and businesses. Outdoor advertising allows you to advertise your products where the ad will be seen by anyone who drives in the vicinity of your store.

The audience for outdoor advertising is growing steadily as people spend fewer hours at home with traditional media and more time on the road and in their cars. Our fast-paced society is on the move. According to a 1995 survey conducted by the United States Government's National Public Transportation Agency:

- 125 million Americans commute to work each day.
- Americans travel 3.4 trillion miles annually, a 143 percent increase over a 40-year period.
- The number of miles driven has nearly doubled in 20 years.
- Daily vehicle trips are up 110 percent since 1970.
- The number of cars on the road is up 147 percent since 1970.

These statistics would seem to prove that outdoor advertising has the potential to reach consumers in very large numbers. We spend more time in our cars (as anyone who must commute to work every day will attest), and what better way to reach people in their cars than with a big, fat billboard alongside the street or a clever ad on the rear end of that bus that's blocking the road up ahead?

Seeing How Technology Has Transformed the Medium

Large-size billboards (or *paints,* as they are called in the business) were once hand-painted in sections on plywood. The wood panels would then be transported to the site of the outdoor sign structure and installed. The really big billboards were done on location by a now nearly extinct species: the sign painter. The problem was that the paint faded, the wood chipped, and the whole board became even more tacky than it already was. It's no wonder that outdoor got a bad reputation in the advertising industry (and throughout the neighborhoods where the ads existed).

But billboards have now gone high-tech. They are digitally printed on vinyl that can be cut to any size and rolled for easy transport. The graphics, regardless of how intricate, can be reproduced with flawless similarity to the original. The process is called *large-scale imaging,* and the colors are true blue and drop dead red and everything in between. If you want to feature a gigantic photo of one of your restaurant's signature dishes on a billboard, you will get precise color and texture from today's advanced outdoor printing techniques. But it wasn't always that way. The quality of your artwork was once in direct proportion to the talent and mindset of the sign painter doing your job. And, as I learned from personal experience, sign painters as a group were (and likely still are) very temperamental.

Measuring the Effectiveness of Outdoor Ads

Because people are spending fewer hours at home, where TV, cable, magazines, newspapers, books, and the Internet all clamor for attention, billboards may be the way to go when it comes to advertising. People are spending more time than ever in their cars — daily vehicle trips continue to climb, and the number of cars on the road seems to grow exponentially. With so many people sitting in traffic jams, those who aren't busy plotting the next road rage incident are stuck with radio and billboards as their only media options.

The fact that billboards are a good way to grab your audience's attention is compounded by the fact that billboards are the cheapest way to reach mass audiences. Prices vary widely, but according to the Outdoor Advertising Association of America, advertisers typically pay a *CPM* (that's the cost per 1,000 viewers) of about $2 for billboards, compared with $5 for drive-time radio, $9 for magazines, and $10 to $20 for newspapers or primetime television.

So how do you know for sure how many people are reading your ads? Billboard cost-effectiveness is measured by the Traffic Audit Bureau, which sends out spotters to sit near billboards and count passing cars. While most advertisers are still local retailers, national sponsors are increasingly using the medium to build their brands. Why? Because outdoor advertising is effective and affordable, and it just sits there pumping out the message 24 hours a day.

Outdoor has been called "a pure advertising medium," and that may be true. Billboards stand alone without the editorial, programming, and competitive advertising distractions found in newspapers, magazines, radio, and television.

Taking Advantage of Your Outdoor Advertising Options

Outdoor advertising takes on many forms. In the following sections, I cover many (but not all) of the outdoor vehicles for sale to retail advertisers. It makes you wish you had unlimited funds, doesn't it?

Off-premise outdoor advertising

Off-premise outdoor advertising encompasses any outdoor sign used to advertise your business that is located alongside a road or freeway, in a mall, on a bus, or flying overhead being towed by a biplane. It is not the sign on the front of your store or your office door.

Permanent paints

Permanent paints are huge structures on which the message is painted on the face or printed on vinyl, which is then attached to the face. As you can imagine, these ads are big and expensive.

Rotary bulletins

Rotary bulletins are the largest of the standard billboard structures, measuring 14 by 48 feet. The advertising copy for rotary bulletins is printed on vinyl or painted on panels, which are rotated or moved between many locations during the term of the contract. They offer the largest impact in the marketplace and are not only big, but costly.

TIP

Other outdoor media formats

The number of different outdoor advertising methods you can choose from are almost infinite. In addition to the ones covered in more detail in this chapter, you can also advertising in the following places:

- Airships (blimps)
- Bus benches and shelters
- Bus interior cards
- Gas pumps
- In-mall kiosks
- Parking meter cards
- Rest areas
- Restroom walls
- Shopping carts
- Stadiums or arenas
- Taxi tops

And that ain't the half of it. Outdoor advertising takes on so many forms that it can, at times, become overly intrusive. If you call a local outdoor advertising company, you'll be able to get a full list of what's available to you. I'd need another book this size to describe them all.

Posters

The industry standard, also called *30 sheets,* posters are the signs you see everywhere. Copy is printed on posting paper and pasted to the face of the sign. Posters measure 12 by 24 feet. Several posters may be purchased and displayed throughout the market to achieve what is known as a *showing* (the number of boards you have purchased and the length of time your advertising will appear on them). Depending upon the size of your showing, posters can be quite affordable.

Junior posters

Junior posters are approximately 6 by 12 feet. They're the same as posters, just half the size. Unfortunately, they are *not* half the cost.

Bus shelter ads

Bus shelter ads are 48-x-68-inch posters in backlit frames that are integrated into bus shelters. They provide 24-hour exposure in heavy-traffic areas.

Bus-side advertising

Bus-side advertising is available in four sizes:

- **Super Kings:** Available only in select markets, these ads are usually located on the traffic-facing or left-hand sides of buses and extend from wheel well to wheel well.

- **Kings:** These ads are also affixed to the traffic side of buses, but they are somewhat shorter in length than the Super Kings.

- **Queens:** These ads are found on the curb sides or right-hand sides of the vehicles.

- **Tails:** As the name implies, the Tails (short for *taillights*) bring up the rear and are quite good for reaching a captive audience (such as you when you're just sitting there inhaling the diesel fumes).

Aerial banners

Aerial banners are in-your-face outdoor advertising at its apex. You're watching a football game, minding your own business, when you look up and see an airplane towing a banner that reads: "Eat a Heap Cheap at Joe's." Aerials are flown over sporting events and other special events of every description, in areas where other forms of advertising are nonexistent. This form of outdoor is also good for birthday surprises when you really want to show off.

Designing Memorable Outdoor Advertising

What makes a great outdoor ad campaign? How many words should you use? What colors work best to attract the attention of passing motorists? Should you use graphics or just stick with hard-hitting copy? Ask a dozen experts and you'll likely get a dozen different answers. But in my opinion, there are two primary measuring factors for outdoor advertising:

- **Impact:** The ability to grab a viewer's attention in a matter of seconds.

- **Appeal:** Persuasiveness and positive response by the viewer to the creative content.

Eyeball-popping creative content, readability, simplicity and clarity of message, and, of course, memorability (just like creative content of any advertising media) are the keys to a successful outdoor ad. The fact that an outdoor ad, at least on a billboard, must be seen, read, and remembered while the viewer is otherwise distracted with driving a car down a hostile freeway makes simplicity and clarity of message the most important part of the equation. You only have a couple of seconds to grab the viewer by the eyeballs, so your copy had better be brief and very fascinating. If you're using a graphic element, it too needs to be unique, relevant, and easy to understand.

I honestly believe that if you can encapsulate your message onto a really good billboard advertisement; if you can project your message quickly and with clarity; if you can generate some truly creative copy (a message that's brief, perhaps funny, and eye-catching), you will have designed your entire ad campaign. If you can boil it down to six or eight perfect words, then you, my friend, have made it so easy on the consumer that you can hardly miss getting his attention. The ad you have written to create a memorable billboard will translate beautifully to any media. It is for this reason that your outdoor advertising copywriting effort deserves serious time and attention.

Using colors wisely

Strong color contrasts between the background and the copy and graphics is absolutely essential. Use primary colors — yellows, reds, blues, and good old black. Use bright shades of colors rather than darker tones, which retreat from the viewer. A bright yellow background and black letters would be the optimum combination (hey, the publishers of this book knew what they were doing, didn't they?). Using colors isn't complicated — just shoot for the best possible readability from a long way off, because that huge billboard looks like a postage stamp from a distance.

Getting help with your outdoor ads

Getting started with outdoor advertising is easier than you may think. For starters, check out the Web site of the Outdoor Advertising Association of America (OAAA), the trade organization for the industry and the epicenter of reams of information about who, what, when, and where. Find this complete informational source at www.oaaa.org. Or call 202-833-5566 to reach a live person at the OAAA who will be happy to answer your questions.

You can also call outdoor advertising companies that are operating in your area, accessible through another great service, the Standard Rate & Data Advertising Source for Out-of-Home. This SRDS book will not only steer you to the right outdoor company, but it will also give you a list of their rates. The book is available for sale in hard copy, at your local library, or electronically at www.srds.com. You can do a search of local companies in a number of ways: by type, geography, or company name. These companies will help you through the complete process: from concept to creation, from printing to posting, and even to tracking your results.

Making your ad readable

Your design should be connected with a simple, clean text in a very readable type font. Prioritize the keywords of your copy and keep your copy short and full of punch. Use humor, but get to the punch line quickly. Vary the font size, avoiding copy set in all capital letters. People are used to reading text in a combination of uppercase and lowercase, so billboard copy should conform to this.

Six words is the most favorable number for billboard readability, but keeping your message that short is often impossible. Try eight words if you must, but any more than eight could be dangerous to the health of your ad budget.

If you're using a graphic element — a picture, drawing, or logo — make it big and keep it simple. Don't force the viewer to search for the message. She won't bother. So make it clear immediately. How many billboards have you seen that, like so many poorly designed newspaper ads, contain enough information to fill an encyclopedia and the advertiser's logo so small you couldn't read it with binoculars? The message is lost in a jumble of words, type fonts, and graphics. The viewer drives right on by with but a confused glance at the ill-conceived board. The ad is a total failure. And the money is wasted.

Keeping it clear

Viewers don't want to be teased; they want to be informed. And with a billboard, they need to be informed in a split second, so don't get too cute. Be clear, concise, and direct. Relate your message to familiar experiences and situations. Emphasize your product or service as the answer to the viewer's prayers. If you're showing the product, make it big, bold, and brazen.

Clarity is more important than cleverness. Don't make the joke so subtle that no one gets it — that will only cause annoyance. And if you do use humor, be sure it is relevant to the experiences and knowledge of your target audience. Don't use East Coast humor on a California billboard. And try to create a tight connection between your product's benefit and its relevance to the viewer's life; create a problem and solve it in eight words or less.

Make it worth remembering

When your goal is to create a memorable ad for any media, imagery is often more important than words. The use of a hard-hitting visual element can generate more memorability for the viewer. Use images that are easily recognizable — like the beer mugs, anvils, and bloody teeth that comprised the signs for saloons, blacksmiths, and dentists hundreds of years ago. Include lighthearted, spirited elements that generate excitement, but try to ensure that the viewer can relate to the person or situation being depicted.

TIP

When all else fails . . .

The sign companies with which you do business have design and production departments whose only goal in life is to make your outdoor advertising successful. They know how to design a board, how to write brief, hard-hitting copy, and where to place your outdoor ads for the optimal impact. The creative specialists in outdoor, like the specialists in any media, understand what works in their particular field.

You will certainly have your own ideas of what you want, and you will likely have at least a copy outline. But you may do well by letting the professionals put the final touches on your creative strategy. This design service is, by and large, available to you at no extra charge. My advice? Take advantage of it.

ANECDOTE

The San Francisco Zoo did a series of billboards that was very memorable, including one that featured a large photo of an anteater and, in black lettering on a white background, the copy: "Eats 30,000 termites per day. Sorry, not available for rent." Now that's creative!

REMEMBER

Above all, make the message simple and easy to recall. Use bright, eye-catching color and brief, well-written copy. You only have a few seconds to make an impact on someone who is already preoccupied driving a car.

Looking at a Success Story

Sometimes a product just cries out for a billboard campaign. It lends itself beautifully to this advertising genre and, with a fairly heavy dose of creativity, it can make all the difference. For example, Chick-fil-A's signature product is the chicken sandwich, served primarily during the lunchtime hours — which means the restaurant chain competes in one of the fiercest battlegrounds, the fast-food restaurant market. When compared to giants such as McDonald's, Burger King, and Wendy's, Chick-fil-A is outnumbered in store count nearly four to one and outspent in media tenfold. Moreover, each of these competing chains has already etched distinct images in the minds of consumers.

Faced with these David-versus-Goliath odds, Chick-fil-A gave its advertising agency, The Richards Group, a tough assignment: Develop an integrated advertising campaign that clearly positions Chick-fil-A as a preferred alternative in the burger-dominated fast food marketplace. In the following sections, I outline how Chick-fil-A used outdoor advertising with great success.

The target audience

The Chick-fil-A target audience differs from the average fast-food clientele, which includes many teens and children. The market for chicken is comprised of more adults, more females, and people with a higher level of education and income than the hamburger market. Customers have a more active lifestyle and are likely to be in white-collar jobs. Mindful of these demographics, Chick-fil-A avoided the usual fast food locations to build their restaurants. Instead, they chose to operate in suburban malls and neighborhoods with a high concentration of its potential customers.

The marketing strategy

In order to efficiently reach the adult, professional, and mobile target audience, the media strategy emphasized outdoor and radio. The budget was allocated: 70 percent outdoor, 25 percent radio, and 5 percent print.

The creative strategy

The Eat Mor Chikin campaign was launched. And it cleverly spotlighted a little known fact: the poor spelling ability of your average cow! On billboards everywhere, one three-dimensional cow statue stood on the back of another cow statue and, with paint brush in hand (or hoof) and black paint dripping down the stark, white billboard background, the cow had scrawled the words "EAT MOR CHIKIN."

The results

During the Eat Mor Chikin campaign, some store sales were up four times over the industry average. It was a thoughtful and clever way to differentiate the Chick-fil-A stores from their burger-dominated competition. Using cows to deliver the self-serving message (I mean self-serving for the cows, who would, of course, prefer we eat chicken rather than beef), Eat Mor Chikin was a brilliantly conceived and executed campaign.

It proves that clever copy and a great creative concept can cut through the advertising clutter like a hot knife through butter . . . or is that chicken?

Chapter 10

Online Advertising: The Newest Game in Town

. . . .

In This Chapter

▶ Using banner ads and e-mail effectively

▶ Determining your campaign goals

▶ Offering customer service — the best advertising of all

▶ Making sure you deliver on your promises

. . . .

The buying of time or space is not the taking out of a hunting license on someone else's private preserve but is the renting of a stage on which we may perform.

— Howard Gossage

Thousands of years ago, a young Piltdown man walked into his cave one day and drew a picture on the wall. Although contemporary scholars disagree as to whether the bottle he sketched contained Coca-Cola or Pepsi-Cola, his intent was clear: Early man had learned to advertise his wares.

Okay, okay . . . I stretched the truth a bit, but the point remains the same. As much as we like to think advertising is a modern invention, it isn't. We keep changing the focus, changing the medium, and honing our skills, but whether you advertise in print, on billboards, or with the newest game in town — the Internet — the objective remains the same: You want to turn a looker into a buyer. The rest is jargon and detail. In this chapter, I walk you through what you need to know about Internet advertising, the latest genre in a seemingly endless array of advertising vehicles.

Identifying the Pros and Cons of Online Advertising

Internet advertising is still in its infancy, and just about every advertiser has a hard time deciding whether online advertising most resembles printed ads, TV ads, or billboards. Actually, online advertisements mix and match elements of each.

Online advertising is like a printed ad because, even online, an ad has definable borders. Think of it this way: As you page through a newspaper, you're never confused about whether you're looking at an ad or an article. Newspaper ads have borders, and most often they're small and don't take up the entire page. The same is true online — most ads are contained within something called a *banner* (a rectangular graphic containing your ad, usually appearing at the top or bottom of a Web page) or something called a *button* (a small banner).

Online advertising is also similar to TV ads because the ad can engage a viewer with motion in the form of animated graphics or video.

Online advertising is like a billboard, too, because both online and outdoor advertising grab attention and notify a viewer about an upcoming event.

Just like any other advertising medium, online advertising has pros and cons. Here are a few of the advantages to using online advertising:

- **You can easily test the market.** If you create a brochure, you have to print and distribute it before finding out whether your campaign is effective. Response (or lack of response) on the Internet is lightning fast.

- **The ad campaign is less expensive.** Because you won't have the costs associated with reprinting and redistribution (as you would in a more traditional campaign), the overall expense of a change is decreased.

- **The ad works 24 hours a day, 7 days a week, 365 days a year.**

- **You can change your online ad much more easily than you can change ads in other media.** When you need to alter your online ad, no printing or taping is required. Just change the HTML that created the online ad and you're done in a matter of minutes.

- **Your customers can see your ad, shop, and buy (if you sell your goods online) all without leaving home.** It's hard to beat that sort of convenience.

- **You can target your audience effectively.** The trick is to place your ad where the "right" customers will see it. If you sell exotic teas, you'll want to place your ad on a site that sells crumpets or cookies, rather than a site that sells motorcycle equipment to bikers. Think like one of your own customers by trying to imagine which sites they're likely to visit. Those sites are where to place your ad.

And here are some of the disadvantages to using online advertising:

- ✔ **It's too measurable.** You can gather more statistics than a baseball team. Worse, some of the *click-through rates* (the number of times the ad is clicked on divided by the total number of times an ad is seen) are low — often 1 or 2 percent or even less. That means hardly anyone who sees your ad will click on it and visit your Web site — or buy. Online advertising is still in its infancy. As of this writing, nobody knows for certain which statistics will prove to be the most valuable. A few years ago, advertisers believed that increasing the number of people who saw an ad would increase the likelihood of a sale. The thinking was that thousands of eyeballs looking at an ad would translate into hundreds of sales. Not necessarily so. A bit later, everyone decided that increasing your click-through rate would increase the number of sales. But that wasn't entirely true either. Currently, advertisers think that the only real measurement of an ad's success is to count the number of people who actually buy a product. The point is that because people don't really understand what works yet, they collect every possible statistic. But not all statistics are useful.

- ✔ **Some major ad agencies (and Wall Street) are losing confidence in online advertising.** The Internet is still so new that the advertising world simply doesn't know yet which advertising methods work best. There is, however, some good news. Few deny that there will be some form of Internet ads (perhaps combined with TV) that will be both powerful and effective in the future. We're learning fast.

Yes, the challenge of winning — and keeping — customers online is great. One problem is the incredible amount of clutter on most Web pages. Readers simply have too much information to digest. Often, they choose to ignore ads — and that is what leads to low rates of return.

Even with its disadvantages, the Internet is turning into a tool that surpasses the wildest dreams of ad execs. It took 38 years for the radio to reach 50 million users. It took television 13 years to reach 50 million viewers. And it took the Internet just 5 years to reach the same number of users — a stupendous achievement.

The Internet is a social technology. As your site grows, you can offer chat rooms and e-mail newsletters. Electronic groups are effective and fun as well. People like a sense of community, and the Internet offers that. In the end, all that interactivity means that you can sell people what they want and not just what is left over in stock. That's not just good — it's right. Happy, engaged customers are the Heisman Trophy of the advertising world.

Setting Goals for Your Online Ad Campaign

The Internet has sped things up, but the basic rules of good advertising haven't changed. Whether you are first or last to market, you need to sustain the basics to succeed — customer service, communication, commitment. Personalized service just about always leads to happy customers. Amazon.com greets consumers by name and offers reading and video suggestions tailored to the individual. People love the notion that someone is looking after their needs and interests.

The first step is to determine your own online advertising direction. Speaking generally, there are three strategies in an online effort:

- ✔ **Branding campaigns,** in which the goal is to get people to recognize your product or company name
- ✔ **Click-through campaigns,** in which you get people to click on your ad in order to be taken to your Web site
- ✔ **Sell-through campaigns,** in which you get people to buy right away

You'll design different banners depending upon your goals — the same banner just won't work for all three strategies. Choose one goal per banner so that you will meet your objectives. Use a good mix of the three campaigns.

Ads that encourage branding

Branding means getting people to recognize your name (in a positive way, of course). The idea is that if someone sees your name enough times, he will remember it later when he thinks about purchasing. For example, a person seeing an ad on TV for a certain type of toilet paper does not leap out of his chair and rush to the store. But he may remember the brand some day when he's *in* the store.

A recent study shows that the primary reason for advertising on the Internet has, in fact, shifted toward branding — and away from Web site traffic-building and sales generation. This strategy makes a lot of sense when you realize that sales resistance is strong when a user is intent upon buying something else.

The drawback to advertising for branding purposes is that the success of a campaign is difficult (if not impossible) to measure. Because of this, some companies decide that branding-type banners are not for them. But I think that's a mistake, because your competitors are out there with their online ads building brand awareness. It's a mistake because branding — whether online or offline — takes time. If you don't make an effort to impress your name on visitors, you lose valuable weeks and months. A person online has thousands of choices, and you want that person to remember your name. The only way to do that is to get it out there.

Ads that encourage click-through

Click-through simply means that when a user sees your ad, he clicks on it and is taken directly to your Web site. When a user clicks through to your site, it means that your ad was so compelling that the user stopped what he was doing on another site and went to visit yours. That's powerful stuff.

The purpose of a click-through campaign is to build traffic to your Web site. One excellent way to think about that to remember headlines in a newspaper. Headlines don't tell you the whole story; they just tell you enough to pique your interest. That's exactly the goal of a click-through campaign: to generate enough interest that your viewers click on your ad and visit your site.

Selling your product is one obvious goal of click-through campaigns (before a customer buys she has to get over to your site). Another reason may be Web traffic generation. Perhaps you have sold advertising space to another company and you've promised that a certain number of visitors will go to your site. Click-through campaigns are also effective if your plan is to build a database of individuals to whom you plan to sell your product in the future. Many businesses currently build such a consumer list by asking people for their e-mail addresses. This is the best sort of customer database, because everyone on the list has asked to be there.

Ads that encourage sales

The point of a *sell-through* campaign (or one that encourages sales) is to drive a sale immediately. Suppose you see an ad for an office supply discount store, and that ad promises useful items on sale for remarkable prices. If you visit that store and buy *only* the items on sale . . . well, that's a sell-through ad that didn't work. The goal is to get you to go to the store, shop around, and buy something else in addition to the sale items. More than that, the ad was probably designed to encourage you to become a regular customer.

To induce a purchase in a sell-through campaign, you will probably have to offer an extraordinary bargain. This is known as a *loss-leader* program.

Sell-through campaigns are appropriate when you want to generate revenue in a hurry. You may think sell-through ads are the only ones worth having, but they really are a short-term strategy, because they require you to always offer amazing sales. Think twice before you settle on this as your one and only ad campaign.

Checking Out Some Online Ad Models

In the dim dark online past (a decade ago) your Web site was your ad — your only ad. Not much was actually sold online, but an Internet presence gave a certain cachet. Businesses placed their sites into the search engines, people came because it was cool, and if they liked what they saw, they called or visited your brick-and-mortar store and bought goods in the traditional way. Web sites in those days tended to be *brochureware* — a simple conversion of product information to language that a Web site could display. No animation, no rich media, nothing. Plain vanilla. But it didn't work very well, largely because customers faced choices that bewildered them and because Web sites couldn't target the right customers.

Here's a piece of trivia for you: The first banner ad appeared on Hotwired. com in October of 1994 — it was an ad by AT&T. Hotwired wondered what the response would be from visitors to their site, and, to their surprise, they did not receive a single complaint. Banner ads were born. Shortly thereafter, someone realized that you could advertise effectively by sending e-mail to people who wanted to know about your products. Electronic newsletters appeared out of nowhere, and a second form of online advertising hit the big time. There are other ad models for online advertising, but banner ads and e-mail are the main ones you need to understand. I cover them in more detail in the following sections.

Deciphering the legalese

Advertisers have been using the Internet to market their wares for a number of years, but the rules are not yet clear. For one thing, the Internet is global, so enforcing laws from one nation on Web sites from another is impossible. But you can keep your nose clean by following a few common-sense guidelines as you advertise online.

✔ Be truthful.

✔ Don't mislead.

✔ Substantiate your claims.

✔ Be fair to consumers.

✔ Make necessary disclosures clear and conspicuous.

If your banner ad promises a free dinner at Charlie's Steak House, you must mention — within the banner — that the purchase of two airline tickets to Florida is necessary before the free dinner is awarded. You cannot force someone to click to your site before learning that a purchase is involved in the "free" dinner. If you offer a free dinner on your Web site, you must place the disclosure close to the offer. You cannot make someone scroll down endlessly to learn that she must buy something first; place the disclosure nearby. Make sure the disclosure is clear and easily understood.

Flying your banner

Placing a banner or *button* (a small banner ad) on someone else's site offers two benefits: It drives visitors to your site, and it gives your product or company visibility on the Web. Banner ads are helpful in building brand recognition.

Knowing what makes a banner good

One thing advertisers have learned is that rich media banners (ones that have graphics with audio, video, and other technology components beyond mere animation) work well. They are simply more interesting than static banners — ones that don't have all these extra features. Rich media banners also take a long time to *load* (appear on the screen), so you don't want the designer of your banner to pile huge amounts of technology into one little ad. If you choose to go with a rich media banner, be sure the *interactivity* (the bells and whistles) are related somehow to what you're selling.

You can drive traffic to your site with cheap tricks, but doing so is unfair. Recently, a certain company designed a banner that looked very much like the error message you receive just before your computer crashes. "Click here," said the ad. People clicked. Many of them thought they had to click or their machine would crash. Instead, they were taken to the Web site of that company. I'm not prepared to say their intention was dishonest, but that idea resulted in a trick that made people feel foolish. My advice is to sell honestly.

Determining the quality of a banner depends largely upon which ad strategy you have chosen. You'll want a different sort of banner depending upon whether your goal is branding, building Web traffic, or selling. If your goal is to build brand awareness, you'll want something attractive and catchy so people will remember. You'll want your company name and/or product prominently displayed. You'll want something simple and short. Find a good slogan so that your ad pops out of the Web clutter.

If you're aiming at a click-through campaign (that is, you want to drive traffic to your site but not necessarily to make an immediate sale) you want to pique interest fairly. You can, for example, put up a banner that advertises free dinners, and in doing so, you can have a phenomenal click-through rate. Millions will visit your site, but that's one of those cheap tricks — unless you are actually prepared to give free dinners to everyone who visits your site.

For a click-through ad, keep in mind the following tips:

- **Remember to say "click here" in your banner.** You would be surprised at the numbers of banners that fail to tell a viewer what action to take.
- **Make it short.**
- **Use the word *free* in your ad.**

- ✔ **Pose a question.** Questions encourage people to click, but you want it to be a compelling question, such as "What three things do all best-selling novels have in common?"

- ✔ **Be sure that people feel as if they will get something they want by clicking on your ad.** "Click here to get a free personalized estimate of your social security benefits with private accounts" is much better than "Click here for information about social security." People do not want to merely visit another Web site; they want to feel that a click will bring them value. Give it to them.

- ✔ **Make your banner interactive.** We all like to be involved, and your viewers are no different.

- ✔ **Change your banners frequently.** If a user hasn't clicked after three visits, he isn't likely to do so in the future.

- ✔ **Create a mystery**. Curiosity is an extraordinary motivator. Suppose you are in the computer peripheral business and you sell keyboards. Of course, we all know that the top row of a keyboard contains these letters: QWERTYUIOP. Now to create a mystery in your ad, ask people to guess the longest word that can be typed using only those letters. I know a lot of people who wouldn't be able to resist clicking over to your site to learn the answer, but I'm sure *you* would never fall for such a silly trick, now would you? (By the way, the answer is not *typewriter*. Oh no, that would be too easy. It's *Rupturewort*, a West Indian plant.) People love to discover intriguing facts — and they will click over to your site to do just that.

If your banner ad is part of a sell-through campaign, you need a fast-loading banner. The point of a sell-through campaign is an immediate sale. How can a slow-loading graphic accomplish that goal? It can't. Create a sense of urgency. The words "Last day of sale" will help. For a sell-through campaign, do all the things you would do for a click-through campaign, except don't create a mystery. You want good strong information so someone will buy as soon as he reaches your site.

Finding a banner designer

Before you start looking for someone to design your banner ad, be sure to find a few samples of banners that you like. Let a designer know what you want to do. In the same regard, know whether you want a branding campaign, a click-through campaign, or a sell-through campaign.

To find a designer:

- ✔ Ask your friends.

- ✔ Ask your Internet Service Provider (ISP) for references. (See Chapter 11 for more information on ISPs.)

✔ Check out the list of banner designers at
www.bannertips.com/designersForHire.shtml.

✔ Search online for "professional banner design."

No matter how you find a designer, ask for references — and check them out.

Placing your banner

You can go about getting your banners and buttons on a Web site in several ways. I cover them in the following sections.

Using ad networks

A number of sites will place your banner ad for you. The big advertising agencies use DoubleClick.com (www.doubleclick.com). If you have a large company and a budget to match, DoubleClick.com is a great option.

But you can also check out other sites known as *banner exchange networks*. With these sites, you have to display banner ads for other companies on your company's Web site, in exchange for them putting *your* banner ad on *their* sites. The cost is lower and makes this option worth considering. Microsoft has a useful exchange program. (You can go to www.bcentral.com. Then click on "Improve marketing effectiveness." From there, you can learn about their free services.) You can also find a banner exchange program at bpath. com. (Go to www.bpath.com. Choose your country. From there, click on "banner exchange.") You can also search the Web for "ad networks" to come up with a huge list of sites that will carry your ads for free.

Placing it yourself

If your customer base is well-defined, you can find appropriate sites and approach them yourself. A simple way to do this is to search the Internet using a few keywords of interest to your customers. (You're looking for sites that share interests or content similar to your own.) You'll get a list of sites that may be appropriate for placing your ad. Check them out and ask if you can place your banner on their site for a fee or even if you can simply exchange banners at no cost to either party (called a *reciprocal link*).

For example, suppose you sell baseball cards. Go to a search engine and type in "baseball" or "sporting goods." The list that comes up under either search may have a site perfect for you. Don't type in "baseball cards" as your search term because the sites that appear there are your *competitors*. They won't want your banner on their sites, and you don't want their banners on your site.

Although this approach can be effective, it takes time and an ability to negotiate a fair price.

TECHNICAL STUFF

Pay schedules

Online ads have three major pricing structures:

- **Cost per thousand (CPM):** This is the cost of an ad for every 1,000 times the ad is displayed. These ads are sold in bulk and cost anywhere from $20 to about $60. Most of the time, when you buy a CPM, your banner will appear on big, highly trafficked Web sites. Sometimes this type of pricing structure is called *pay per face,* but it's the same thing — the cost of 1,000 impressions. (An *impression* is the number of times an ad appears on a Web page.)

- **Cost per click (CPC):** You only pay for this if someone clicks on your banner ad and is taken to your site. Be a little careful before plunging in to this type of ad. Your audience *will* be better targeted, but the cost is higher and you'd better be able to convert these visits to sales if you want to make money. Expect to pay anything from 5 cents up to 50 cents per click if you go with a place like ValueClick.com (www.valueclick.com). Sites like this buy unused ad space on prime locations. Some companies won't sell by CPC because the quality of a banner is a determining factor in how much they earn, and it's a factor those sites cannot control.

- **Cost per transaction (CPT):** You pay when you make a sale. This choice offers great accountability, but you will pay a significant percentage for this type of fee structure. This is also known as *cost per action* (CPA).

Finding out if your banner is working

After you run your banner ads, find out how effective it is. You can do this by using several kinds of statistics:

- **Impressions:** The number of times an ad appears on a Web page.
- **Click-through:** The number of times people select/click on your banner or button.
- **Click-through rate (CTR):** The number of times the ad is clicked divided by the total number of times an ad is seen.
- **Conversion:** The rate at which some goal is achieved (sales or orders or traffic building, for example).
- **Hit:** Every component of a Web site viewed by a visitor. If you have one Web page with 20 graphics and a visitor looks at all of them, you will have 21 hits.

In general, the conversion rate is the most important statistic. Number of hits is largely meaningless, but I include it on this list because you will hear the term everywhere. Don't be fooled. You are interested in click-through rates and conversion rates rather than just the number of impressions.

Are banners and buttons effective?

If you get a 1 or 2 percent conversion rate, your banners are performing at or above normal. That's dismal, you say. Well, yes it is, but consider the whole story before rushing to judgement.

When so many dot-coms failed that we started to call them dot-bombs, online ad impressions still increased exponentially and reached an all-time high in December 2000 — the height of the panic.

Plus, with so many more ads out there now, the conversion rate is bound to be lower. Not all companies spend the time or effort to care about the right kind of banner put in the right place to do the right job. So good banners and buttons can be very effective.

Banner bashing is popular. Maybe it's right, too. I can't guarantee you that banner advertising will wind up being the online ad model that works. But I do think incorporating banners into your overall advertising strategy makes sense.

You can get these statistics in several different ways. If you join a program (such as the one at www.tradebanners.com), you can either buy *banner placements* (a fixed number of impressions) or you can trade ad space on your page for ad space on someone else's Web site. When you join a program, you will be given access to individualized statistics that you can view any time you want. You can find out how many times your ad has been seen and also how many times people clicked over to your page. To get the conversion rate, you will have to work with your Web host (the supplier of your e-commerce software).

You can also buy log analysis software or even hire a company to track your data and provide you with customized reports. You can find companies that provide log analysis by typing the keyword "log analysis" in any Internet search engine.

E-mail advertising

E-mail is the sweetheart of the current advertising models. It's cheap. It's fast. It's effective. Recently, response rates for *permission-based advertising* (where you ask the customer before sending e-mail) beat the heck out of banner-ad click-through rates. Currently, e-mail response rates are an astonishing 11.5 percent.

Why is e-mail so successful? Because it's a form of dialogue. Your customers can respond to you, a real human being, instead of watching a Web page.

Think of an e-mail campaign as being an extension of your other advertising strategies. There's no point in replacing them entirely, but you can add the hottest sizzle in town by using e-mail. The reason e-mail is hot is that you can target so effectively. You can be wildly creative — embedding audio and video and interactive capabilities in your messages — for relatively little expense.

Collecting lists

If you want to use e-mail in your ad campaign, you're going to need e-mail addresses of people to send your messages to. Start by asking your regular customers for their e-mail addresses. Those who want to receive ads from you will comply — and you don't want to bother the people who don't want to give you their e-mail addresses.

You can also collect information from those who visit your site by asking them for their feedback. Inquire about their interests. Ask them for their e-mail addresses. Offer discount store coupons or tickets to a local show to people who give you information. **Remember:** The data people give you is valuable, so you may want to give a little something in return for the information they give.

You can also buy lists containing thousands of e-mail addresses. But I hate this method because the people on those lists have not asked to be there. If you send unsolicited advertisements, you're sending *spam* (unwanted e-mail). Spam is unkind, unfair, and counterproductive. Plus, response rates on these kinds of e-mails are low.

Publishing newsletters

E-mail newsletters are an increasingly popular Web phenomenon. Offer a newsletter on your Web site and allow people to sign up. Then, once a week or once a month, send out information about your business — information that will help the customer. Be generous with your tips and information pertinent to your business. Word will get out that you offer good value, and people will come.

A holistic veterinarian I know started her newsletter over a year ago, and it's a winner. Each month she sends out a newsletter via e-mail that is chock full of tips for animal health. And her business has increased dramatically.

Using e-mail successfully

E-mail can be a strong part of your overall advertising campaign. Be sure to follow these tips:

- **Ask for e-mail addresses.**
- **Never send unsolicited e-mail.**
- **Keep records of all registrations forever.** Sometimes, years later, people tell you they never signed up. With great courtesy, show them their original registration and the date you received it.

✔ **Always offer a chance to opt out.** In each e-mail, tell people how they can stop receiving the mail. Make the instructions clear and prominent.

✔ **State your privacy policy.** Tell people their e-mail addresses will never be shared or sold. And keep your word.

✔ **Appoint a real live person to handle problems and inquiries.** Your goal should be to respond to each e-mail within 12 hours. Sooner is better. Another good idea is to have an automated reply that is sent immediately and lets the person know his message was received. Be sure to follow up with a personalized reply as soon as possible. Many (if not most) ISPs offer the ability to respond automatically.

✔ **Keep your list secure.** Make sure that the recipients cannot see each other's e-mail addresses. Learn to make an alias list and put that list in the blind carbon copy (BCC) area when sent.

✔ **Check the e-mail you send out for typos, misspellings, and so on.** Put your best foot forward.

✔ **Choose your subject line with care.** Make it provocative — and make it sound like something other than an ad. "Make money fast," _doesn't_ work. "A unique opportunity to improve your business," _does_ work.

✔ **Avoid closing down communication.** I once had an e-mail correspondence that left me infuriated. I was about to buy a new car, and I wanted my new baby to be perfect. I requested (by e-mail) a certain color that I had seen on another model by the same auto manufacturer. I received an e-mail in response that stated I couldn't have my car in that color. Well, okay, but the infuriating part was that her note had a postscript that read, "Have a nice day!" With that one line, the salesperson declared the conversation over and closed down communication. _Never_ close off communication with a customer.

Understanding privacy concerns

Some people argue that the Internet has destroyed our personal privacy. Think about it a minute. Zillions of bits flow across the wires every hour, and some of those bits are about _you_. Do you really want your private information readily available? Do you really want your medical records open to every doctor in the world? Even if your own physician is magnificent, can you trust all the others? Do you want your financial records open to every banker? Do you want your social security number flying around the ether?

When you ask customers for private information — their e-mail addresses and street addresses, for example — you need to treat that information with the utmost care. Ask for as little information as possible. You probably don't need to know your customers' income, their marital status, or the number of children they have.

Have a privacy statement on your site and stick to it. Let your customers know they can trust you.

Fostering relations with the press

You may be surprised at how eager reporters are to find you. Many communities, even small ones, have a newspaper or newspaper section devoted entirely to local business. But you can make it easy or hard for reporters to write about you. Think of media coverage as free advertising — always a good thing. Here are a few tips to improve your relationship with the press:

✔ **Have a Web page devoted to press releases.** What? You don't have any press releases? Well, write some, or hire a local writer to whip up a few for you. Then e-mail them to newspapers and, at the same time, put them on your Web site. A press release does not necessarily have to be printed in a newspaper. You can simply put a few on your Web site. That helps a reporter find out exactly what you do. Put your newsletters on your Web site, too.

✔ **Ask your local chamber of commerce to have a link to your Web site.** Reporters look at city pages to see what is new and interesting from a local angle. If your site is there, they're more likely to visit it.

✔ **Make it easy for reporters to contact you.** Have your phone number and address prominently displayed on your Web site. Some businesses even have a special phone number for reporters to call for an interview.

✔ **If you see a story about your business specialty and your business was not included, befriend the reporter who didn't mention your business.** Call him or, better yet, send him an e-mail telling him what parts of the story you liked best. Then mention that you are an expert in that field and would love a chance to tell your story. Most reporters (especially freelancers) try to sell three articles for every story idea. In other words, they reuse ideas and just change the slant. Why? Because writing a story takes research, and reusing old research is easier than studying some new subject. Usually, the reporter will need at least one new interview subject for the new slant. Make a friend of the reporter, and the next time, he'll remember you. Bingo — a free ad.

Today the return on investment is high for e-mail advertising. One reason is that there are few upfront costs — an enormous advantage. But it may not always remain so cheap and easy. For one thing, your e-mail will start competing with hundreds of other e-mails jamming someone's inbox. And people will grow less tolerant as time goes by. Some ISPs and other e-mail service providers have already made blocking programs available to protect their clients. It's called *spam blocking,* and the idea is to allow clients the choice of filtering their mail. Advertisers may eventually have to pay for the chance to slip past the guards. That's not necessarily a bad thing. Sometimes paying a little more decreases the competition.

Affiliate programs

Affiliate programs (also known as *partnership programs* or *associate programs*) are one of the hot new advertising models. The concept is simple: You contract to place ads on your site, and you are paid when a visitor to your site clicks through or purchases something from another site. Affiliate programs are carefully targeted to the interests of your visitor. If you have a Web site dealing with antique furniture, you will *not* want to become an affiliate of a sporting good site, for example. Affliliate programs are good for sites that are narrowly focused — and there are zillions of topic-specific sites. Amazon.com was the very first affiliate — they offer a percentage of the sale if one of your visitors buys from Amazon.com after clicking on their link from your site.

One drawback, if you are considering becoming an affiliate, is that, frequently, a visitor who clicks through to another site will not return to yours. There are, however, ways to ensure that a visitor actually remains on your site even though he has clicked on an ad. If you are not an HTML expert, hire a Web designer to help you accomplish this.

Find out more about affiliate programs by visiting www.associate programs.com or www.quickclick.com.

Offering good customer service

Customer service is the best advertisement of all. It's the prime cut, the sweet spot of retaining customers — and attracting new ones. Customers want human contact; they crave it, in fact. Exchange e-mail and have a cool Web site, but when your customers write or call to ask a question, give them a straight-up answer as quickly as you can.

Be yourself. You have your market niche, and you don't need to be all things to all people. Do what you do and do it well, and they will come. The hottest trend in business today may be the change from product-based marketing to customer-based marketing. Your customers are your gold.

Chapter 11

Web Sites: If You Build It, They Will Come

• •

In This Chapter

▶ Deciding whether a Web site is right for you

▶ Knowing the features of a successful site

▶ Being aware of what you want out of your site

▶ Finding and hiring a Web designer

▶ Getting the word out about your Web site

• •

> *In the ad game, the days are tough, the nights are long, and the work is emotionally demanding. But it's worth it, because the rewards are shallow, transparent, and meaningless.*
>
> — Author Unknown

You've worked to build your business, and now — like tens of thousands of others — you're wondering whether you should go online by creating a Web site. Do you need a Web site? The answer is yes, you probably do — especially if your goal is to expand your business. Millions of people not only have access to computers but are quick to use the Internet for research. For some, a business isn't real unless it has a Web site. When I need a product or service, I check the Web even before I open my phone book. It's fast, it's easy, and, as a consequence, a business that has a Web site is more likely to attract my attention. Having a simple but well-thought-out site is, in itself, a form of advertising — even if you don't plan to sell online right away.

In this chapter, I walk you through the steps along the Web site pathway, answering some common questions as I go. What makes a Web site good? If you build it, will they come? Is it easier and cheaper in the long run to hire a

Web designer? The dirty little secret is that creating a good Web site isn't as hard as technical people would have you believe — if you know what you want and are willing to commit some cash. The first step is making the decision to do it. As Shakespeare may have asked about e-commerce, "To e or not to e. That is the question." And in today's world, the answer is yes.

The real question is this: Is a poorly executed Web site better than no site at all? Stated simply, the answer is a resounding no! In many cases, a Web site is the first impression a customer will have — and everyone knows the importance of good first impressions. A poorly designed Web site with inaccurate information or spelling errors strikes a blow to a business image. If you build a Web site, make it a good one. In this chapter, I show you how.

Taking a Look at the Pros and Cons of Web Sites

If you choose to take your business online, you're in excellent company. The latest surveys show that about 150 million people worldwide are already accessing the Internet. In the U.S., 36,000 brand-new users go online *every* day. Most of these people won't become your customers, of course, but why not attract *some* of them? In addition to collecting new buyers, a Web site can offer real service to current customers. If 20th-century advertising efforts pulled in *new* consumers, then 21st-century advertisers have determined to serve long-standing customers. Service is the key — and a Web site can help.

Before you dive into the Web world, take a few minutes to consider what you want out of a Web site, and what a Web site can do for you. Here are some of the advantages that Web sites bring:

- **A Web site will improve your image.** Face it — just about *everyone* in business has a site. If you don't, you want to make sure you've intentionally chosen not to do so, and be sure your reasons are sound.

- **A Web site can help your business — and your customer list — expand.** When you have a Web site, you can essentially have a storefront in every city, town, and village in the world. Anywhere people have access to the Internet, they can have access to your business. Your customers are no longer limited to the people in your neighborhood — the world is yours for the taking.

- **A Web site can reduce some costs.** You can put information on your Web site that you may normally put in an expensive brochure. People who visit your site can get information quickly, and you save printing and mailing costs. Everybody wins. Large companies have saved millions by putting their product documentation and user manuals online. In addition, a Web site can minimize support costs. Every time a customer finds an answer to his question online, that's one person who won't have to call to ask for the hours or location of your store. Think of it this way: You can increase your profits by bringing in more money, but there is a second way to improve your bottom line — spending less.

✔ **A Web site is available 24 hours a day, 7 days a week, 365 days a year.** Your Web site works for you even when you're are sick or on vacation. When your customers want to buy, your Web site is there to take their order.

✔ **A Web site offers customers a choice.** They can call you, they can visit your storefront, they can send faxes, and they can e-mail you. Adding a Web site means they can visit you at your Web site as well. Offering more choices puts the customer in control. *Remember:* Service is not just a goal — it's a trend, and a worthy one at that.

Now that you're sold on the advantages of a Web site, take a few minutes to consider the drawbacks as well:

✔ **Sometimes having a Web site gives visitors the impression that they'll be able to buy online.** If you don't have an online store, some visitors will be disappointed.

✔ **If you include an online store in your Web site, many customers will not be willing to send their credit card information over the Internet.** Some fear being ripped off. Others prefer shopping in person; they like to see products before they buy, in order to judge their value.

✔ **Having a Web site does not ensure success.** You'll have to work for success on the Web as hard as you work for it in your traditional store. Not even large merchants and their advertising agencies are sure how to make money on the Internet.

✔ **A Web site can be a time and money sink.** That's why knowing what you want is essential. Think first; act later.

Building a Good Site

If you decide to go the route of having a Web site for your business, you need to know what makes a site successful. So what makes a site good and what makes a good site better? Three qualities of excellent Web sites stand out:

✔ They are clear of purpose.

✔ They are easy to navigate.

✔ They portray the image you most want to communicate.

People go online to accomplish some purpose. The best sites enable people to get what they want quickly.

A few years ago, in a nationally televised vice presidential debate, a candidate asked two questions that became the objects of derision. "Who am I?" he asked, "and why am I here?" It's too bad people laughed at him, because his questions contain wisdom. You would be astonished at the number of commercial Web sites that don't explain their own purpose to a visitor. When people arrive at a Web site, they want to know the purpose of the site immediately. Are you selling something? If so, what? Are you offering information? Fine, where is it? Often, you can clarify your reason for existence with a simple tagline under your company name or logo (for example, "Margie's Muffins — Selling pastries to discriminating palates").

Easy navigation requires a thoughtful plan, but the extra effort pays off. People become impatient when they click endlessly and never seem to get where they want to be. You can help them by offering no more than a few choices per page. Divide your home page into broad but easily understood categories such as "Products we sell," "Frequently asked questions," "Press releases," and "How to contact us." **Remember:** A customer who gets lost on your site is a customer who will not return.

Your own Web site should carry the same image you portray in your bricks-and-mortar (traditional) store. Get your logo out front. Project an image that reflects the goals of your store. And get your selling message out there immediately — the customer doesn't have time to be teased.

Expressing your message clearly

A person who arrives at your site is interested not only in knowing what you do, but also in what you can do for him. Tell each visitor what benefits you offer — don't make them guess.

Use short paragraphs. Not only are short paragraphs attractive, but few people enjoy wading through an intimidating document full of big blocks of text. Prioritize your content. Put your most important and timely information at the top. Step up and be bold about the most exciting content.

Think of each person who arrives at your site as your one and only customer. Don't make him do all the work. Keep it simple. Avoid confusion.

Focusing on content

Content is the single most important reason people visit a site — they want information. Give it to them freely. Offer something of value.

Omit needless words. That's what Strunk and White said years ago (in _The Elements of Style_), and it's still grand advice today. All content should have a reason to be on your page, so get rid of fluff.

Customers love knowing the latest tips and the most current information, and they're more likely to return to a site when they're fairly certain the content changes regularly. The best sites clearly state when and how often the Web site content is updated.

Visual clues are helpful in communicating time-sensitive information to your audience. If your site features articles on a certain topic, make sure the date is displayed prominently. You may want to post a red arrow next to new information to alert the consumer. You don't want to be flashy (using blinking neon lights, for example), but you _can_ use bold colors with discretion. Good sites also often have an area called "What's New." That's a good spot to highlight promotional information or future events.

Making your site a door, not a window

You want your site to be inviting, like the reception area or lobby of your own business. Offer a visitor no more than four or five choices. When visitors arrive at a site, they immediately try to make sense of it. But they stop trying if they have more than a handful of choices on a single page. Let them know the point of your site right away. Invite a customer in.

Don't make any single page too long. So what's too long? A page is too long if people have to scroll down to find relevant information. If you have a lot of information to share, split it up and put a healthy chunk of information on each page. Each page of content should contain a single conceptual nugget of information. Not six nuggets — one. Clearly, some exceptions to this guideline exist, but on the whole, a single page of information is a reasonable goal.

Check and recheck your spelling and grammar. And carry a theme throughout your site. Make sure each page has the same background and the same buttons to help visitors navigate your site.

I learned a lesson the hard way about trying too hard to impress people. Once I designed a cool background for a friend, and it looked great on my machine with my software. I took it to her home, put it on her computer, and was appalled. My beautiful dark blue background looked garish and ugly on her machine. Different Internet browsers display colors differently, so beware.

Solid backgrounds are best. But if you have a dark background and also use dark text, people will have a hard time deciphering your words.

Cutting down on graphics and audio

Visitors want fast-loading pages, and graphics slow things down considerably. So every graphic on your Web site must earn its place. Is it worth the extra time it will take to load? Using the newest new thing is not always the *smartest* smart thing. Some people don't have fast Internet connections. Others don't want to buy all the software necessary to display graphics and audio and movies. Make your page one that loads quickly.

What is a fast-loading page? One that appears in just a few seconds. Bear in mind that some people do have broadband connections and enjoy sophisticated graphics. So design your site for the appropriate audience.

Be careful before adding audio to a site. Many people do not like having music blare at them unless they choose to listen. Some people surf the Web in their cubicles at work. They (and their bosses) will not be happy if loud noises suddenly scream out. So skip the audio unless it's important to your business — if you sell music, for example, or speech recognition software. And always offer a visitor the choice of whether to listen or not.

Making it easy to contact you

You would be surprised at how many sites forget this simple piece of wisdom: Make it simple for customers to find you. Sprinkle your phone number, address, e-mail information, store hours, and so on throughout your site. Also add a link to your homepage saying, "Contact Us." When readers click on that link, make sure all your contact information is available for viewing.

What you can learn from Goldilocks

People hate clicking and clicking and clicking while never seeming to arrive anywhere useful. They will stay on your site if you give them the information they want within a few clicks. Never force anyone to work too hard to find what they want.

There's a piece of magic involved in creating a good Web site, and it's this: People are just like Goldilocks — they don't want too much information on a page and they don't want too little. They want just the right amount.

How do you know the right amount? Observe yourself or your kids surfing the Internet. What makes you impatient? Slow-loading graphics and long dull pages, I'll bet. On the other hand, if the pages don't contain enough information, you're forced to click too often. You don't want that either. Visit other sites to develop a sixth sense about what is too much and too little. This is not a riddle that technology can solve; it calls for common sense and clear thinking. A good general guideline to shoot for is no more than three clicks before viewers find what they're looking for.

Tell your customers how you will support their needs. Can buyers send e-mail to you? Should they call? Do you have a toll-free number? Reassure customers that you are a real business and not *vaporware*. (Some years ago computer geeks divided the world into two parts. Half the world, they declared, is software, while the other half consists of hardware. Someone noticed, however, that many of these wonder products never actually existed. The term *vaporware* was coined to describe bogus goods.)

Maintaining your site

A good site has links that work. Clicking on a link only to find yourself on a page that says, "Information not found" is just plain annoying. Having broken links can damage your reputation and give customers a reason to question your ability to provide whatever service you are promoting. Remember that the work on a Web site does not end when the page is placed on the Internet. Keep your links and all other information accurate and up to date.

Your site will look different depending upon the software people use. Ask your friends to view your site to make sure it is attractive on other software.

Setting Your Web Site Goals

Establishing goals for your Web site is essential. (How else can you tell if you're succeeding?) Start by imagining your site in general terms. Do you want to amuse visitors? Then your Web site should be catchy and fun. Are you trying to persuade people to support a political cause? Maybe you want serious articles with just a dash of humor in the cartoons. Do you want people to hire your investment firm? You'll want to highlight your credentials in a professional, understated Web site.

Think small. Why? Because it keeps the costs down, and because keeping a site small allows for intelligent growth.

Most people create business Web sites for one of three reasons:

- ✔ To offer information.
- ✔ To offer some form of interactivity, such as e-mail or customer support.
- ✔ To offer a full-blown online store.

Visit the sites of your competitors. What do you like and dislike? What do they offer? How can you make your site different from and better than theirs? Make a list of competitor services and add to it the things that will make your site more valuable to the customer.

When you're setting goals for your Web site, ask yourself the following questions:

- ✔ **How big do you want your site?** Do you envision your Web site to be large, with many pages, or smaller and more compact? With a larger site, you will want to consider tools that allow people to search your site to find what they need. Unless you have a very large business already, go with a smaller site that can grow with your business.

- ✔ **How soon do you want your site up and running?** Hiring a Web designer can add weeks to your schedule, so planning ahead is smart. A word to the wise: *Not* hiring a Web designer can add *months* to the schedule, unless you're already a competent designer. Just be sure to put a limit on the amount you're willing to spend.

- ✔ **What audience do you want to reach?** If you sell rock music, your site will, and should, look a lot different than if you're selling flowers. Does your audience have access to the latest technology or will they be reluctant to try anything flashy? Prepare a list of what your customers want. What is important to them? Don't give them what *you* want. Give them what *they* want.

If you choose to create an online store at your Web site, keep in mind that customers want exactly the same thing they want in a traditional store. They want to locate goods easily. They want decent prices and quality merchandise. They want to get in and get out as quickly as possible. They want items to be in stock and accurately priced. Oh, and they want *service,* including guarantees and the ability to return what they don't want. Your customers must trust you, or they won't buy.

Sorting Out the Elements of a Web Site

Although thousands of pages have been written about Web sites over the past decade, here is essentially what you will need to get your site up and running:

- ✔ A domain name (such as Yahoo.com or Amazon.com)
- ✔ Site design and construction
- ✔ A Web site host or Internet Service Provider (ISP)

Choosing a domain name

Your domain name is a very important part of your Web site's success. If you choose a name that's catchy and easy to remember, your customers will come back time and time again. If the name is long or hard to remember, they may forget about it before they even get there.

In general, when you're choosing a domain name for your Web site, pick one that's directly tied to your business. For example, if your business name is Main Street Flower Shop, you could try MainStreetFlowers.com.

Keep in mind that domain names are a very hot commodity. People snatch them up all the time, so the name you want may already have been taken by someone else.

For more information on choosing the right domain name for your business, as well as for tips on buying the name you want, check out *Domain Names For Dummies* by GreatDomains.com, Steve Newman, and Susan Wels (published by Hungry Minds, Inc.).

Designing a site

Doing your own Web site design can save you lots of money, *if* you already have the skills. Are you a good graphical designer? Do you know how to transfer that knowledge to the computer? Do you understand HTML (hypertext markup language — the language used to display stuff on the Internet)? Do you know how to create fire-eating content? Can you take all your beautiful pages and put them on the Internet? Well, then, doing it yourself is the best choice for you.

For the rest of us, there are two choices: using templates and hiring a Web designer.

If you're interested in finding out more about Web site design, check out *Creating Web Pages For Dummies,* 5th Edition, by Bud Smith and Arthur Bebak (published by Hungry Minds, Inc.).

Using a template

A *template* is a boilerplate pattern that produces a certain type of finished product. Using templates in your Web design lowers costs and ensures consistency throughout the Web site. A Web site template may include such items as a menu, buttons to pass from one page to another, graphics, and sample pages that you can customize. It may have a template to describe your company history, the items you are selling, or special services you offer.

Before using a template, consider two issues:

> ✔ **Templates can provide professional-appearing pages, but you must use only those choices available in the package.** In other words, if you want individuality, templates are not the right choice.

> ✔ **Many templates take time to learn.** Templates may be cheaper than a designer in terms of cash layout but costly in terms of time.

You can get templates from some ISPs and you can also buy them from Web design vendors. Ask your ISP if it provides Web site templates.

Hiring a Web designer

If you don't have the skills and don't want to learn them now, or if you want a professional and personalized site online quickly, then hiring a Web designer is a good way to go. It is also usually — although not always — the most expensive alternative.

To get started, check out the following sites for lists of Web designers in your area who may be able to help you:

- **AAADesignList.com:** www.aaadesignlist.com
- **The List:** webdesign.thelist.com
- **LookSmart:** www.looksmart.com

Wait, you say! Finding a Web designer is one thing, but how do I know if the developer is any good? Not all Web designers are created equal. If you choose to hire a designer, you want her expertise, yes, but you also want your own ideas steering the boat.

Here's what you should expect from a good Web designer:

- **Several sterling references.** Be sure to call the references and ask how well the designer worked with the customer. Did the designer meet expectations? Was the schedule met? Were there unexpected costs at the end?

- **A trail of good Web sites.** Examine the work of the designer by visiting several Web sites developed by that person. Are the pages attractive? Are the sites easy to navigate? Do the sites have a look and feel appropriate to the Web site? Do any sites take an inappropriate time to load?

- **A clear list of what is and is not provided in the Web design project.** Will the designer put your site on the Internet for you? Will the designer notify search engines that your site is available? Will the designer create a logo for you, or do you have one already? How many pages will your finished site contain? Will the graphics be custom-designed or taken from a graphics package?

- **Does the designer know how to optimize your site for the search engines?** Find a Web designer who understands how to optimize your site so that customers can find you.

- **A delivery schedule.**

- **Milestones.** Will the designer give you a chance to approve or disapprove of the site at each step along the way?

- **A clear estimate of the costs — *all* the costs.**

- **A professional product.** The various pages on your site should all have a unified look and feel. Graphics should be tasteful and not too large. No single page should be so long that a visitor has to scroll way down to get to important information.

Your designer should expect professionalism from you, too. Here is what your designer can expect from you. Be sure you're providing it:

✔ **A clear sense of purpose.** You should communicate the way you want your site to look and feel. Flashy? Understated? Jam-packed with information?

✔ **The content for your site.** A Web designer cannot be expected to know your business as well as you do. You must provide logos, information, or whatever you have promised to the designer in a timely manner.

✔ **A list of a few sites that you particularly like.** The sites don't have to be in your same line of work, though.

✔ **A mind that's made up.** If you change your mind a little bit, that's to be expected. But no one can work with a person whose mind isn't made up.

✔ **Prompt payment.**

When you find a designer you like, you'll have several types of contracts from which to choose:

✔ **Hourly:** If you choose an hourly contract, make the reporting schedule frequent so you will know exactly how far along the designer is at any moment. You don't want to be caught by surprise. Be sure to reserve the right to cancel the project if your expectations are not being met.

✔ **Not to exceed:** Under this type of contract, the developer will estimate the cost for you and will probably charge by the hour, but the designer agrees not to go *over* a certain cost. If the developer has misjudged the estimate, he absorbs the cost.

✔ **Fixed price:** This contract is a flat rate. You and the designer agree to a single price for the entire job. Know exactly what you will receive on a fixed price contract. The number of hours your designer takes to complete the project is of no concern to you. Whether the designer finishes your site in a single day or a month, you pay the same rate.

✔ **Cost plus:** In this type of arrangement, you are billed for all costs, plus you will pay a fixed fee or a fixed percentage on top of the costs. Some developers subcontract part of the work to other people, and you will be required to pay the fee.

✔ **Design to fee:** Under this kind of contract, you tell the designer how much you are willing to pay. In return, you receive the best Web page possible for that price.

These various financial arrangements are the same for any design job — Web sites, print, collateral, whatever. You can mix and match or create other types of agreements as you and the designer see fit. Most designers require a payment before the project begins. Keep that initial payment as low as possible.

Make sure you include a payment schedule in your contract, no matter which type of contract you use. If speed is important to you, add a schedule incentive. For every week the project is late, deduct a percentage (about 5 percent). If the project is delivered early, add a bonus to the fee. Never ever make the final payment before the work is fully completed and you are satisfied. Also include a cancellation clause in the contract. You want to be able to cancel at your discretion at any time. (You have to pay for anything completed up to the point of cancellation, of course.) The developer will want a cancellation clause, too. That's only fair.

Finding an ISP

Internet Service Providers (ISPs) are everywhere, and you have many options to choose from. Here are some questions to ask of ISPs when you're shopping for one that works for you:

- **What kind of technical support do you offer?** You want someone available to help you 24/7/365. Do they have a toll-free number? Is technical help available via e-mail? *Remember:* Technical support never seems that important when you're signing up, but it becomes the most important thing in the world when your Web site crashes.

- **How many e-mail accounts will I have?** You may need multiple e-mail addresses if you have several employees. Take stock of what you think you'll need — now and in the future — and keep this in mind when you choose an ISP.

- **Do you have traffic limitations?** Some ISPs have restrictions on the number of visitors you may have to your site. Popular sites may be zinged with unexpected costs. Find out what additional costs you will incur if you go over the limit. The goal is to attract lots of people to your Web site, so an ISP that charges you for doing precisely what you're striving to do may be one you want to avoid.

- **How much disk space will my site be allowed?** Tell the ISP whether you think your site will have numerous pages or just a few. Be sure to mention whether your site will have lots of graphics as well. This information will help the ISP choose the correct package for you. Most hosting packages offer at least 25MB of disk space, which should be plenty. That works out to about 500 Web pages — give or take a few.

- **Do you keep backups?** System crashes can kill your business. If the ISP says its system never crashes, don't believe them. What you want them to say is that, on those rare occasions when their system crashes, they keep backups on another machine. Along the same lines, ask if the ISP has a backup power supply onsite.

✔ **Do you offer site statistics and log files?** This information is helpful if you want to keep track of how many visitors you have and which are the most (and least) popular pages on your site. You can find out how long each person stays on your site and where they came from — all very handy information.

✔ **Do you offer high-speed Internet access?** Most people connect to the Internet using a modem, but small to medium-sized businesses often depend on high-speed access. Ask your ISP if it supports digital subscriber lines (DSL), integrated services digital network (ISDN), cable modem, and T1 and T3 connections. Does the connection work at all times? Are there peak hours? Can you get a refund for downtime?

✔ **How many users per modem do they have?** You don't want busy signals all day. The more access numbers, the better.

✔ **What software is required of you?**

✔ **What is the cost for the service?** Do they offer hourly or flat-fee rates? In general, a flat fee is better because you won't have to keep one eye on the clock as you work. If you are absolutely sure you will not go online frequently, the hourly rate is preferable. Remember that a lot of people begin by thinking they won't be online much. Then they figure out how to use the Internet and decide they love it. In most cases, go for the flat fee.

✔ **What is your privacy policy?** Some ISPs sell the e-mail addresses of their clients. Unless you like getting lots and lots of spam in your inbox, you don't want this.

✔ **Do you offer Web hosting?** If the answer is no, find another ISP. Web hosting is simply the capacity to host your Web site in addition to giving your business Internet access.

✔ **Do you have templates available to help me build my site?** Some ISPs offer simple boilerplates to fill out (called templates). You provide information pertinent to your site and the template creates the correct HTML for you.

✔ **Can you help me find a Web designer/developer?** Many ISPs keep a list of Web designers because they realize that most people don't want to bother with learning HTML. These Web designers can create a Web site tailored to your individual requirements. Hiring a pro is a good way to go unless you are determined to master mounds of technical information.

✔ **Will you buy and register a domain name for me?** As ISPs discover more about what their customers want, they offer more services. In days gone by, you used to have to find an available domain name and then buy and register it. For a small fee, ISPs can take care of this little headache for you.

✔ **Do you offer shopping carts?** A *shopping cart* is what enables a buyer to select more than one item and pay for them all at the same time. If you're certain you will *never* want to sell online, you can ignore this question. But the answer could prove important if you think you may want an online store later.

✔ **What e-commerce software do you have that can help me build an online store?** Do they offer secure services for the customer? The current standard is called Secure Sockets Layer (SSL). Ask if the ISP offers it. SSL protects your customer's private information, including his credit card number. You don't want to operate an online store without it.

Promoting Your Site

If you build it will they come? Having a Web site does no good if nobody can find it. You can promote your site in a couple ways — online promotion and offline advertising. And you'll need to do *both* to get the word out.

Online promotion

A *search engine* (or directory) is a tool (such as Yahoo! or AltaVista) for combing the billions of Internet pages to find the information you need. One problem with search engines is that they're so incredibly thorough. Even the simplest search can return millions of *hits* (sites that fit your search criteria). Another problem is that no single search engine covers the entire Web. That means you will receive different answers to the same question on different search engines. You can view that as an annoyance *or* as an opportunity. I choose the latter outlook, because it gives me more chances to succeed — to get my site listed in such a way that anyone can find it.

Don't worry about getting your site listed on more than eight or nine search engines. Almost everybody has a favorite search engine anyway, and people aren't going to check 47 search engines to find you. Each person will check one or maybe two of the major engines, so there is no point in bothering with the little ones.

Each engine ranks sites using different criteria — and those criteria change frequently. The formula used by the search engines to rank sites is highly secret, but some common elements never change. Search engines rank sites high in any given category if the site follows a set of rules. This is why finding a Web site developer who understands how to optimize your site for the search engines is so important. If you run a furniture store specializing in antiques, you want people to be able to look under *furniture* and *antique* and *antique furniture* and have your business appear near the top of the list. A good Web designer can make sure this happens.

To make it easy on your Web site developer, tell him to optimize only for the following search engines and directories:

- ✔ AltaVista
- ✔ Excite
- ✔ Google
- ✔ Infoseek
- ✔ Inktomi
- ✔ Lycos
- ✔ WebCrawler
- ✔ Yahoo!

Search engines take six to eight weeks to index new sites, so you will have to be patient. Make sure that your Web site developer submits your URL (Web address) as soon as possible to decrease the wait.

Offline promotion

You can do a lot offline to let people know you have a Web site, too. Make sure your staff knows what your Web address is and ask them not to be shy about passing it around. Put your URL on everything:

- ✔ Brochures
- ✔ Business cards
- ✔ Direct mailers
- ✔ Newspaper ads
- ✔ Radio and TV commercials
- ✔ Stationery
- ✔ T-shirts, pens, tiepins, and magnetic refrigerator stickers
- ✔ Your storefront sign
- ✔ Your telephone answering machine or voice mail message

Six ways to drive people *away* from your site

Want to rid yourself of pesky customers and make your Web site a total disaster? Here are six excellent ways:

☛ **Put lots of silly graphics on your site**. People love spending their time waiting for your page to load. They are especially amused when some of the graphics flash on and off and cause them eyestrain.

☛ **Don't mention your product or how much it costs until you are forced to explain what you sell.** Be sure not to mention how and when the merchandise will be shipped.

☛ **Make your customer hunt for ways to contact you.** Putting your phone number in tiny print does the trick nicely. Be coy about your store hours, too.

☛ **Use the element of surprise.** Make information inaccurate or vague.

☛ **Throw in misspellings and grammatical errors.**

☛ **Make sure your links don't work.**

Or you can do just the opposite of the above and enjoy the hits of happy customers. It's up to you.

In other words, put your URL everywhere you would put your telephone number or street address. It's just as important to your business's success.

Give people a reason to visit your site. Offer something free, whether it be information about an amazing diet or a free T-shirt. Most people who see your URL on a billboard will not rush home to view your site unless something is in it for them. Offer convenience. Offer online ordering. Offer *something,* or no one will bother.

Part III

Developing a Plan That's within Your Budget

The 5th Wave   By Rich Tennant

"Hey! Frank Malloy! You still advertising diving equipment?"

In this part . . .

Sometime in the process of developing your advertising plan, you will need to sit down and crunch numbers. You have to find out whether you can afford all the great ideas you'll come up with. Your goal is to create an advertising campaign with a good chance at success, and to do so within a budget you can comfortably live with. Doing this can be a tricky juggling act — sort of like keeping a couple of bowling balls and a chain saw in the air at once. On the one hand, you want your ads to have an impact, which means you'll want to place those ads on mass-appeal media (as opposed to unappealing media). On the other hand, high-impact mass media costs money, which you may not have in infinite amounts.

To put the problem another way, you want to find a happy medium between devising an ad plan with a foolproof chance at making a successful impact in your marketplace, and going to debtor's prison. You're on the horns of a dilemma (and those horns can be quite painful). So in this part, I give you some guidelines to help you plan your budget and show you comparisons of how other businesses allocate advertising funds as a percentage of their gross sales.

I know it's a cliché, but it's true: You must plan your work, then work your plan.

Chapter 12

Setting and Working within Your Advertising Budget

I know half the money I spend on advertising is wasted, but I can never find out which half.

— John Wanamaker, Philadelphia department store magnate

Companies like Procter & Gamble, General Motors, and McDonald's spend more on advertising each year than the average small to mid-size business could ever hope to gross in a lifetime. No one knows (and the companies aren't telling) what their ratio of advertising budget to gross income actually is, but you can bet it's high. These companies have spent a king's ransom successfully positioning their products to be top-of-mind with the entire buying public — and it costs them a yearly fortune to maintain this *branding* of their products. If one of their products begins to slip in overall sales, they throw $25 million in extra advertising funds at the problem without a second thought. The total amounts of their ad funds are simply astounding (Procter & Gamble, for example, spent $4.7 billion on advertising in 1998 alone).

You, on the other hand, will very likely look upon your advertising dollars as a seriously important personal investment — an investment that (shudder!) comes right off the bottom line and, therefore, will never be a part of your hard-earned take-home pay. For this reason, you need to do some careful planning as you decide what percentage of your gross sales you can realistically afford to spend for advertising. You don't want to overdo it, but you can't skimp too much either. As with many things in life, balance is what it's all about.

A good place to start when you're setting a budget is in examining your goals. If you want to become the Big Dog, if your driving ambition is to elevate your business into an industry-leadership position and blow your competition away, then of course you will need to spend a lot more money than if you were satisfied with just getting by. In this book, I make the assumption that you want to do much better than just getting by — you wouldn't be advertising at all if you didn't want your business to grow and prosper. But in order to see the kind of success you're after, you need an ad budget.

Over half of new businesses fail within their first two years. This depressing statistic is probably due to a number of things, but a lack of working capital is usually at the top of the list. Most businesses start out with great hopes and limited cash, and it's the hand-to-mouth reality of a startup that kills most of them. When people open new businesses, they often forget to set aside enough money for a large enough ad budget to get their name out there. You can invent a better mousetrap, but not having enough working capital to afford to tell the world about it is like trying to tow a boat with a rope.

Knowing How Much to Spend

So, what dollar amount, or percentage of gross sales, should you invest in an advertising budget? The question is a very tough one. And although I can give you some guidelines, only you will be able to answer it in when it's all said and done. After all, it's your money.

To get an idea of what typical businesses spend on advertising, I asked several of my agency's clients what percentage of gross sales they spend. Not a single one of them could give me straight answer to my question. They had each used a different formula to arrive at their budget number, and they each planned their advertising expenditures using different criteria.

Our agency has one retail client who spends as much as 10 percent of gross sales on advertising. Although this percentage may seem high, some businesses *must* spend that amount in order to compete, and I've worked for clients who spent even more. On the other hand, I've seen businesses spend 2 percent or less on advertising — and, in the case of very small companies, some don't spend even that much on a sustained basis. According to a radio station manager I know, the average retail business spends somewhere between 3 and 7 percent of gross sales on advertising.

You can use these figures as general guidelines to help you set your own advertising budget, but keep in mind that each business is unique. What works for one company may not work for another. When in doubt, follow this simple rule: Spend as much money on advertising as it takes to make and sustain an impact in the marketplace, but don't spend so much that you run the risk of putting yourself into financial jeopardy.

You can begin the process of setting a budget by trying to come up with some answers to the following question:

- How big is your business?

- How much yearly income does your business generate?

- What do you want to accomplish with your advertising, and how much will that cost?

- What is your competition spending?

If you're in a highly competitive business, such as wireless phones, tires, or the car business, you need to step up to the plate with some serious bucks in order to hit a homerun in your marketplace. Your competition is spending their brains out, and you will have to do the same. On the other hand, if your business enjoys a unique status in your market, if you provide merchandise or a service that people cannot find elsewhere, then you'll be able to get away with much lower spending.

If your budget is too limited to make an impact in the market on a daily or weekly basis, stash your cash until you're having some special event or sale and then attack the media full-force. In advertising, you're better off having a big voice once in a while than a weak voice every day.

Coming Up with a Plan

You probably went into business to succeed — and that means that you'll do whatever it takes to reach this lofty goal . . . as long as it's legal and within fiscal reason. But in order to succeed with your advertising — or with anything in life, actually — it helps to have a plan of action. In this section, I help you get started in coming up with a plan that will work for _you_.

Looking at your competition

A good step to consider when devising your advertising plan, and planning the extent of your budget, is to try to find out what your competition is doing. Do you see ads for your competitors in the newspaper on a regular basis? Call the paper and ask for its retail display ad rate in order to figure out how much the competition is spending to advertise there. Do you hear competitors' radio commercials often? Call the station's sales department and ask about its rates. A salesperson will likely tell you _precisely_ what your competition is spending so she can talk you into doing the same thing. Does your weekly mail bring coupons or brochures from your competition? Find out what those ads cost. (In Part IV, I give some guidelines and relative costs for all media, but you can pin it down even further with a few well-placed phone calls in your own area.)

Why should you want to know what your competition is spending? Because this information will give you some basis for planning your own budget. Forewarned is forearmed, which in this case means that gathering information about the other guys will help you make a quantified judgment as to how much you'll need to spend in order to compete with them. If you own a mom-and-pop hardware store, you may have a tough time generating a budget that will compete with the monster-size warehouse stores — but don't panic. Simply outspending the other guy (or even trying to keep up with him) isn't the whole answer.

You may be relieved to know that you can spend a lot less than your competition and still make more of an impact by being a bit more creative with both your message and your media buying. You *can* make up for a lack of money with an abundance of creativity and careful — no, make that *diligent* — media negotiation and spending. You can also make your available advertising budget stretch if you don't waste any of it on irrelevant media that will bring you little or no business.

Regardless of the limits of your ad budget, and if you are trying to reach a broad audience, accept this as a given: You *can* afford mass media. You *can* afford to buy radio commercials, ads in a mass-circulation daily newspaper, spots on broadcast television and cable stations, even ads in the regional editions of major magazines. This media may, at first blush, appear to be unaffordable. But, regardless of the expense (which may be less than you think), when you consider how many people you'll be reaching, it's the smartest way you can spend your money.

What you *cannot* afford to do is fritter away a limited ad budget on questionable media, like the dozens of ads you find in your mailbox every day, that are better suited for wrapping fish than they are for attracting new customers to your business. The old saw "You get what you pay for" will never be truer.

Identifying your target market

If you own a skateboard store then you're going to target teens rather than senior citizens, right? And you'll find those teens, not reading the newspaper or looking at direct mail pieces, but listening to very narrowly programmed radio stations and watching certain TV shows. If, on the other hand, you're selling luxury cars which are purchased primarily by affluent adults over 55, you will do well to place ads in the Business section of your paper, and to buy spots on radio stations programmed with news, talk, oldies, or classical music. Just a little bit of thought into who your target market is and what forms of media they pay attention to can save you lots of money and tons of grief.

By identifying your primary target market, you can do a better job of narrowing your media buys, which will lead you to a bottom-line budget figure that makes sense. This information will also help you when it comes time to design and write your ads. Teenagers, as you know, speak an entirely different language than do adults, so not only must you buy the media they are attracted to, you also want to write and design your ads to attract their attention in the first place.

Knowing your product

What you're selling will help you determine what media you should be buying. Are you selling tires? Then your primary media will be print, because you need to list all those different brands, sizes, and prices in those long columns of itsy-bitsy type. You may also call attention to your print ads with some radio. And, if you want to show how clean and beautiful your shop is, you may consider some TV. Direct mail, if it's a stand-alone piece for you and you alone, can be somewhat effective as well.

Are you selling a professional service such as accounting, financial management, or consulting? Then you'll want to look at news, talk, or another radio format listened to by business people. If print is in your ad plan, then the local business journal, or the Business section or main News section of your newspapers are good bets.

If you're selling beauty products, or run a hair or nail salon, you'll need to find your target market by buying on radio stations that can prove to you their audience composition includes mostly women. Women also read the newspaper Business page in great numbers, as well as the Entertainment, Society, and main News sections. And dozens of television shows — and even entire cable stations — are targeted toward women.

What I'm getting at here is that you must narrow your focus in order to get a handle on the amount you will need to invest in advertising, by identifying your primary market segment. There's no sense in taking the shotgun approach when a well-aimed rifle shot will find more of who you're looking for — and for a lot less money. If you're selling a female-oriented product, you don't want to waste too much of your ad budget advertising to men, and vice versa. Sure, there will be some spillover, and there's nothing you can do about that. But targeting your media buys as narrowly as possible will save you money in a big way.

Maximizing Your Budget

You need to spend enough money on advertising to make an impact in the marketplace. You need to make some noise, be heard above the din of other advertising messages. But you don't want to spend more on advertising than you can comfortably afford. Making the most of the money you have can be a difficult tightrope act.

One of my clients, whose advertising budget remains steady from month to month regardless of ups and downs in sales, preaches consistency as the number one rule in his advertising plans. His philosophy is simple: In order to compete, you must be heard. You want consumers to think of your business when they're in the market for the products you sell, so you should at least have *some* advertising presence at all times. His thinking is, over the year, it all averages out.

On the other hand, not everyone can afford to have an advertising presence year-round. You may not even need to be out there every day. By virtue of your unique product or service, you may be able to do a fine job by only advertising special events or sales on an as-needed basis. This kind of advertising requires a bit more planning and creative media buying in order to get the job done, but it's a workable option for many businesses.

Finally, many businesses simply don't have enough money to do much more than advertise when they absolutely have to, such as Christmas or back-to-school times.

Whichever of these groups you fall into, keep in mind that you can save big bucks in many different ways, several of which I outline for you in the following sections.

Creative and production

Creative and production are areas that, with just a bit of good writing and skillful execution, are perfect places to save money without sacrificing effectiveness. Your ads can look and sound like champagne, even though your budget can only afford beer. You don't need to spend a small fortune producing a television commercial to sell something that could easily be explained in a well-written and cleverly produced radio spot. Nor do you need to buy a full-page, four-color newspaper ad when a small-space, black-and-white ad with a killer headline and graphic will likely attract as much or more attention. And you needn't waste money on a so-called celebrity spokesperson to pitch your business on radio if you can hire an actor to imitate a famous voice.

I once produced a series of radio spots for a chain of Bay Area health clubs that, although we most certainly never mentioned the character's name, starred the voice of someone who sounded a lot like Conan the Barbarian. Want a voice? Call your ad agency, or look in the Yellow Pages under "Talent Agents."

You can save money on advertising production if you begin with a clever concept and good writing that take cost-effective production into consideration from the very beginning. In other words, don't write a TV spot that must be filmed beneath the Eiffel Tower if you can't afford to send a film crew to France. Putting together a radio spot using French music, European traffic sound effects, and an actor with a believable French accent might be a bit more cost-effective. If you do it right, the listener will add the mental image of the Eiffel Tower for you, free of charge.

Okay, so you're not planning to do a full-blown commercial shoot in Paris, but you may be tempted to write and produce a TV spot because you feel your product is so darned "visual" that the consumer simply must see it to appreciate it. Here are two truths to ponder before you bite off more than you can chew:

- ✔ Television production costs more than radio production.
- ✔ Radio *can* conjure "visual images" in the mind of the listener if it's used correctly.

Armed with this information, why not write a radio commercial that is filled with visual imagery and costs only a pittance to produce as compared to a TV spot? These mental images (*the theater of the mind,* as I call it) can be more effective than showing the actual product. A chain of furniture stores my agency handles hasn't done television in years because we proved to them that radio can effectively paint mental pictures of the various furniture pieces they're selling. With the same amount of dollars they were spending on one or two broadcast or cable TV stations, they are now buying time on a half-dozen radio stations — and their business has never been better.

Begin by planning a creative concept that can, at the same time, be produced inexpensively and is clever enough to be heard above the roar. Easier said than done, you say? Perhaps. But it is not impossible, and it can be quite a bit of fun. Besides, why would you want to do boring advertising? Consumers don't want to see or hear any more boring advertising — they're already saturated with it. They'd much rather see or hear clever, funny, memorable ads that, more often than not, will jolt them into responding. This type of advertising is what you should be shooting for.

Using the media you can afford

I get into the meaty parts of media negotiation, planning, and buying in Part IV. But for now, I help you consider a few of your options as you formulate your budget strategy. This section may give you some pleasant surprises, or at least dispel some of your beliefs about media affordability.

Radio

One of the top-rated news/talk-radio stations in the Bay Area sells primetime ads (during the morning and evening commute) for prices in the $1,000– to $1,500-per-spot range, but its late night (midnight to 6:00 a.m.) ads can be had for as low as $100 a spot. I actually know of one local business that buys the late-night time slot on this station and pays for the commercials with $100 bills. The beleaguered station sales rep has to schlep over to his office to collect the money this guy pays in advance for whatever number of spots he can afford on any given week. This strategy may sound a bit hokey, but advertising on this station during the late-night time slots really works for this guy. He has a presence on a major station, which gives his business an aura of prestige, and he gets it on a surprisingly low budget. So, what is the moral of this little story? On radio, you don't need major ad bucks in order to sound like you do.

Another affordable way to buy radio is by taking advantage of the *package deal,* which includes a certain number of prime spots, a few mid-days, a few overnights, and a few *rotators* (spots that the station may run anywhere it likes). Radio stations usually tell you they'll sell these packages to you for only "$50 a spot!" or whatever the amount — this is referred to as an *average spot cost.* And that's true if you look at the average cost of the ads when grouped together. But because you'll reach a lot more people during the morning commute than you can hope to reach at 3:00 a.m., an average spot cost isn't the best way to analyze the cost effectiveness of package deals. You're better off asking the station rep how many *gross impressions* the spots in the package will generate — that number will tell you how many people will actually *hear* the ads, which in turn will help you decide if the package is all that it's cracked up to be.

Newspaper

In the area of print, you don't need to buy large ads in order to be noticed. Take a look at your daily paper and you'll see that, in most cases, the smaller ads are placed at the top of each page — they sit atop the large space ads. This is just the way the newspaper's layout department does it, for some reason. Now, while I can't deny that the eye may be first drawn to the largest ads on a page, it stands to reason that if your message is clear enough and presented in a clever way, and if your ad is positioned near the top of the page, with a good headline and an eye-catching graphic element, you'll probably get as good a response as the guy whose big, fat ad is sitting beneath yours and contains none of the above.

Cable TV

Cable television is an affordable media, but if you use it, you need to be diligent about a few details. Here are some questions you need to ask before you buy:

- ✔ On which of the cable channels will my spots run?
- ✔ At what times will the spots run on those channels?
- ✔ In which zones will my spots run?

Sound confusing? I'll tell you how confusing it really is: Cable TV has been known to reduce a professional media buyer to tears. And a seasoned ad agency accounts payable manager once said he'd rather schedule a root canal than try to decipher a cable station's invoice. Here's why: Every cable company is selling ads on a hundred or more different channels, each channel is programmed to reach a separate and unique market segment, and each channel is broadcast into various zones within the overall coverage area. So, although eminently affordable, particularly at a paltry two bucks a spot in some cases, make sure you know precisely what you're buying.

Broadcast TV

Broadcast television can be affordable in certain time slots. One chain of auto-repair shops for which I have done work buys one or two 30-second commercials daily on the early morning news show (6:00 a.m.) and the early fringe news program (5:00 p.m.) on the local ABC-TV station. Because he's on these local news shows every day, and because these shows are very reasonably priced, he has a substantial television presence (at least with the people who watch those shows) for less than $5,000 a month.

Bottom line: Go bargain hunting

You want an advertising presence in media that gives you your best chance of attracting large numbers of customers. The various media options listed in this chapter are only a few of the many ways you can save money and still buy media that will do you the most good. In Part IV, I provide even more information on the various forms of media and how to buy them.

Concentrate your available dollars in good, solid media — even though you may not be able to afford to buy prime-time or full-page ads. Don't toss away your money on cockamamie "deals" offered to you by off-the-wall media that no one will pay attention to. In other words, don't buy a rotten egg when you can afford a lovely omelet.

Go bargain hunting. Your local media, even some of the national media, have some great deals.

Late night, early morning, even midday time slots may offer just the kind of programming that will be viewed by your target market. And these time slots are priced within the budgets of most local advertisers (so *that's* why you see all those car dealer ads at those times).

National magazines

Yes, unbelievably, you can afford to buy ads in big-time magazines like *Time, Newsweek, Sports Illustrated,* and the like by buying advertising in what's called their *regional editions.* You can place your ad in one of these publications, or a predetermined group of publications that is sold as a package, for relatively small amounts because all of the big magazines break down their circulation (and actual printing) into zones or regions. For instance, you can buy an ad for the circulation of the entire Bay Area, or break it down to just your city. Some magazines will also sell you a *cover wrap*, sort of like a book's dust jacket, which can be a fairly prestigious way to get the word out there!

Although magazine advertising is a rather dramatic vehicle for a local business to use, it doesn't cost nearly as much as you think. When you can buy a big-time publication that allows you to pay only for your *sphere of influence* (the area from which you can reasonably expect to attract business), you can afford to at least look like a major player. So, if you want to impress the neighbors and keep up with the Joneses, pop a full-page into *Time* magazine. That ought to get their attention!

Chapter 13

Boosting Your Budget with Co-Op Programs

In This Chapter

▶ Getting clear on what co-op advertising funds are

▶ Finding suppliers who have funds you can use

▶ Being aware of the different forms co-op funds take

▶ Applying for, and receiving, co-op money

*M*any suppliers, manufacturers, and distributors of various major products and goods have advertising money set aside for use by their retailers. These funds are called *cooperative advertising* (*co-op* for short). The term *cooperative* means just what it says: If you spend some money, the manufacturer will also spend some money — the two of you cooperate to get the advertising job done.

Another form of cooperative funding is called *vendor money.* Vendor money is *in addition to* any co-op funds you may be entitled to. It's usually passed along to the squeakiest wheel — the clever retailer who knows it exists and has the cheek to go after it. Vendor money has no strings attached; you receive it either in the form of cash, or as a discount on future purchases.

After you've located the funds you need, you'll have to run an obstacle course on your way to collecting them, providing all the proof the vendor requires that you actually ran the ads. Then, and only then, will you receive your co-op funds in some form or another. Co-op funds are paid in strange and unusual ways including, but not limited to:

✔ Cash reimbursement

✔ Additional merchandise

✔ Discounts off future merchandise purchases

No matter what form of co-op payment you receive from any given supplier, always keep one thing in mind: It's found money — money you wouldn't otherwise have if you hadn't gone to the trouble to ask for and earn it.

Although co-op advertising is sometimes very complicated, frustrating, confusing, and time-consuming, it is well worth the effort. Co-op funds are a wonderful thing when you can add these extra dollars to your own advertising budget and use them to make a much bigger splash in your market. In this chapter, I give you the information you need to put co-op funds to work for you, demystifying this often-confusing part of the advertising arena.

Knowing Who Uses Co-Op Funds

Each week, you probably receive one or more multi-page, color brochures from your local supermarkets. These brochures are filled with this week's bombastic specials on everything from soft drinks to bathroom tissue, dog food to deodorant — and they usually contain coupons you can use when you shop at their stores. These newsprint brochures are almost entirely paid for with co-op funds provided to your local grocer by the companies that produce the dozens of items listed inside. Each of the manufacturers, suppliers, or distributors pays for the percentage of advertising space it receives in each brochure. For instance, if the toilet paper company is getting one full page of a 20-page flyer, it tosses 5 percent of the total cost of the brochure into the pot. By advertising only those products that will provide co-op funds, your grocer can, in theory, produce and distribute these weekly brochures without spending a dime of his own money.

The manufacturers and distributors that supply the grocer provide a certain amount of co-op money based on the total amount of their products the grocer purchases. If the grocer buys 1,000 cases of creamed corn for a special price, then advertises "dramatic savings" on that merchandise in his weekly mailer, he may get $1,000 in extra co-op funds as part of his deal with the creamed corn supplier. And you can bet that the grocer won't buy 1,000 cases of any particular brand of creamed corn unless he also gets a boost of co-op money from the supplier to help him peddle it.

When you add up all the items advertised in these flyers, you can be sure that someone in the grocer's advertising department spent a heck of a lot of time finding and figuring out what money was available from which suppliers, and how to collect and spend it. A local chain of supermarkets for which I have done advertising work has a full-time person who does nothing but handle co-op funds.

The grocery business is just one example of who takes advantage of co-op funds and what they must do to collect it. The formulas for computing co-op are as diverse as the companies that offer it. And there's always a catch — there's no such thing as a free lunch (free creamed corn, perhaps, but no free lunch). The retailer (you) must adhere to certain rules and make certain purchases in order to qualify for and collect co-op money. But do not be dismayed — it's worth it!

Grocery stores aren't the only businesses that take advantage of co-op advertising funds. Virtually any retail business you can think of is selling products for which co-op ad funds are available. If you look around *your* store, you may be able to identify products from big-name manufacturers who, in all likelihood, have co-op or vendor dollars set aside to aid you in selling these items. If you don't take advantage of the money that's out there, that money is most likely shared by company executives as bonuses. This may sound self-defeating on the part of the manufacturer, which should be doing all it can to sell product, but corporate executives often have other, shall we say, *personal* motives. Why not put that money to work for you instead of letting it go to line the pockets of the corporate bigwigs?

Many retailers either don't know co-op money is available, or they find the thought of collecting the funds too daunting. For this reason, a lot of available cash is left on the table because retailers think they have better things to do than fill out forms and adhere to certain rules in order to collect a few extra bucks to throw at advertising. You can work this situation to your favor, however, by taking advantage of the money your competitors aren't seizing for themselves. Yes, it's work. But when you receive a nice check from one of your manufacturers, or some free goods, or a big discount off your next purchase, the extra work will have been well worth your time and trouble.

Finding Out Which of Your Suppliers Have Co-Op Funds Available

The suppliers of many of the products that you sell most likely have available advertising funds that they will be happy to provide you — if you follow their sometimes convoluted rules and go to the trouble to ask for it.

I have one client who told me that, in his first ten years in business, he never applied for co-op advertising funds because he didn't know they existed. Not a single manufacturer from whom he was buying merchandise had bothered to tell him they had co-op funds available to augment his very limited ad budget. So what's the moral to this story? If you want co-op funds, you have to ask! Look at all the brands you're selling, read every factory invoice, calculate what you're spending with each of your suppliers, and go after them for ad bucks. Chances are, co-op or vendor dollars are available from at least *some* of the companies who supply you with inventory.

Each of the vendors who sell to your store has assigned a sales representative to work with you. You are visited by these people on a regular basis — of course you are, they want to sell you stuff! These sales reps are a great place to start the process of finding co-op funds. Even though these people may not be inclined to offer information on co-op funds on their own (because of some bonus arrangement they may have with their employers), they'll definitely tell you about them if you ask.

If you get a positive response from one or more of these sales reps, get the lowdown on how you should go about collecting some of this money. Ask what you will need to do to qualify for funds, and what, if you do qualify, you will be required to do in order to receive a check. If the manufacturer's rep tells you there are no co-op funds available to you, press the issue and ask if there are vendor dollars (which have no strings attached other than a few initial qualifiers).

You may also want to talk to the marketing and/or advertising managers of these suppliers — these are the people who control the advertising funds (including co-op money), which means you can get your answer straight from the horse's mouth. If the marketing or advertising manager says the company doesn't offer co-op funds, show how smart you are by asking for vendor dollars. This question will definitely get a marketing or advertising manager's attention because, chances are, he's never mentioned these available dollars to anyone.

If you're working with an ad agency, ask them what their experience is with businesses similar to yours, and where these other businesses may have found co-op money. Agency people know where the bodies are buried, as they say in the ad biz. I even know of one group of radio stations in my area that has a co-op department for the express purpose of helping its direct advertisers find money they may not otherwise have known was available to them. Of course, the radio stations benefit from this found money, too, because the companies spend that money advertising on their radio stations.

One way or another, ask as many people as you can think of within the various companies you deal with about co-op funds. Unless you're selling something obscure like arts and crafts made by individuals, you'll quite likely find some hidden money somewhere.

Understanding the Rules, Regulations, and Restrictions

Each of your suppliers will have a unique set of rules to which you must adhere in order to collect even a dime of co-op funds from them. The rules and restrictions set up within co-op programs can be so complicated that you may wonder if these suppliers want anyone to even *try* to collect. But even though the restrictions can be a bit off-putting, if you follow the rules to the letter, you will be rewarded with either some extra cash to invest in advertising, or some additional merchandise with which you can make a big, fat profit. All in all, the pain is worth the gain.

If you work with an ad agency, they may be able to help you navigate the rules and regulations. My agency, for example, deals with several clients who count on co-op advertising funds to either augment or completely provide their advertising budgets. Because these accounts have hired my agency, we do all the work of collecting the funds for them. It's one of the services we provide, and we do it month after month for multiple accounts (each with different rules of collection). Collecting co-op funds can be time-consuming, but if you know the rules and follow them, you can do it without much trouble.

When you're working on your own, without an agency, you'll need to do the legwork yourself. In the following sections, I walk you through the process of using co-op funds — and collecting your money.

Co-op funds may be earned (and accrued) over a specific period of time and carry with them a deadline for use. It's knows as "Use it or lose it." Make sure you find out about any deadlines imposed by manufacturers on the use of their available co-op advertising funds, and be sure to spend the money before it disappears.

Getting your ads pre-approved

For the purpose of example, let's assume that you own a paint store. One of your major manufacturers has told you they will co-op an advertising campaign to sell 1,000 gallons of Putrid Peach paint they have lying around. They tell you that, if you will contribute some of your ad bucks (you pick the amount you think it will take to dispose of this paint within a reasonable amount of time), they will match you 100 percent up to $5,000. Your total ad budget could, therefore, be $10,000 — more than enough to buy some local radio time and a couple of big ads in the newspaper.

Advertising cooperatives: Not the same as co-op funds

Advertising cooperatives are a different beast altogether. Unlike co-op funds, advertising cooperatives *cost* you money. But it could be the best money you'll ever spend, because you'll enjoy high-quality production and your fair share of the clout of a substantial combined media budget.

Advertising cooperatives (also known as *dealer ad groups*) are common in the franchising business and the automotive business. The franchise business learned a long time ago that it could do a much better job at advertising if it asked each of its franchisees to pony up a percentage of gross sales, which would then go into a war chest where it would accumulate until there was enough available cash to do a large-scale media buy for all the franchises together. An individual store couldn't hope to do advertising on a scale to match the combined budgets of many stores. Strength in numbers is the name of the game.

The advertising cooperative's money is also used to employ the services of an ad agency that produces top-quality TV, radio, and print advertising, as well as in-store, point-of-purchase display materials, and in the case of food franchises, menus, banners, bags, and so on. If you are in a business that can take advantage of the media buying power and quality production provided by an advertising cooperative, be sure to get involved. Your business will most likely benefit.

Your next step is get your ads preapproved by the manufacturer. In most cases, you will be required to have all your advertising preapproved by the factory to make sure they adhere to the manufacturer's co-op guidelines. Your supplier may have an approval form for you to fill out. Along with this completed form, you will be required to submit copies of radio scripts, a cassette tape of the final produced commercial(s), and at least a rough layout (plus a copy of the final, finished copy) for your newspaper ads. The manufacturer's advertising or marketing department will then either send you a stamped approval as is, or advise you to make certain necessary and required changes. They may also simply advise you of the required changes and stamp and sign the approval "Approved with changes." Be sure to follow their co-op rules and guidelines carefully, making whatever changes they request.

Never run co-op advertising without first obtaining signed preapproval from the supplier.

Getting proof of performance

After you've made the requested changes to your ads (if there were any), you need to make sure to get what's called *proof of performance* from the media, which is really just verification that you ran the ads as you said you would.

To return to the paint store example from the preceding section, when you buy your ads from the radio station, advise them that you'll be using co-op funds (they'll usually know precisely what information you will need). Let them know that you'll require the following verifications and co-op information with their invoices:

- ✔ **A notarized copy of your finished script listing the number of spots run and the total dollar amount those spots represented in your total media buy.** If you are using more than one script, each script will need to be notarized with the above information.
- ✔ **A notarized or certified invoice listing the run times of each spot, the title of the script for each spot, and the total dollar amount of the buy.**

Advise the newspaper how many *tear sheets* you'll need to provide for the manufacturer (tear sheets are copies of the actual printed page on which your ad appeared — the manufacturer will let you know how many you'll need to provide as proof of performance). The newspaper will provide those tear sheets along with their notarized total invoice.

Submitting your co-op claims package

You make the requested changes, the ads run, the campaign is a success, and hundreds of people with questionable color sense fight their way through your doors. The Putrid Peach paint is history. Now you just submit the entire package — the signed pre-approval form, the notarized media invoices, the notarized radio scripts, the cassette tape of the finished radio spots, and the newspaper tear sheets — to your supplier along with your written request for reimbursement of the promised percentage of the campaign.

There. Wasn't that simple? Now all you need do is wait for the co-op check to arrive in the mail. And, there's a bonus in the above scenario — you also got rid of that disgusting paint color!

Part IV
Buying the Different Media

The 5th Wave
By Rich Tennant

"You can fool some of the people all of the time, and all of the people some of the time. But it takes a staggering advertising budget to fool all of the people all of the time."

In this part . . .

The chapters in this part give you a real-world look at negotiating with sales reps and buying advertising schedules on the various media for your retail business. The advice I give here is done under the assumption that you want to save a few dollars wherever possible. I also show you a few tricks of the trade and give you a good understanding of the buzzwords you will encounter along the way.

Chapter 14

Purchasing Ad Time on the Radio

- -

In This Chapter

▶ Knowing which stations are best for you

▶ Paying attention to the demographic you're selling to

▶ Weeding through the data you hear from sales reps and getting to what counts

▶ Reading a radio station's invoice

- -

An idea can turn to dust or magic, depending on the talent that rubs against it.

— Bill Bernbach

Radio stations target their programming to attract very specific audiences. You can find stations formatted for everyone from teenyboppers to Baby Boomers, from cowboys to classical music aficionados. There are stations that feature hits of the '50s, the '60s, or the '70s; stations that broadcast only news; Spanish language, country, jazz, or good old rock 'n' roll stations. Radio has something for everyone. So, before you get down to the nitty-gritty of negotiating and buying a schedule for your radio ads, you need to do a little homework to assure that your schedule will run on the station best suited to attract customers to your business, customers who will want to buy what you're selling. If you're selling pickup trucks, for instance, you'd probably be better off advertising on a country music station than on one that plays only classical. If, on the other hand, you own an art gallery or jewelry store, the classical station may be just the place for your ad bucks.

Radio audiences tend to be very loyal to their favorite stations, sticking with their favorites not only out of choice, but out of habit. They're also loyal to many of the advertisers on their favorite stations, so finding the stations that can deliver the best audience for your commercial messages is definitely worth the effort.

In this chapter, I help you figure out which stations to advertise on, guiding you through the terminology you'll hear from the people selling you the ads. I also let you know how to read a broadcast media invoice to figure out if you're really getting the ads you paid for. And I let you know how you can stretch your advertising budget — and get something for yourself at the same time.

Finding the Best Radio Station for Your Ads

You probably have your favorite radio stations — ones you've programmed into your car radio. And you probably know of other radio stations that you specifically avoid, because what they play just isn't what you like. If you use these personal likes and dislikes as a starting point, you're well on your way to selecting the stations that are right for your advertising dollars. Without even knowing it, you've already done much of your research.

Knowing what you like and don't like helps you find the station that's right for your ads because you're aware that each station appeals to a certain audience. But the stations you listen to may *not* be the ones that your customers listen to. So don't limit your advertising to just the stations *you* like. If you do, you could be missing out on a huge section of your target market.

Many car dealers use a very clever (some might say, diabolical) method of market research in order to determine which radio stations to advertise on: They check the pre-set stations on the radios in the cars brought in for service. This is a very shrewd way for them to find out the listening habits of their customers.

If you aren't in the car business, instead of running outside to check the pre-sets on your customers' car radios while they shop in your store, do an informal survey. Ask your customers this question (and word it just this way): "What is your favorite radio station?" The answer to *that* question is the one you want to take to the bank. After you've surveyed a few dozen people, a pattern will begin to emerge and you'll have a good idea which stations to consider for your advertising. If a station is appealing to your existing customers, it will likely be a good bet to attract new ones.

Narrow your list to three or four stations, call each one, and ask to speak with someone in the sales department, preferably the Sales Manager. Tell each salesperson that you are considering placing an advertising schedule on their station, and set some appointments. Yes, it's unavoidable: You need to invest some time and listen to sales pitches from several stations, but it will be time well spent. The stations you call will assign the sales call to one of their sales reps, probably a new hire who is trying to build an account list (their top people will be too busy servicing their existing accounts and taking long lunches).

Ask a lot of questions of the reps you meet with, both about the strengths of their station and about their competition. Clarify who their target audience is, and decide if it meshes with your target (see the following section for more information). Talk about how you will be defining the success of your campaign and what your expectations are. One of the stations will stand out in your mind because that station's sales representative did the best job of finding your comfort level. Buy the stations (that's ad speak for "buy an ad on the stations") that have convinced you they can deliver your prime demo, tell them you'll be watching the results very carefully, and then put your commercials on the air.

If you make a mistake — if the stations you choose don't do the job you expected — chalk it up to experience and take solace in the fact that soon, very soon, you will be contacted by every other station in your market. Yes, as sure as death and taxes, after you have placed an ad on one station, you will be contacted by all the others. Station reps spend most of their time listening to competing stations in order to hear which advertisers are buying which stations. If they hear a commercial for your store, and you're not already buying their station, you *will* be contacted.

Figuring out which demographic you're after

Who are your customers? Men between 18 and 35? Women between 35 and 54? Teenagers? Whatever demo you're after, there is very likely a radio station in your market programmed specifically to reach that narrow audience segment. The problem is, the station that is programmed to appeal to your prime demo may not enjoy the best ratings in the market and, therefore, may not be your best buy. Picking the right stations is a complicated process, and, more often than not, you will ultimately need to take a giant leap of faith when finally placing your buy. But a good place to start is with the most current ratings of all stations — information you can get from any and all of the sales people who will call on you. If, on the other hand, you are located in a small market with but a couple of stations, you don't need to sweat this stuff.

The unique breed called "Radio Reps"

I have often wondered what possesses an otherwise likeable, intelligent, often attractive, sometimes educated, person to chose radio sales as a career. Is it because they're masochistic and enjoy being told *no* day after day? Or, is it the opposite? Is it because they won't take no for an answer — never have (just ask their mothers), never will (just ask their sales managers) — and God help the person who has the impudence and audacity to dare utter such a negative word to them? Or is it because they simply enjoy putting on a suit every day and driving around town in a used BMW trying to sell something that, to most people, is an abstract idea (they are selling air, and air is usually available to most of us at no charge).

I have also pondered how radio reps explain to their parents what they do for a living. How do they elucidate to their dear moms and dads, who spent a fortune putting them through college where they earned a degree in something obscure like Mass Communications, that they are now gainfully employed selling *air*. "That's nice, dear," I can hear Mom saying, "but isn't air free?" "Well, actually, mom, I sell . . . time," the proud, but misguided, radio rep would reply. "Time?" Dad would exclaim. "But isn't time something that sort of just happens? How can you sell time?"

Radio reps (and television reps) do sell air and time, the vernacular for paid advertising on broadcast media. But, in all fairness, they do *so* much more than that, and if their parents only understood, they would be extremely proud. Because, you see, radio reps also do lunches and take meetings. (I can remember when we used to "have" lunch and "attend' meetings. Nowadays, we *do* and *take*.) If you're a big advertiser with a sizeable budget, you can eat free lunches every day for the rest of your life.

That's the good news. The bad news is, you'll be having lunch with a radio rep every day for the rest of your life. And if you become overexposed (as I am), they will begin to blur in your memory because, by and large, radio reps, regardless of sex, are interchangable; both the men and the women dress in suits, mousse their hair, wear earrings, drive BMWs, are annoyingly enthusiastic, call everyone "babe," and won't take no for an answer!

I deal with dozens of broadcast reps every working day (I have known and enjoyed some of them for decades), and I can assure you that the following observations are spot on: If you spend a sizeable amount of your total net worth on his station each and every month, your broadcast rep will call you every day; send you flowers on your birthday; send your spouse flowers on his or her birthday; give you a reasonably good bottle of wine each Christmas or Hanukkah; furnish you with free tickets to Major League baseball games, concerts, and movies; give you scrip good for food and booze at reasonably good restaurants; take you golfing as often as you like; and never take no for an answer.

But the day you finally decide to cancel your contract and try another station, then say no when your rep begins to whine, and mean it . . . you'll never again see or hear from that person you were convinced was your new best friend. You see, not only do radio reps *sell* time, they also must manage their own time very judiciously. They, like all of us, only have so much time, and they endeavor to spend most of theirs making money — preferably, tons of money. So the day you are no longer part of their income stream, then you, my friend, are history — all because of a sad truism in the advertising business: no budget, no friends.

Radio stations break down the various demographics into seven different age groups for both sexes. Ask the stations you are interviewing to show you a demographic profile of their listeners; this will give you a clear picture of whether a particular station will be a good fit for your business. The demographic groups surveyed by stations are:

- Men 12–17
- Women 12–17
- Men 18– 24
- Women 18–24
- Men 25–34
- Women 25–34
- Men 35–44
- Women 35–44
- Men 45–54
- Women 45–54
- Men 55–64
- Women 55–64
- Men 65 and older
- Women 65 and older

When presenting to you, most stations will use ratings for a category called *Total Adults, 25–54*. This figure is an extrapolation of the totals for three separate age groups of both sexes.

Often, a station will show you their ratings based upon total persons 12 and older. You'll most likely find this information in a sales piece in the media kit. Be aware of what you're looking at as you sift through this information. You don't want to base your media buy on such a broad audience composition; you want to see the various age groups separated into the categories that I list in this section, so you can be assured that your prime demo is well represented in a station's listenership. And, besides, how much spending power do 12-year-olds really have? (In truth, a lot more than their parents would care to admit, but still not as much as adults.)

The most current station ratings are published every quarter in what is known in the ad biz simply as a *book*. The research is done and the books are published by companies like Arbitron, which is the largest and most recognized ratings service. Smaller markets have their own ratings services, which are less expensive and therefore more attractive to small market stations.

The ratings services use different methods to rate the stations, including radio listening diaries, which are maintained by individual listeners, and random telephone calls within the survey area. Personally, I don't think the research is always accurate (how can the listening habits of a few hundred accurately represent the listening habits of millions?), but it's all we have, and so we live with it. Just don't accept one ratings book as the gospel, because it isn't. Most stations will provide you with copies of some of the research contained in these rather voluminous, extremely expensive books, and what you want to know specifically is how their station (against all stations within the market) ranks in numbers of listeners who are in your prime demographic target group. There is no need for you to subscribe to a rating service, and even if you wanted to spend the money I doubt you could anyway, but your station reps will gladly share the information with you — especially if the latest research makes their station look exceptionally good.

My agency's media director will not usually buy any station based on a single rating book, regardless of how well the station ranks overall. She tries to use a four-book average as a starting point, but with all the day-to-day changes in most markets you often have to look at the most current information. Otherwise, you're looking at irrelevant data. Getting a four-book average isn't always possible, because small markets may only have two books per year (and some only have one). If you can get a four-book average, you will be able to see how a particular station has fared throughout an entire year (and believe me, station ratings can change dramatically from book to book, from month to month). And here's the best part: When you ask the sales rep for this information, you'll totally intimidate him with your insider knowledge. Most station clients don't know these books exist.

Making sense of quantitative and qualitative data

In order to choose the right stations on which to place your commercials, you should look through all the data that the reps provide (and if they don't provide it, ask for it). This data falls into two categories:

- ✔ **Quantitative data:** The actual numbers of audience members, used to accurately measure market situations. In plain language, the number of people listening to a given station.

- ✔ **Qualitative data:** The type of people, or various components of an audience, used to determine the quality of responses to expect from an advertising message. In other words, what kind of people are listening to a given station and what types of products are they likely to buy.

Putting station events to work for you

Radio stations love to throw parties. They create special events at the drop of a hat. Most of the larger stations even employ a Promotions Director, a vivacious, enthusiastic person who could just as easily become a Cruise Director. They will do promotions like a remote broadcast at your store, in which their on-air personalities broadcast from your lobby or parking lot inviting listeners to "Hurry to XYZ Company and get your free station T-shirt and bumper sticker." These special events can be a great traffic builder, occasionally attracting real customers in addition to the ones just wanting the free stuff.

Ask your station rep what kind of promotions the station can put together to benefit your business. If you're spending a fairly sizeable budget, you will probably get this type of promotion for free.

Radio stations also participate in community events such as street fairs, outdoor concerts, and college campus events. They set up their booths or park their electronics-packed vans and then broadcast and hand out free stuff. Many times they will sell sponsorships of these events, as in, "The big downtown chili cook-off is sponsored by [Your Store Name Here]. Come down and meet the nice folks and pick up your free T-shirt, coffee mug, and key chain." If you can benefit from one of these sponsorships, and if the event is relevant to your business somehow, then go for it. These events are usually priced quite reasonably and include multiple on-air mentions (in the form of 10– or 15-second announcements, or *mini commercials*), which will enhance your advertising schedule.

Most stations prepare a *media presentation folder* to leave with you after they have made their initial sales pitch. These folders will include lots of qualitative research custom-assembled to demonstrate how their station will deliver just the audience your individual business is after. The qualitative research is done by outside companies and can get into excruciating detail. Using an individual station's audience as a sampling, these reports will list everything from audience employment status to occupation, from education to household income, from home ownership to number of children — more than you ever wanted to know, believe me.

The amount of research data that's available to you from radio stations is amazing. My agency doesn't need to subscribe to any of the ratings services or buy the books they produce each quarter; the various stations we deal with are only too happy to provide us with anything we need. And they will be eager to supply you with whatever *you* need in order to help you decide which stations you will entrust with your hard-earned advertising dollars. The information may, at first glance, look a bit ponderous, but do read through it. It's very interesting stuff.

Cume, ranker, and rigmarole: Talking the talk of radio advertising

At the end of this book is a glossary of radio terms, but the terms you may hear bandied about by radio reps in order to confuse you (while also attempting to convince you that their station is the perfect match for your business) are ones you need to know. In the following sections, I cover a few of the most common.

Cume

Cumulative audience (or *cume* for short) is the total net unduplicated audience accumulated over a specific period of time, as in the total audience of a station during morning drive time. You don't really need to know how many people are listening to a station, but you do need to know how many people *in your target demographic* are listening. If, for instance, you want to reach men 25 to 34, you don't care if the station has a cume of 250,000 when most are women and only a very few are within your target demo.

Be wary of station reps who proudly sell cume. In many cases, cume doesn't mean anything — it's too broad a measurement. On the other hand, stations can certainly give advertisers *cume by demo,* which is the total unduplicated audience, measured within a certain timeframe, of members of a particular age group of either men or women or both — a much more relevant measurement. A station can and will give you their cume for men 25 to 34, for instance, if that is the primary demographic group you're after. The cume measurement can be compared with newspaper circulation: It is comparable to the number of people who receive the paper, but it doesn't tell you how long they spend reading it.

When you *don't* care enough to buy the very best

Just to confuse you (and to contradict myself), I will tell you now that it's not always necessary to buy the top-rated stations. Why? Because the top-rated stations are so darned expensive you can blow your whole budget without coming close to achieving your frequency goals. And the leading stations may not deliver the prime demo you're after anyway. The top-rated station may cost $1,000 a spot for morning drive (in some markets it's a lot more than that). But the second and third place stations may each cost half or even a third of that price. So, you can buy the silver and bronze winners of the ratings Olympics and get twice to three times the number of spots and listeners. You achieve frequency, and you're not forced into bankruptcy. It's a beautiful thing.

Cume is a valuable measurement; it just doesn't tell the whole story. Because this is radio and you're going for *frequency* (the number of times an audience member will hear *your* commercial), you need to know the amount of time people spend listening to a station (*time spent listening* is shortened to *TSL*). A station with really long TSL and a smaller cume (that is, fewer people tuned in but who stay with the station for a long period of time) is likely to have better average quarter hour (AQH) ratings than a station with a large cume and a small TSL (such as an all-news format where many people tune in but get only the news, weather, or traffic report they're after and quickly switch stations).

Ranker

A *ranker* is a computer-generated report showing a selected demographic audience of each radio station in a given market, ranked from highest to lowest (for example, how many women 18 to 35 listen to each station in a market). A ranker can be based on cume ratings, AQH ratings, share, or whatever. By using *qualitative* data to create a ranker, nearly every station in a market can show you that they are number one — they simply manipulate the data to highlight their own strengths, as in "We're number one with women 35-plus who have purchased perfume within the past year." Of course, if you're actually looking for women over 35 who have purchased perfume recently, buy that station in a heartbeat!

Beware of rankers, because each station will put its best foot forward and bring you a ranker based on parameters that will make it look its best.

Dayparts

Radio stations sell advertising time in various chunks referred to as *dayparts*. Naturally, morning drive time (6:00 a.m. to 10:00 a.m.) costs a lot more than midnight to 6:00 a.m. because you're reaching more people during the former. When you buy a schedule, you can either pick only prime time or make the more frugal choice and buy a schedule that includes spots in various dayparts, plus *rotators,* which are spots run in the best times available throughout the 12– to 24-hour period. A rotator may run at midnight, but sometimes you get lucky and it runs in the middle of the day, or possibly in drive time. It all adds to your frequency, so regardless of what times your ads run, you'll reach *some* listeners.

Reading the Fine Print

When you've made your decision to buy a radio schedule to advertise your business, the station sales rep will present you with a proposal and a contract for your signature. The proposal will come after the initial meeting, but before you agree to the buy. Study the proposal carefully but stop right there! Don't sign anything until you sit down with the rep and try to grind out a better deal. Radio can be made much more affordable if you just do a little horse-trading. Don't be afraid to ask for some free stuff. The rep will expect it and will likely have something in his pocket (something that the sales manager has preapproved just in case you ask) that will sweeten the pot.

The contract, which will be delivered or sent to you after both you and the station management have agreed upon the terms (and free stuff) that have been hammered out between you and the sales rep, will show how many spots you will be getting, in which dayparts those spots will run, and what the total cost will be. The contract will be broken down to show the cost of each commercial message you're buying. Some dayparts are cheaper than others, so the spots will have different costs.

If you wanted to know how much a newspaper ad would cost you, the newspaper sales rep would show you a *rate card,* a printed sheet on which you could see the precise costs of each and every column inch (although newspapers also offer so many discounts that the rate card is simply a start-ing point — see Chapter 16 for more information). But when you're trying to find out how much a radio schedule will cost you, the sales rep won't show you a rate card because, on most stations, no such thing exists — buying radio time is always negotiable. And for that reason, when buying radio time, you shouldn't accept the first proposal as presented to you; you should always shoot for something better, for something extra. Nine times out of ten, the station will add something in order to get your name on the dotted line.

My agency buys millions of dollars' worth of radio time every year, and I don't think we've ever bought a schedule "as is." We negotiate with the sta-tion for additional spots at no additional cost. If that doesn't fly, we ask for better spot positions in more desirable dayparts (we'd rather our spots run in the morning drive daypart than from midnight to 6:00 a.m.). If we're turned down on that request, we ask for free *billboards* (10– or 15-second announce-ments that are like mini-commercials). Our media buyer is continually looking for something extra from the stations — and you'll benefit from doing the same. Getting extras from a station is often easier if you're willing to sign a long-term advertising contract, such as an annual one.

Your contract promises that you will receive a certain number of spots — some in morning drive, some in midday, some rotating in the best times avail-able throughout the day, and some midnight to 6:00 a.m., for example. When you receive your invoice from the station, do what is known as *post analysis:* Check the times your spots ran (all of which are listed on the invoice) and compare the *actual* run times to the *promised* run times. If there are any dis-crepancies, you are owed *make goods,* which are free spots given to you by the radio station in order to fulfill all contractual promises.

Don't get bored with your commercial

Because you're probably going to buy a 13-week radio schedule, you may be tempted to ask the station for *run times,* wherein the station will call or fax you every day with a list of the actual times your spots are scheduled to run (within a few minutes). Most new advertisers ask for run times because hearing their commercials on the air is kind of fun. But if you tune in several times a day to hear your own spot, you'll soon get very bored with it. Keep in mind, however, that the other listeners, the people who may actually become your customers, will *not* get bored with your spot, because they're not hearing it every single time it runs. So don't get all twitchy about changing copy every week. You can run the same copy for the full 13 weeks without boring anyone except yourself. Besides, the average listener won't actually "hear" your spot until she's listened to it at least four times (that's why you need to buy frequency).

Of course, a 13-week schedule is also a good opportunity to rotate two or three different commercial messages, broadening your sales pitch. So, if you have the time and the inclination, knock yourself out and write several spots.

Many advertisers don't go to the trouble of doing post analysis. I do, however, and I continually find errors and always obtain make goods on behalf of my clients. Honest mistakes are made. Even though I'm sure the stations won't do anything to cheat you, you should still examine the invoices carefully and hold the station responsible for any errors and omissions.

Reading a station invoice can be a challenge — they are sometimes quite confusing. But *do* go over them carefully to assure yourself that you got what you paid for. The invoice you'll get from the station is divided into columns. All the spots in your schedule are broken down into the following categories: day of the week (for example, Monday), date (November 6), length (60 seconds), actual time/title of ad (6:56 a.m., Inventory Closeout), rate ($450).

If your spots are being paid for by a supplier on a co-op advertising program, you also want to check your invoices very carefully to assure that the stations have supplied you with all the requirements for co-op reimbursement. You won't get paid your co-op funds if you don't send all the paperwork! You will have provided the stations with copies of your radio script(s) (see Chapter 13 for co-op guidelines), and now you want to make sure the stations have notarized your scripts and certified your invoice as proof of performance.

Many of my agency's clients are co-op based. So around the tenth of each month, when the broadcast invoices begin to arrive in the mail, frustration and disappointment arrive with them. Even though we have been dealing with multiple radio stations for years on behalf of these co-op based clients, and even though the stations know that our accounts require notarized, certified scripts and invoices, they still occasionally send us incomplete invoices. Inevitably, we receive invoices from some stations that do not include notarized scripts. I then have to call the offending stations to get the problem resolved, cajoling them in order to get the corrected paperwork. Be diligent in studying your invoices from broadcast media.

Being Patient While Waiting for the Results

Radio is a *frequency medium,* which means that every listener must hear your commercial message at least four times before she remembers it. Yes, regardless of how creative you have been and how brilliantly you have written your message, your commercial may have no effect whatsoever until the average listener has heard it four times. The newest research shows that due to the increasing amount of advertising clutter, advertisers in most markets need to shoot for what's referred to as a *four frequency.* People are bombarded with advertising messages to the point where they tend to tune them out (3,000 advertising messages each day according to the latest research). But when any given listener hears your spot at least four times, your message will slowly begin to sink in. If what you're selling is appealing to that listener, she may then respond to it and become one of your customers. The station can show you how many spots you will need to buy and how much money you will need to spend, in order to achieve a four frequency (reaching their average listener a minimum of four times).

On radio, you're better off buying a minimum 13-week schedule in order to accomplish the frequency you need and to assure that your commercial message reaches enough listeners to make your cash outlay worth your while. That's three months to make an impact. You don't absolutely *have* to buy a 13-week schedule, of course. You can step up to the plate with a heavy one-month budget and still accomplish the desired frequency. But, if you can afford it, I recommend the tried-and-true 13 weeks. Hearing your commercials over a longer period of time ultimately gives you a presence with the listeners. Your name and message begin to sink in, which is precisely why you're advertising in the first place.

No matter how many weeks of radio advertising you can afford, you need to give your ads time to work. You may even want to try something called *flighting,* where you commit to, say, two weeks per month on a station, then evaluate your results after three months. ***Remember:*** Consistency is the key. You can run ads one week a month, if that's what you can afford — as long as you stick with it.

The 72-hour window

Why do you suppose there are so many car dealer ads on radio (or any other advertising medium, for that matter)? It's because car dealers understand and endorse the concept of frequency, because of what they call the *72-hour window*. What is a 72-hour window? Car dealers know that when a person, any person, finally decides to buy a new car, he will buy that new car within 72 hours of making the decision to do so. Remember how hard it was to wait for your birthday? Well, we're all still kids at heart, and we want instant gratification. It is because of the 72-hour window that car dealers need a continual radio presence.

For example, Bob finally decides to buy a new car. Prior to making that buying decision, every dime that every car dealer spent on advertising was wasted on Bob, because Bob wasn't in the market for a new car and he ignored all those car ads. And after Bob has purchased his new car, every dime that every dealer spends on advertising will once again be wasted on Bob. But, while Bob's 72-hour buying window is open, every dealer needs to be on the air in case Bob tunes in and happens to hear one of their commercials. That's why you hear so much car advertising on the radio. All those car dealers are waiting for Bob to make up his mind.

In addition to frequency, you're also interested in *reach*, the number of people who will be exposed to your messages over the course of your radio schedule. Reach, when revealed to you by a station, is usually shown as a percentage, not a number. If your schedule shows a reach of 5 percent men between 25 and 34 years of age, then that is the percentage of all the men ages 25 to 34 within your market whom you are reaching with your schedule.

Taking Advantage of Client Incentives

From October through December of each year, radio stations enjoy multi-millions of dollars in additional revenue from political, automotive, and retail Christmas season advertising. Between politicians attempting to get elected, car dealers trying to clear inventory, and every retail store in the known universe hoping to get a piece of the Christmas shopping pie, broadcast sales reps can just sit in their cubicles and answer the phone. As a matter of fact, most stations become so saturated with advertising that they're literally sold out — meaning you couldn't get a new commercial on the air even if you wanted to. This feeding frenzy also results in sky-high advertising rates for the final quarter of each year.

But, at the stroke of midnight on New Year's Eve, the worm turns. And that is the time when smart advertisers negotiate some very attractive deals with stations. Broadcasters know that first-quarter ad dollars are harder to come by. The competition gets fierce, and stations have to work harder for their money. It's first-quarter incentive time — the mother lode.

Nearly all radio and TV stations offer first-quarter incentive packages. These packages take many forms but usually involve free commercials, promotions, even all-expenses-paid trips to destinations around the world. Buy one spot, get two spots free. Buy two spots, get one free. Buy a January schedule at full price, get February and March schedules for half price. Spend a certain amount over the three-month period and fly off to Europe, Mexico, or Hawaii. The variations on the theme are endless, but the bottom line is simple: During the first quarter, you'll get a lot more bang for your buck. And people don't quit listening to radio on the first day of January, so taking advantage of what the stations have to offer makes sense.

Stretch your budget to the max during this new year bonanza. If you're paying $150 per spot but getting another spot for free, you're actually paying only $75 per spot — which means you're getting twice the impressions for half the usual price. And, don't forget: Radio is a frequency medium. It takes three or four of your commercials heard by the same person to make an impression, so the more spots you can run the better.

If, after your first quarter ad schedule has run and been paid for, you get to board a plane for a week or more of free rest and relaxation at some exotic resort or European capitol . . . well, you deserve it for being so darned smart! Advertising agencies as well as their clients can earn free trips via first-quarter incentives. My staff, our clients, and I have traveled all-expenses-paid (air, luxury hotels, and most meals) to London, Paris, Hong Kong, Africa, Hawaii, Mexico, and New Zealand. We've even cruised down the Danube River through Germany, Austria, Slovakia, and Hungary — all in return for buying first-quarter radio or television-broadcast packages. Hey, you're probably going to spend the money anyway. Why not get something extra in return?

If a client incentive package is offered to you, and if you can afford to commit to an extended contract, grab it. Stretch your budget while taking advantage of some great deals and wonderful trips.

Chapter 15

Getting Your Ads on Television

• •

In This Chapter

▶ Paying attention to the programs you advertise in and the audience you reach

▶ Working with the sales rep to get a contract you can both agree on

▶ Figuring out whether cable advertising is worth your time and money

• •

Television is a device that permits you to be entertained in your living room by people you wouldn't have in your home.

— David Frost

*B*uying an advertising schedule on television is a confusing proposition. Where can you find viewers? Where do you spend your money? The television audience is fragmenting, thanks to the hundreds of choices available with broadcast, cable, and satellite dish technologies. The major networks' share of total viewing audience has been shrinking for a long time, and few see any reason to expect the erosion to reverse. No single network, station, or program seems to dominate anymore — people simply have too many viewing choices. Viewers can choose among the big four networks (ABC, CBS, NBC, and FOX), independent stations, and the numerous channels offered by cable and satellite systems. The Internet, DVDs, VCRs, and on-demand systems like TiVo are vying for viewers' attention and siphoning them away from TV.

Consumers now have such a mind-boggling variety of choices that reaching them in large numbers is nearly impossible (unless you have unlimited funds, and even then you have no guarantee). As a matter of fact, it's not only difficult to *reach* viewers in large numbers, it's getting more impossible to *find* them in large numbers. The uncertainty of where to locate substantial numbers of television viewers has even professional media buyers confused.

When you jump into this grossly uncertain media pool, you need to search for a reasonable share of the total television-viewing audience (especially those who are in the demographic group you're after), combined with afford-able advertising rates somewhere in your local television market. In this chapter, I help you do exactly that.

Buying the Programming, Not the Station

Virtually every TV station will offer at least a few programs that deliver your target audience. Unlike radio, in which each station delivers pretty much the same type of listener throughout the day, television demographics vary widely from program to program. Think about your own TV-viewing habits, and you'll see what I mean. The same station that airs *Monday Night Football* also airs a three-hour block of soap operas during the day — and those who watch the former probably don't watch the latter.

Don't get locked into thinking of television in terms of stations. Think instead in terms of programs and types of audience. If you have several stations in your market, you may find that the best way to reach your target audience is to buy one or two programs on each station.

You're buying the programs and the audience, not the stations. So, be sure your target market is clearly defined before you contact the television stations in your market.

Requesting a media kit

Contact the TV stations in your area and request what's known as a *media kit*. A media kit is basically a brochure package with information on the station. It should give you some general information about their coverage area, their programming strengths, any special programming they are known for, their history in the market and other sales-type stuff.

Be sure the media kit includes a program listing, usually called a *program grid*. This will give you an idea what types of programs the station airs throughout the day. When you have reviewed this information, and given yourself a brief overview of the station and its programming, you'll be better prepared to have a serious meeting with the station sales rep.

Prime time programming? Probably not

Depending on the size of your media market, you will likely find that if a show won a Golden Globe or Emmy Award you probably can't afford it. Commercials on the top-rated sitcoms and dramas can be very expensive, even on a local level. But don't despair: You can find some affordable time slots in and around well-watched programming — affordable enough to give you a presence in your local market even though your ad budget may not be quite as large as that of General Motors.

If, on the other hand, you are situated in a smaller advertising market, you may indeed find that prime time programming fits neatly within your budget parameters. The smaller the market, the cheaper the spots.

By doing just a bit of research you may also find that cable stations and *independent stations* (those stations not affiliated with major networks), offer a good variety of programming with both loyal audiences and reasonable spot costs. Your local network-affiliate TV stations have affordable early-morning talk shows and morning news programs with good ratings and loyal viewers. Daytime soaps and talk shows, especially if your target demographic is women, are a great buy. And the early-evening local news and early fringe will bring you a good return on a modest investment. My agency runs commercials on *Jeopardy!* and *Wheel of Fortune* on the San Francisco ABC-TV affiliate for very reasonable prices as part of a larger buy.

Meeting with a sales rep

After you've looked through the media kits provided by the stations in your area, and after you have some idea of the kinds of programs you'd like to advertise on, arrange to meet with a sales rep from each station. This meeting is a fact-finding mission for both of you. When you meet with the sales rep, be very clear about your objectives, your target demographic, your business trading area, and anything else you feel is relevant in helping her put together a potentially successful schedule for you. Be sure she understands your expectations, as well as how you plan to measure your results.

Be sure to ask lots of questions. Any sales rep who isn't willing to help you understand her station and the television market as a whole isn't someone you want to work with.

The sales rep should be motivated to help you develop something that works for your business within your budget parameters, so that you will continue to advertise. If you don't feel that the sales rep who comes to meet with you is the right fit, call the station's sales manager and request someone else. You don't want personality differences or a lack of trust to stand in your way when you're trying to make an objective decision about your advertising.

Affordable dayparts

You may be buying television by dayparts and not by specific programs. Buying by dayparts is a great way to save money because it gives the station some flexibility, which allows them to charge a lower rate. Just be sure that all or most of the programs that are included in the daypart you're buying make sense for your type of business. Some of the standard dayparts you will be looking at include:

✔ **Morning news:** 5:00 a.m.–9:00 a.m.

✔ **Morning:** 9:00 a.m.–12:00 p.m.

✔ **Daytime:** 12:00 p.m.–3:00 p.m.

✔ **Early fringe:** 3:00 p.m.–5:00 p.m.

✔ **Early news:** 5:00 p.m.–7:00 p.m.

✔ **Access:** 7:00 p.m.–8:00 p.m.

✔ **Prime:** 8:00 p.m.–11:00 p.m.

✔ **Late news:** 11:00 p.m.–11:30 p.m.

✔ **Late fringe:** 11:30 p.m.–1:00 a.m.

Keep in mind that these dayparts (including their time ranges and names) may vary slightly from station to station, so always be sure to clarify what the time period is. If your sales rep gives you a proposal by daypart, also be sure to clarify what the programming is during those blocks of time (or refer to the program grid that came in the station's media kit).

After you've met with the sales rep, she will go back to the station and work on a proposal, sometimes called an *avail.* Occasionally, a sales rep will bring a proposal or avail to your initial meeting, but usually she will want to meet you and gather some information before making recommendations. A typical proposal will include the following information:

✔ The programs or *dayparts* (time periods) during which your ads will run (see the nearby sidebar, "Affordable dayparts," for more information on dayparts)

✔ The number of times per week your commercial will run in each program or daypart

✔ A rate for each program or daypart

✔ A weekly or total cost

Some stations will have a special schedule already prepackaged for new advertisers or clients with smaller budgets. These types of schedules usually give you one cost for the whole schedule, as opposed to individual rates per daypart or program. They usually have names like *New Business Package* or *Retail Package.* These packages can be a great way to get started, but be sure you're aware of what they include, as well as any limitations or restrictions involved. If the schedule includes a limited number of commercials in the areas or programs you're interested in, you're probably better off paying a little more for fewer, but better targeted, commercials.

Negotiating Successfully

When you have the station's proposal in front of you, you may find some points that you'd like to negotiate. Negotiating doesn't have to be an adversarial process — and it's almost always more effective if it's not. In the following sections, I fill you in on a few of the rules I have developed for myself over the years as I've negotiated with television stations.

Everything is negotiable

If you think the rate is too high, ask if there is any flexibility in the rate. If the sales rep can't go lower on the rate, ask if she can add any bonus (free) commercials to the schedule. If she can't add any bonus commercials to the schedule, ask if she can add any *billboards* to your schedule. Billboards are essentially your logo with a "brought to you by" mention (for example, "This news brief is brought you by XYZ Cleaners").

If you've offered some points of negotiation and haven't gotten anywhere, it's perfectly all right to say, "You know, I just don't feel comfortable with this schedule as it is. What else can you suggest?" You don't have to explain any further. The sales rep's job is to come up with something that makes you feel comfortable enough to move forward.

Tell the sales rep you want to do business with her station

Let the sales rep know right up front that you want to do business with her and her station. This makes the deal hers to lose (which is something she doesn't want to do), and it gets her on your side right away. If she knows she's close to getting your name on a contract, you will get a lot more of her effort than if she believes you're just as likely to buy an ad on another station. So, be positive, and use phrases like, "Your news rate is just a little bit too high for me to buy the number of commercials I need, but I'd really like to use the station. What else can you do?"

Let the sales rep know that your advertising schedule must work

The sales rep needs to be aware that you will be monitoring your results closely. After all, if this ad campaign works out well, you will be doing a lot more advertising with the station (and if it doesn't, you won't). Knowing that you're monitoring your results offers the sales rep further incentive to make sure your campaign is as effective as possible — and it also lets her know she will be held accountable if it isn't.

Consider the time of year

There is considerably less demand for TV ads in the first quarter (January, February, and March) and the third quarter (July, August, and September) than in the rest of the year. January, July, and August tend to be the lightest months of all. Therefore, stations have a lot more flexibility in the first and third quarters, and you will be able to push a bit further for a better deal during those times. On the other hand, if you're trying to buy time in the busiest months, you may not be able to negotiate much at all (although it's always worth a shot).

Ask for promotions and other deals

Television stations have a variety of promotions going on all the time. In addition, they have the ability to design a traffic-building promotion specifically for your business. As you negotiate the advertising schedule, be sure to ask what else the station may be able to do, in addition to the advertising schedule, to help you achieve your objective. (These additional bonuses are sometimes referred to as *value-added* deals.)

Get better rates with annual or long-term contracts

Often, stations can offer you better rates, or other incentives, for making long-term commitments. Some of these incentives may include a pool of bonus commercials to be added to your schedule throughout the year, as availability permits, or free trips to be utilized by business owners in exchange for spending a certain dollar amount on advertising.

Stations may put your commercials into a *bonus pool* if you sign a long-term contract. The bonus pool consists of unsold commercial air time — a "pool" of time into which certain station clients will, as their commercials reach the front of the queue, enjoy free spots. Bonus-pool members even receive a monthly statement showing the exact times these free spots ran. Bonus pools can end up giving you a lot of extra impressions over the course of a year.

In addition to the bonus pool, many stations reward long-term commitments with yearly *client incentive trips*. These are all-expenses-paid journeys to select destinations throughout the world and are usually done in a first-class manner. If you step up to the plate with a sizeable commitment, you will often be wined and dined lavishly to make sure you stay with the station year after year.

Incentives and lower rates can be great opportunities, if the campaign already makes sense. Just be careful not to make commitments you wouldn't make otherwise just to get something for "free."

Everything can be preempted

As you evaluate your options and negotiate with stations, keep in mind that nearly all television commercials can be preempted. This means that if a certain program is a sellout (meaning more people want to advertise during the program than there are spaces available), some advertisers may choose to pay a higher rate than you're paying just to get in. When this happens, in order to make room, the station starts dropping advertisers from the program based on their priority or *section code* (a ranking, usually 1 through 9, of the various rates paid by advertisers, which determines each advertiser's priority). If you have purchased your spots at level 5, usually the cheapest rate for local advertisers, you will be told up front that your rate is preemptible, so there shouldn't be any surprises. The *issue date* (when an advertiser bought a schedule) is also a factor. The last one in is the first one bumped. If you're having a sale next weekend, you want to be sure that you don't negotiate rates so low that all of your commercials may get preempted. Believe me, it has happened. On the other hand, if you have some flexibility, getting bumped may be less of a concern and you should go for the cheaper rates.

Your station sales rep will get a preemption list daily for all of her clients, and part of your negotiation is making sure she knows what you want done with your bumped spots. The options generally include the following:

- Run the commercial in the same program on a different day or week.
- Run the commercial in a comparable program.
- Credit the cost of the commercial back to you.

Before you sign your contract, be sure to discuss with your sales rep what will happen when your commercials get bumped, so your invoice is not full of surprises!

Stay within your budget

One of the biggest mistakes new advertisers make is trying to buy too much. You will probably be faced with more programming that fits your demographic than you can afford to buy. Instead of trying to stretch your budget to cover as many of these options as possible, you're better off doing the opposite.

Choose one or two (maybe even three) options and buy those programs or dayparts as heavily as you can. Reaching *some* potential customers effectively is better than reaching a whole bunch of viewers ineffectively.

Of course, every rule has an exception! If you have the luxury of doing image advertising, where your goal is just to let people know you're out there, you can go ahead and sprinkle your commercials around. Some stations will even allow you to buy *all-day rotators,* which will air as time permits. These spots can be a very inexpensive way to go, but remember that there are no guarantees of when, or if, your commercials will air.

Compare and evaluate several stations

When you're thinking about buying ads on TV, talk to more than one station, if you have that option. Not only will you have a basis for comparison, but you're also more likely to encounter a sales rep you really like. And working with a sales rep you like is important, because station sales reps can be your greatest source of information.

When you're evaluating TV stations, don't assume you're comparing apples to apples. Television stations have a wide variety of ways to present their audience figures. The two most common numbers you will see are *household ratings* (how many individual households with TV sets are tuned into a particular station) and *demographic ratings* (how many people within certain demographic groups are tuned into the station). Stations sometimes use household ratings because they look so much larger — households usually consist of multiple individuals in a variety of different demographic groups all lumped together. However, if your target demographic is women between the ages of 25 and 54, what difference does it make to you how many *households* you're reaching? You just want to be sure you're reaching the women in your target demographic. Whenever possible, be sure you're looking at the ratings for your target demographic, and if the proposal isn't clear, *ask.*

Talking the Talk, So You Can Walk the Walk

As you become more comfortable buying television ads, the station will undoubtedly start to get technical on you — especially if you're working with more than one station. As the stations become more competitive with one another, they will begin bombarding you with more and more detailed ratings information. This research data they will share with you is designed to show their stations in the best possible light, while making the competing stations look inferior. So you need to have a basic understanding of what stations are presenting to you, and where these numbers come from.

Unlike radio, which is measured almost continuously, television audiences are measured primarily four times per year. The four ratings periods are February, May, July, and November. These periods of measurement are called *sweeps,* with May and November being the most important. The top ten national markets (New York City, Los Angeles, Chicago, Philadelphia, San Francisco/Oakland/San Jose, Boston, Dallas/Fort Worth, Washington D.C., Detroit, and Atlanta, in that order) are also measured in January and October. Selected top markets are also *metered,* which means that audiences are measured on a daily basis via reports called *overnights.* (The overnights let you know whether the latest reality show beat out that high-rated sitcom last night.) However, in most markets, television has to live and die by the basic four measurement periods (the sweeps) during which networks air their best programming and when local stations promote themselves most heavily. That's why you rarely see reruns during the sweeps periods. Sweeps months are when the TV stations pull out all the stops, bringing you all-new episodes of your favorite shows.

A.C. Nielsen is the company responsible for collecting ratings data for television in nearly every market across the country. They do so through *diaries* — books that are completed by members of randomly selected households listing which shows they watched and when. Nielsen also uses *meters,* which are electronic devices attached to a randomly selected number of televisions across the country. Meters measure whether the TV is on or off and keep track of which stations are being viewed. Meters are only capable of providing household information on what programs are being watched, because there is no way for the meters to determine which household member is actually watching. The nitty-gritty demographic information is collected through the diaries. Some televisions are even equipped with *people meters,* electronic gadgets activated by individuals in the household when they're watching television and deactivated when they turn the darn thing off.

In any given market, the total number of persons or households with access to television is referred to as the *universe.* The viewing levels are described as HUT (short for *homes using television*) and PUT (short for *persons using television*). So, if someone were to say, "Television rates drop in the summer because of the decrease in HUT," it would mean that, in the summer, fewer homes are using television and people are watching television for fewer hours each day.

When stations present their numbers to you, the data will most likely be in one of two forms: rating or share. *Share* refers to a station's percent of the television audience at that time. For example, if a station shows you an 8 share for men 25 to 54, for their 11:00 p.m. newscast, that means that, of all the men between the ages 25 and 54 who are watching television at 11:00 p.m., 8 percent of them are watching *that* particular station's news. *Rating,* on the other hand, refers to a station's percentage of the overall universe, whether they are watching television at that precise time or not. For example, if a station says their 11:00 p.m. news program delivers a 2 rating for men 25 to 54, that means that, of all the men between the ages of 25 and 54 in the survey universe, 2 percent watch the 11:00 p.m. news on that station. Ratings for individual stations can be expressed as a percentage (2 percent of all men ages 25–54) or as a real number (7,500 men ages 25–54), but share is *always* a percentage. Because rating relates to the entire television-viewing universe, and because share relates to the HUTs or PUTs, the share percentage is always larger. So if you compare one station's share to another station's ratings, you will be comparing apples to rutabagas and will not get an accurate picture. As much as possible, you want to be sure you are comparing the same measurement on each station.

To get even more technical, stations *source* (or survey) their audience information in one of three ways. Here is a brief outline of each:

- ✔ **Actual:** This is the number exactly as it was reported by Nielsen research. If a station gives you a February Actual, that means the number came from the most recent February rating book.

- ✔ **Projection:** This number is adjusted based on a standard mathematical formula, which is the same at every station. A *projection* is the HUT or PUT level from the time of year you're planning to advertise multiplied by the share percentage from the most recent book. This number, called a PJ (short for *projection*), is used often by professional media buyers and stations. It is considered a good measurement because it utilizes the most recent information but adjusts the data to the time of the year to account for seasonal variances in the viewing audience.

- ✔ **Estimates:** Estimates can literally be anything. If a station has a new program, moves a program to a different time, is running a special, or just feels they were shortchanged in the rating book, they will use an estimate. An estimate will be presented as a number, footnoted with a lengthy rationale for why the station thinks the program will deliver that rating number. Unless estimates are all that is available, I don't recommend using these numbers in your research of stations. If an estimate is all you have, let the station know that you will hold them to that estimated number. If the program falls short in the next rating book, they will need to air additional commercials for you to make up the difference.

You may be wondering, "What would be a good rating? Can't you give me a guideline?" Unfortunately, because ratings and shares are percentages tied to population and market competition, there are no guidelines that work across the board. In a market with lots of competition and a large population, ratings will be smaller than in a smaller market with fewer viewing choices. As you get more comfortable comparing stations and programs using the information provided in this chapter, you will soon get a feel for what constitutes good ratings in your market.

Determining Whether Cable Advertising Is Right for You

In addition to broadcast or over-the-air television, most markets have the option of cable television. Unlike broadcast television, which is free to anyone with a TV set and an adequate antenna, cable television is transmitted through a network of underground cables and is a subscription-based service. Cable subscribers have access to additional premium channels, which cannot be received over the air (although some are available with satellite systems). Some examples of cable channels, or networks, include ESPN, CNN, HBO, A&E, HGTV, and MTV, to name just a few.

Keep in mind that not all cable channels are commercial channels that accept advertising, and not all are available to local advertisers. Check with your local cable company to find out which channels in your area are available for local retail advertising.

Cable offers the visual impact of television without the broad reach. Because so many cable networks are available to viewers, each one has become highly targeted and reaches a very specific audience. So, if you have a sporting goods store, you're probably going to focus on sports-related networks, like ESPN, Fox Sports, or ESPN 2. If, on the other hand, you own a day spa, you will probably focus on networks more appealing to women, such as HGTV (Home & Garden Television) or Lifetime. Not all situations are this clear-cut, of course, but the point is that cable networks have very specific target audiences, making it easy to eliminate those that aren't appropriate to you and to concentrate on the ones that better fit your target demographic.

In addition to targeting your customers by specific network, some of the larger markets offer cable advertising by *zone*. Zones are individual geographical areas within a cable system's total sphere of influence — small pieces of the cable pie. This allows smaller advertisers to buy advertising only in the zones immediately surrounding their place of business. The San Francisco Bay Area, for example, has 11 regional cable zones as well as several sub-zones. So, if you have a clothing store in a particular San Jose suburb, you can buy cable advertising in the zone that covers just those households that are located nearby. On the other hand, if you have a chain of auto parts stores, with locations in various cities throughout the Bay Area, you can place your advertising in all zones, or *market-wide*.

Working with a sales rep

So you're thinking that cable sounds pretty good and you'd like to explore it further. But you're frightened by a nagging thought: Do you have to meet sales reps from each network? Luckily, your local cable company will have an advertising department, and a sales rep from that office will be happy to sell you commercials on any or all of their available networks, and in any or all of their zones. Depending on your local cable operator's agreement with the networks, they will be able to insert your commercials on several networks, or on just a few. However, in all markets, the programming and the commercial inventory is controlled by the network, not the cable company.

Your first step is to contact the cable company and set up a meeting with an advertising sales rep. This meeting is an opportunity for him to learn about your business in order to prepare a proposal, but it is also an important opportunity for you to find out what options are available to you in your market. At the conclusion of this first meeting, you should know what networks are available to you locally, whether your market is zoned, how much local control there is on where your commercials can air, and anything else unique to buying cable advertising in your neck of the woods. Your sales rep will want to come back with a proposal, and this is where it could get tricky.

Beware the bookkeeping nightmare

Cable is an extremely flexible and targetable way to advertise your business. You can choose the networks and narrow your buy to the geographic zones that you feel best target your potential customers. A word of caution, though: The more complex your buy — the more networks and specific zones you choose — the more complex your invoices will be. Talk with your sales rep about this upfront so there are no surprises when your bill comes. You may find that you receive a separate invoice for each network included on your schedule, as well as for each zone, so be prepared! This can be an overwhelming amount of paperwork and has been known to make even a professional advertising Accounts Payable Manager break down into uncontrollable sobbing.

Cable advertising has a reputation for sometimes being really cheap, and there is a reason for that: It is not uncommon for cable reps to sell very broad *rotators* (spots run during available times, rather than prescheduled times, at the discretion of the station) over a single network or across several networks. They have so much commercial inventory that they may as well sell it for something! However, although just $2 or $3 per commercial (yes, cable time sometimes sells for a seemingly paltry amount) sounds too good to pass up, believe me it isn't. If you are advertising power drills, and your $2 commercial runs in a 3:00 a.m. program on the Women's Network about getting in shape after you've had a baby, you just threw away three bucks. If your entire advertising schedule is made up of these cheap rotators, the likelihood of your commercial airing in prime time and on an appropriate network is slim. Cable companies don't give the good stuff away, and when you realize that fact, you will soon see that cable is not always as "cheap" as it seems.

If you want to buy a spot during the Major League Baseball Championship Series or the Stanley Cup Finals on ESPN, you will pay a premium. If you buy a rotator on ESPN, hoping to land in this well-watched programming, you will be disappointed. You definitely won't end up in the game. You may end up in the pre– or post-game, but then again, you may end up in the Introduction to Knitting or Celebrity Skeet Shooting hours. Don't risk it.

Hitting the bull's-eye with cable

Cable's biggest strength is its targetability, so use it. Buy programs or time periods on the appropriate networks, as specifically as you can. Then ask the sales rep to include some really cheap (or free) rotators in addition to your negotiated schedule. You can always check your invoices to see where and at what times the rotators ran and decide if they're a worthwhile investment.

These cheapo rotator commercials can be a great way to enhance a schedule, but they should never be the meat of your campaign. *Remember:* If it seems too cheap to be true, it probably is. You get what you pay for.

Doing the math

One thing you should become educated on before you commit to any cable advertising is *market penetration,* the percentage of the total television households in your market that subscribe to cable. This topic is an important one to ask about before you evaluate the potential effectiveness of cable in your market. Your cable reps have this information (and so do your broadcast television reps, who will use it to steer you *away* from cable).

ANECDOTE

You don't *always* get what you pay for

I once produced a TV spot for a Volkswagen dealer specifically targeted to women between 25 and 49. The 30-second spot featured an on-camera pitch by a well-dressed young woman who stood near the car in a lovely outdoor setting and outlined the many virtues of the new Jetta. She explained why it was perfect for the driving needs of busy professional women on the go. Our media department very carefully picked only cable programming for women — Lifetime, HGTV, and stations like them. We bought a fairly heavy schedule and anticipated good results.

A week or so later, whilst having lunch at a sports bar, I glanced up at the TV above the bar to watch a show called *The Lumberjack Olympics,* which was being televised on ESPN 2.

Big, burly, sweaty guys in bib overalls and hobnail boots were chopping trees to bits with incredibly sharp axes, climbing trees in ten seconds, doing log rolling, and performing all sorts of other macho feats of strength and dexterity. Guess which 30-second spot was the very first one I saw? Yep, our businesswoman selling VW Jettas.

The moral of this story is simply this: Read your cable invoices very carefully to make sure you get what you paid for. In fairness, I must report that the spot I saw on ESPN 2 turned out to be a bonus spot and free of charge. However, free or not, it didn't do us one bit of good, because you could bet there wasn't a female viewer within a thousand miles of that programming.

Market penetration information, as it applies to cable, is important for a couple of reasons. First, if the cable penetration in your market is 50 percent, that means that the top-rated cable network in your market has the potential to reach only half of the total households in your area. That also means you're eliminating half of your market right off the bat. Then, looking at the remaining 50 percent who are cable subscribers, you need to narrow them down by demographics and geography, if applicable, in order to come up with the actual number of potential customers you'll be reaching with your commercials.

By the time you slice and dice these numbers, they can end up fairly small. In fact, most cable networks (even the strongest, such as TNT, A&E, and TNN) do not deliver enough audience consistently enough to show up in the Nielsen rating book. And because they don't deliver enough audience to show up on Nielsen research, most cable companies use their *own* research, which is cable-specific.

Cable-specific research is fine, as long as they don't try to compare their research numbers to "over-the-air" television. Broadcast television ratings are based on a market population of total television households. Cable ratings, on the other hand, are based on a market population of *cable* households. This number can be *much* smaller than the total universe for television, depending on the cable penetration. Obviously, if cable does not penetrate 100 percent of the television households in the market, they would be at quite a disadvantage if they used the larger universe as the basis for determining their ratings. So, they use the smaller universe of cable households. And for this reason, you cannot directly compare broadcast television ratings and cable ratings. If you do, you're comparing apples to rutabagas again.

Before you sign a contract, do the math to see whether advertising on cable makes sense for your business. Let's say your market consists of 100,000 television households. The cable penetration is 60 percent, which means 60,000 households have cable. The morning news on your local NBC affiliate, a broadcast television station, does a 2 household rating. The cable network, CNBC, has a morning news program, which also does a 2 rating, but with *cable* households. The 2 rating on the local NBC affiliate represents 2,000 households (2 percent of 100,000 households), while the 2 rating for CNBC represents just 1,200 households (2 percent of 60,000). So if you advertise on the broadcast station, you reach 800 more households than if you advertise on the cable station, even though both of them have a 2 household rating.

Although cable television delivers a smaller audience then over-the-air television, this does not have to be a disadvantage for you as an advertiser. After all, cable is usually less expensive, which means you can buy more commercials. In addition, cable can offer excellent targeting opportunities, both geographically and demographically.

Chapter 16

Snagging Ad Space in Print

. . . .

In This Chapter

▶ Knowing where to run your ads

▶ Maneuvering the minefield of print ad pricing

▶ Working with a sales rep

▶ Getting the best deal possible

. . . .

One advertisement is worth more to a paper than 40 editorials.

— Will Rogers

I have good news and bad news. The good news is that newspapers actually have easy-to-read (albeit somewhat difficult-to-understand) rate cards on which are listed the various costs for various ad sizes. The bad news is that the rate card is nothing more than a starting point in the media-negotiation and –buying process, because newspapers have created so many permutations of their basic (or *open*) rates that even a professional media buyer has trouble deciphering them in order to come up with the most frugal media buy. And after you discover the nuances of one publication's rates and myriad discounts, you can then call the next publication and start all over again finding out about theirs — no two newspapers' rates and discounts are alike. (I think they do this just to totally confuse us and to give their salespeople a reason for being.)

In this chapter, I show you how to select the right print publications for your particular business, and how to negotiate with those publications after you have narrowed down the list. Pay close attention, because newspapers have more discount rates than there are stars in the heavens — and you don't want to pay one dime more than you have to.

Deciding Where to Run Your Ad

When you're ready to get your print ad out there for the world to see, the first thing you need to do is choose a venue. This task may seem like an easy one, and sometimes it is. You can choose among major daily newspapers, weekly papers, entertainment-oriented newspapers, trade publications, magazines, mailing inserts, and on and on. Your mission is to choose the media that your potential customers are reading. How do you accomplish that?

Although you may be tempted to put your ads in the publications that *you* read (after all, they're the ones you know), your ads will be a bigger success if you put them where your customers will see them. Talk to people in your target audience — your customers. Ask your current customers how they chose your store or business, how they decide to buy, what publications they read, which sections of the newspaper they turn to first, and which media they are likely to respond to when shopping around for what you're selling.

With a little hip-pocket market research — where you ask a lot of relevant questions of people who already know your store — you should be able to pin down the publications into which you should be inserting your ads.

Figuring Out How Much Your Ad Will Cost

After deciding where you're going to put your ad, you need to figure out what the ad is going to cost you. You'll do that with the help of a sales rep (see the section "Finding a Good Sales Rep" later in this chapter). But before you go into a meeting with a rep, you need to know a few things about how print ads are priced. Somewhere in the mists of time, all newspapers made the diabolical decision that no two advertising pricing schemes would ever be the same.

Print ads are generally priced by multiplying the number of columns wide, by the number of inches high, by a dollar amount for each column inch. For example, a quarter page ad in most newspapers is 3 columns wide by 11 inches high, which makes it a 33-column-inch ad. If the open rate for your local paper is $50 per column inch, you will have an ad that will cost you $1,650 for one insertion.

Unfortunately, it's not always that simple. Here are just a few of the seemingly infinite variations possible to that simple pricing structure:

✔ The initial $50 per column inch rate can change for numerous reasons because it is the *open rate* (the rate paid by a new advertiser who will only run an ad one time).

✔ If you are willing to commit to running your ad multiple times over a certain time period, you can reduce the open rate by as much as 50 percent.

✔ Discounts are often given for new businesses, minority-owned businesses, first-time advertisers, political advertisers, nonprofit groups, and so on.

✔ If you're willing to commit to three ads per week, and if you're also willing to make a substantial dollar commitment over an extended time period, you will dramatically reduce your rate per ad.

✔ You may qualify for more than one of the above discounts — for example, if you are willing to commit to a long-term buy and you are also a nonprofit.

TECHNICAL STUFF

Cost per thousand

The cost of reaching the consumer via print is often expressed in *cost per thousand* (CPM), the cost to you if you want to reach 1,000 consumers with your advertisement. For instance, coupon booklets are usually target-mailed to groups of 10,000 households. To have your ad included in a one-time mailing of a coupon booklet to a particular group of homes may cost you $275, resulting in a CPM of $27.50 ($275 divided by 10). In that same market, you may find that running an ad in a daily newspaper may give you a much different CPM. For instance, to run a print ad that includes that same coupon may require a 3-column-by-2-inch ad (6 column inches). That ad priced at an open rate of $80 per column inch would cost you $480. If the newspaper boasts a circulation of about 300,000, your CPM is only $1.60.

But hold on there! There is much to consider, much to factor in. First, depending on which section of the paper your ad runs in, only count on about 20 percent of the paper's total circulation actually *seeing* your ads. Second, a small coupon ad positioned on a full page of newsprint is dramatically different (read, *dramatically less effective*) than a color coupon printed and mailed to consumers in a coupon booklet.

What's the moral of this story? CPM is an important consideration when evaluating the cost of print advertising. However, you need to consider other factors if you want to compare apples to apples. My suggestion is to always factor in the variables, stir in some gut feel, and do the math so you're aware of the CPM. Then use all these various aspects to make more sense of a sometimes-confusing media choice.

Usually newspapers offer what they call *pickup rates*. A pickup rate is a discounted rate given in return for running the same ad two or more times in the same week. For instance, if your first ad runs in the Sunday paper, a pickup rate may be quoted to you by your newspaper rep as follows: "Our pickup rates are 20, 30, 40, then 50, 50, and 50." That's their way of saying that if you run your ad a second time in the same week, you will receive a 20 percent discount; a third insertion in that week gets you a 30 percent discount; a fourth insertion gets you a 40 percent discount; and for every time you run the ad in that same week after that point, you will receive a 50 percent discount. And the discounts apply to all ads run. The discounts definitely have a way of adding up! The ad in my example earlier in this section, which I priced at $1,650 for a single insertion, ends up costing $594 at the end of one week if you run it multiple times — which gives you a discount of 64 percent!

Ad pricing is complicated, confusing, convoluted, and intimidating. The only way you can be sure you're getting the best rate possible is to tell your rep, in no uncertain terms, "Give me *all* available rates."

Finding a Good Sales Rep

If you're buying print media, you will, for better or worse, need to deal with sales reps from the various publications — newspapers, magazines, Sunday supplements, coupon books — into which you will be inserting your ads. Sales reps come in many shapes, sizes, and abilities ranging from "nearly comatose" to "able to leap tall buildings in a single bound." So, unless you own a portable defibrillator and can strap it on quickly, you want to look for a rep who is a high achiever.

Never cold-call a publication

Imagine that you're a first-time advertiser looking to get information about a certain publication. Now imagine telephoning that newspaper's retail advertising department and, because you have no one's name, asking to speak to just any sales rep. The really good reps are busy taking orders, or they're out in the field generating new orders, or they're visiting their many clients and taking care of business. So who answers your call? Yep, the rep who's lazy, or a rookie without clue, or the guy who's waiting around the office hoping the phone will ring.

Don't give your advertising account to just anyone. Do everything you can, regardless of the size of your budget, to work with the best sales rep in the department. When you want a job done right, as the saying goes, give it to a busy person.

Go straight to the top

When you're interested in buying an ad with a particular print media, you don't just have to take the sales rep that the receptionist transfers you to when you call the front desk. You can find one who works for you, one you does his best to get you what you need. Picking the right rep can mean the difference between a successful, mutually profitable relationship with an advertising partner, and a frustrating and possibly expensive disaster.

A great place to start is by calling the publication's sales manager. Explain your needs and the kind of person you'd like to work with — tell her you have been disappointed by some other media reps and would like to work with her best sales rep, someone who's sharp and motivated (and hungry); someone who will actually return your phone calls on the same day; someone who carries a cellular phone and pager; someone who's available to help you solve last-minute problems; someone who will be your advertising partner; someone she would be proud and confident to have you work with.

Although this strategy has no guarantees, you're much more likely to get someone who works hard for you than you would be if you just called and told the sales manager to send someone out to see you. The person the sales manager assigns to you after you give her some parameters (which will imply that you're no rookie to this media-buying game) will probably be given some very specific instructions about what your expectations are, rather than just being handed a yellow sticky note saying, "Call this guy."

Ask for referrals

Another method for finding a good sales rep is simply to ask for referrals. You can save yourself a lot of wheel-spinning and grief by taking advantage of insider knowledge. The two best sources for referrals are sales reps for competing publications and your own friendly business competitors.

Sales reps, even though they're competing for the same advertising dollars, tend to know each other, hang out together, belong to the same clubs. High achievers are going to be friends with people similar to themselves. Birds of a feather, and all that.

Your business competitors, at least those with whom you are on speaking terms, can be another great source of insider information. Because you are in business, you probably know your neighbors, friendly competitors, suppliers, and so on. Some of them are undoubtedly placing advertising with the same publications you are looking to employ, and they can steer you toward sales reps you will enjoy working with, as well as warn you of sales reps you should avoid.

Becoming a Formidable Buyer

Buying ad space in the many print media requires patience and tact — and a bit of conniving — at least if you want to get a good deal. In this section, I provide some helpful hints on getting the most for your money when it comes to print ads.

Acting as though you're buying an ad reluctantly

If you're thinking about placing a print ad, you've probably decided to use a particular newspaper and you may already know, for example, that you want to run a quarter-page ad every Saturday for the next six months. If you were to walk into a meeting with a sales rep and tell him what you're looking for, he would probably pull out a rate card, listing all the standard rates for ads of various sizes. But if you pay the rate-card rate for an ad, that's essentially the same as paying full sticker price for a car at your local dealership. And, if you're like me, you ain't gonna do that!

Buying reluctantly is all about not revealing all your cards to your sales rep. So when you meet with the rep, convey something like the following:

> I've been considering several different types of advertising, including advertising in your newspaper. I have a great deal with the Yellow Pages, I plan to buy some local radio, and I'll be sending out a monthly coupon with a direct-mail house as well. I just wanted to find out from you whether your newspaper may be able to round out my media buy and complement what I already have in the works.

Emptying a sales rep's bag of tricks

Like most people, you probably have had the experience of someone trying to sell you something that you didn't really want to buy. Whether it was a time-share condominium in Mexico or a new car at the dealer down the street, the common (and happy) denominator of this excruciating experience was that the longer you *resisted* the initial offer, the better the deal got.

Believe me when I say that all media sales reps carry with them a bag filled to the top with tricks to be used to close deals when the need arises. If you've done your job, you will eventually get a much better deal than you were offered originally, and in turn, you will have stretched your ad budget.

This language sends out a strong message to the rep, a message that states that you aren't just a pushover and that the rep will have some work to do in order to get your business. The rep doesn't need to give you a big, fat sales pitch. You have shown, in your speech, that you know what you're doing, that you'll expect to be treated differently than other new advertisers, that you're not about to pay full sticker price, and that, bottom line, you want a deal. That's a powerful message!

Don't just stop with good opening remarks. If you're meeting in your office, leave a few business cards from this rep's competitors lying around your desk along with pages torn from the Yellow Pages on which you've scribbled notes with a red marker. Reps have a notorious talent for reading upside-down, so anything you leave on your desk *will* be read. Ask the newspaper rep if he thinks radio advertising is still a good value in your area. Prearrange to receive a phone call in the middle of your meeting and say things like, "No way! I'm not paying that rate. That's ridiculous!" You have now set the stage for the sales rep to come back to you with a convincing pitch that his publication is not only the right media for you, but also one of the most affordable. Now is the time to sit back and listen. Let the rep go to work, and never give him the slightest hint as to which way you're leaning. And when he has quoted you the best rate he can personally offer, refuse it and send him back to his sales manager for an even better one.

During my decades in the advertising business I have worked with hundreds of clients, big and small, and I can tell you that owners of small businesses, whose ad budgets are comprised of their own, hard-earned money, are instinctively reluctant buyers. As a matter of fact, in my experience, the smaller the account the more client service (read, *hand-holding*) is involved. These people correctly perceive their ad budgets as "real dollars" subtracted off the bottom line (that's their take-home pay) and they want to know how every nickel will be spent. Conversely, employees of large companies, who are spending corporate advertising budgets, tend to view those dollars as an abstraction, also tend to be lazy with their buying, and are, therefore, much easier to sell and service. If you are spending your own money for print ads, I probably don't need to tell you to be a reluctant and careful buyer, but I'm reminding you to do so just in case.

Making your sales rep think he's got competition

If you don't create at least the appearance of a competitive situation, you won't receive the best price available. In other words, even if you're *not* talking with other sales reps from other media, you need to make your sales rep *think* you are. You need to introduce the possibility of competition (and reality) into the lives of your sales reps. You can accomplish this feat in countless ways, a few of which I outline in the following sections.

Ask for more

The mere mention of competition is usually enough to send your sales rep running for her pencil sharpener. The simplest method is to study the rep's first offer and then, casually, but with confidence, simply ask for more. If she offers you four ads for $1,000, tell her you need six ads for the same price — or you'll be forced to get quotes from other sources. You may not get exactly what you ask for, but I guarantee that you will get *something*.

Wheel and deal

Call all the competitors, get quotes and bids, and then let them tear each other apart. Show reps their competitor's proposals and let the various reps analyze their competitors' bids. Then, sit back and watch the back-stabbing games begin. This game is despicable, but it works to your own advantage. It may get a little bloody, but I guarantee you'll get the best rates and combo deals available from each and every publication.

Make an arbitrary change

If you've been using a particular newspaper for an extended period of time, make a surprise and very arbitrary change. Then when your sales rep drops into your office to get your monthly order, tell her you've decided to place your ads in another paper or switch your budget to radio this month because her competitor has offered you a deal that you simply couldn't refuse. Naturally, your rep will be shocked and dismayed, and she will very likely lay a huge guilt trip on you by whining something like, "Gee, I thought we were working so well together."

The rep will then do one of two things: Go out to her BMW (they all drive very tired BMWs), run a hose from tailpipe to interior, start the engine, and leave this world in utter despair. Or return to her cubicle where she will have to tell her sales manager that she has lost your business this month. She will then be instructed to go back to your office and do whatever it takes (offer lower rates, more insertions, better page position, whatever) to win back your business. What you hope is that your sales rep chooses the second option — not only does she go on to lead a long and happy life, but you get a good deal on the next month's ads at the same time.

Complaining when the time is right

If one of your customers bought a brand new whatchimacallit from you at a premium price, then took it home, used it once, and it broke, I guarantee that you would quickly see that customer back in your store, whatchimacallit in hand, ranting and raving for either an exchange or a refund. Or if you yourself ordered something from a catalog that turned out to be less than advertised, you'd get onto the customer service line in a heartbeat and complain loud and clear until you were either sent another item or given assurances of a full and immediate credit to your account. Complaining is sometimes the only way to get what you want (more so everyday, it seems), and you should use this tried-and-true technique to assure that your print budget is always maximized. Newspapers don't go out of their way to make mistakes; it's simply a fact of life.

If anything is wrong with the placement of your print ad, don't be shy. Get on the phone and chew out anyone who will listen to you. Start with your rep and move right up the chain of command until you find satisfaction. If you ad falls on a page that was printed a bit light because the roller was running out of ink, complain. If your ad is buried in some obscure section of the newspaper that you didn't contract for and would never select if given a choice, complain. If your ad was scheduled to run on Friday but didn't run until Saturday, complain. If your ad is sandwiched between two of your competitor's ads, complain.

Most publications have a fairly liberal policy when it comes to giving their customers *make-good ads* (ads that try to make good on the publication's promise to you). Rather than making a good customer angry about some fairly common mistake, the publication will usually give you another free ad to make up for anything you're unhappy about.

If you don't complain, whatever it is you *didn't* complain about is bound to happen again. In any newspaper, there is good, great, and just plain lousy ad placement (or position). Most ads are placed in a section and on the page in a random and somewhat arbitrary fashion. The people who do the actual layout of the finished paper start with a stack of ads and a pile of pictures and stories, and assemble the newspaper. Your well-timed complaint can cause your rep to hand-carry your ad back to that department and ask the nice folks for a favor. To further my point, if you and your competitor *both* get lousy ad placement, and the other guys complain but you don't, then your competition will get the make-good ad, your competition will get better placement next time, and, because of all this, your competition will have an advantage over you.

You can significantly stretch your print advertising budget by not pretending you have lockjaw every time a publication screws things up. Loud and vociferous complaints will get you two things: make-good ads and better ad placement. The value of free make-good ads is fairly easy to determine, and a well-placed ad can be worth twice that of a poorly placed ad. In short, your ad will do a heck of a lot better if it's positioned where someone can actually see it!

Most papers will, sadly, give you a legitimate reason to complain at least once every ten ads you run. Newspapers just have a talent for getting it wrong, perhaps because of the sheer volume of ads they run each day. It is logical, therefore, that you could stretch your ad budget by 10 percent simply by not being shy.

Part V

Beyond the Basics: Making Use of Publicity, Premiums, and Events

The 5th Wave   By Rich Tennant

"There you go Mr. Mellman. As agreed, every bird I sell over the next 12 months will be trained to say, 'Hello', 'Pretty bird', and 'Mellman's Carpet World'. Some of the birds have trouble with the word, 'carpet'. It comes out 'crapet'. That gonna be a problem?"

In this part . . .

Publicity — sending a press release to a publication in the hopes of getting some free ink — is most certainly a form of advertising. Premium items — the giveaway refrigerator magnets, key chains, mouse pads, and coffee mugs you know and love — are definitely forms of advertising. And promotions and events — whether radio station–invented or created by you — are also unique forms of advertising. As part of an overall ad campaign, each of these can increase your exposure in the marketplace. And in this part, I show you how to make them work for you.

Chapter 17

Publicity and Public Relations

· ·

· ·

There is no such thing as bad publicity except your own obituary.

— Brendan Behan, Irish playwright and poet

Although closely related, public relations and publicity are two different things. *Public relations* (or PR for short) is the ongoing process of promoting yourself and talking yourself up. *Publicity* is the occasional process of using a much bigger tool (usually in the form of media) to promote yourself. Here's a simple analogy illustrating the difference between public relations and publicity: If your business sponsors a Little League team for kids who live near your store, *that* is public relations. You are endearing yourself to the kids' parents (the public to whom you're trying to relate), who may, as a result, become your customers. If, on the other hand, you send your local newspaper a written story bragging about your Little League sponsorship in the hopes of having it printed, *that* is publicity. You're now blatantly (some would argue, cleverly) trying to endear yourself to everyone who subscribes to the paper. A public relations campaign may cost you money — uniforms and equipment for your Little League team, for example — but publicity, for the most part, is free (the media doesn't charge you to publish or broadcast your story).

The publicity blitz I conceived to put the Pet Rock on the tip of everyone's tongue (see the nearby sidebar) was accomplished at absolutely no cost. I never spent a dime to advertise the product and the national and international publicity was free. I must admit that I had the advantage over other inventors: I had an advertising and public relations background and knew the various steps to take to obtain free publicity. But you're in luck! I'm sharing these insights with you in this chapter.

ANECDOTE

The Pet Rock: A publicity phenomenon

One fortunate day in late 1975, my idea for the Pet Rock was quickly transformed from a novelty gift item with an uncertain future into an international retail phenomenon. It was a day that proved, without a doubt, the incredible power of publicity — a day that forever changed my life. It was November 10, 1975, and a half-page publicity story about the Pet Rock and a photo of its inventor (me) were featured in the influential *Newsweek* magazine.

At the time, I was looking to jumpstart the introduction of the product to the retail gift trade (but I was unable to afford a huge advertising budget), so I wrote a publicity story about the Pet Rock, and sent it, along with photos of me, the product, and its packaging, to the major weekly news magazines. The Pet Rock was a highly unusual product, and I wasn't sure what to expect from the mass media, but I kept my fingers crossed.

Maybe it was a slow news day. Or perhaps the tongue-in-cheek qualities of both the product and the publicity story attracted the editors' attention. Whatever the reason, *Newsweek* printed my story, even embellishing it a bit, and the rest is history. Even better, the story included the important fact that the prestigious Dallas-based Neiman-Marcus department stores had purchased a test order of the product at the Fall New York Gift Show. It was the turning point in putting the Pet Rock alongside the hula hoop in the Fads Hall of Fame. The *Newsweek* story gave the item media credibility, and the Neiman-Marcus mention within the story gave it retail credibility. The media followed the lead of *Newsweek,* and retailers followed the lead of Neiman-Marcus. No media wanted to be left out of this crazy story; few retailers dared ignore the product.

The Pet Rock, in my opinion, was more of a media event than it was a sales event. Although we sold (literally and figuratively) tons of them, the media attention generated by the product far outweighed the sales produced. During its five-month retailing life span (yep, that's all it had), the Pet Rock was referenced in nearly every daily newspaper in the country, most major magazines, all network national news programs, *The Tonight Show* and other late-night talk shows, most radio talk shows, and international media such as the BBC. I was personally interviewed hundreds of times, sometimes doing two interviews simultaneously with a phone to each ear. The Pet Rock, thanks to the initial story in *Newsweek,* generated multimillions of dollars of free publicity that, as amazing as it may seem, continues to this day. Over 25 years later, I am *still* contacted by major media to comment upon new novelty items that purport to be, but aren't, "this year's Pet Rock." The Pet Rock has become a part of the lexicon, a permanent piece of Americana. I quit saving the press clippings decades ago.

The moral of the story: Do not doubt the influence of publicity. Use it to your advantage, and you shall prosper.

Starting an Ongoing Public Relations Campaign

From the sponsorship of a local Little League team to allowing local service clubs the use of your store or conference room for their meetings, PR can take many forms. Public relations is just that — relating to the public, which, in this case, means your current and future customers. Your PR effort doesn't have to be grandiose and expensive — it can be modest and still be highly effective. If you own a pet-supply store, you can offer free dog-training classes or low-priced vaccination clinics (these could also be defined as *promotions*). If you own a restaurant, you can offer your banquet room free of charge to the local Toastmasters or Rotary Club (of course, you'll charge them for the food and beverages). And regardless of your business, you can offer free goods for charity auctions or buy ad space in the high school yearbook, ticket books for worthwhile raffles, and so on.

One of my clients, a furniture store owner, donated a very expensive dining room set to a local fundraising auction and, as a result of his generosity and the ensuing publicity, he has been enjoying new cash customers from the sponsoring club ever since.

The trick to PR is to do good works for the community while gaining at least a subtle recognition for yourself and your business. The nice folks who donate lavishly to the arts do so, of course, out of a generous, selfless sense of civic duty. But God help the person who misspells their names in the program!

Unlike the immediacy of a press release, where you're looking to get a story published right away, PR is a continuing process just as your advertising campaign is (or should be) a continuing process. Your PR campaign is an integral part of your entire communications course of action and is no less important than a blockbuster TV or radio commercial or a full-page ad in the local daily. And, if yours is a small to mid-size retail or service business, a solid PR effort in your community is doubly important. A well-planned PR campaign will keep your name in front of your customers (and prospective customers) even when they're not being totally blown away by your advertising skills.

If you're in business, you're probably already conducting a PR campaign in your community. You buy this, donate that, sponsor this, offer that — and perhaps sometimes wish you had your money back so you could add it to your advertising budget and get some measurable return on your investment. But PR is a necessary evil to the success of a small business. The huge corporations donate en masse to the United Way or other charity clearing houses. The smaller local businesses (that's you and me) get hit for the raffles. Even if a group wanted a large corporation to donate to their fundraiser, they couldn't get past the front desk receptionist in a monolithic office building. But with a small business, all the Girl Scouts have to do is walk through your front door and, *boom,* you've bought yourself a bunch of cookies.

Consider PR part of the cost of doing business, and take heart — in many cases you will reap the rewards (the Girl Scouts' moms and dads may throw some business your way to thank you for your kindness). Consider also that, if you *don't* buy the raffle tickets and donate to the charity auctions, you could incur the negative side of public relations. Public relations of this sort is a double-edged sword; you may get tired of all the local service clubs and charities continually putting the touch on you, but not participating may be worse than a few minor annoyances. The people selected as members of the fundraising team by these organizations are chosen because of their tenacity. They don't know how to take no for an answer and, if you do say no, they have very long memories.

So how do you make friends and influence people; create understanding, acceptance, and awareness of your business or product; and gain a favorable response from your marketplace? Know what messages you want to communicate. Think about what your various audiences need to know about your product or service. What is it that makes what you sell better than, or different from, anything else consumers can get elsewhere? Are there audiences who should know about your community involvement, your environmental record, your particular expertise that adds value to your sell? Should people know about the comprehensiveness of your offer, key endorsements you have received, the credibility of your investors, the partnerships you've formed, or the promotional tie-ins you provide with other organizations?

Your messages should directly answer the question: "Why should anyone care about what you offer?"

When you know what you want to communicate through your PR, how do you go about delivering that message? You can use many different vehicles for communicating with the audiences you want to reach. Here's a list of potential communications vehicles:

- Publicity or press releases targeted to mass/trade/community media (see the section on publicity later in this chapter for more information)
- Article reprints of publicity you have received from various media, which you then mail to specific lists
- Professional-quality photography to accompany your press releases
- Volunteer participation in community and charitable organizations or foundations
- Scholarships you have awarded and that carry your name
- Seminars, speeches, and lectures you give to various groups
- Web site and Internet postings of publicity you have received
- Contests you sponsor that carry your name
- Newsletters you write and send out on a regular basis
- Donations of products or services to community causes, events, and clubs

Your list of communications vehicles that will get your name in front of the public is limited only by your own imagination.

The big boys do PR well, don't they?

With expensive PR firms at their disposal, giant corporations and prominent national figures are nearly immune to public relations disasters, right? Wrong! Even the world's major brands and most famous names stumble when it comes to PR.

The San Francisco public relations firm of Fineman Associates (www.finemanpr.com) selects, compiles, and publishes an annual list of the ten worst PR gaffes. The "winners" are companies that have been caught up in avoidable blunders that caused adverse publicity. The image damage was done to self, company, society, and others — and it was widely reported by the national press that year. Fineman's lists are published each year in various newspapers and magazines. Watch for them. They're not only funny, but very instructional.

Using Publicity Wisely

Most people understand the power of favorable news coverage, whether it is *The Wall Street Journal,* the local daily, *Time* magazine, local radio or TV, an industry trade journal, or a community weekly paper. Restaurants receiving positive media coverage are swamped with phone calls for reservations. Companies get a flood of orders for their well-reviewed widgets. Designers become "hot." New respect is derived from customers, competitors, family, and friends. Apart from the single article or broadcast segment you may notice and envy, what you may not realize are the many benefits that an organized and continuing publicity effort adds to your other marketing efforts. If you're using paid advertising, articles in which you or your company appear help infuse your campaign with credibility and detail. Plus, publicity adds reach and frequency to your message that you may not otherwise be able to afford.

Publicity can be a wonderful and highly productive thing when handled correctly. But just like anything, if you don't have a strategy for what you're doing, you may flounder. In this section, I fill you in on how to write a press release and get it seen by a big audience.

Writing an effective press release

The backbone of publicity is the press release. A *press release* is a news story written by someone other than the editors and reporters of the media to whom it is submitted for publication. It is, when written properly, a valuable tool for businesspeople, because it can generate what amounts to free advertising. And when your press release is printed in your local paper, it becomes an endorsement of sorts by that publication. Your potential customers will see the story that you either wrote in its entirety or outlined for rewriting by the publication and think it has been written by the paper.

Press releases have one purpose: to get you free publicity (a form of advertising) by informing the media that your company has done, or will do, something newsworthy. Here are just a few of the subjects you could use as a basis for a press release:

- A promotion or new hire
- A purchase of a competitor's business or a merger
- A community project your company has sponsored
- An industry award won by you or one of your employees
- The introduction of a new product or service
- A new location or the addition of a branch office
- A highly successful year or quarter
- A change in corporate policy or a new affiliation

If you've won a prestigious award, you have a newsworthy story. If you've promoted one of your employees to an important position or if your business has won an important contract, you can send a brief release to the Business Editor of your local paper. If you have invented and are introducing a new product, by all means send a story to the paper. The bottom line here is to send news that may be of interest to a broad audience.

One of the all-time PR blunders

In the late 1980s, television newsmagazine *60 Minutes* did a story about the so-called "unintended acceleration" of Audi automobiles. The story was a result of a woman who drove over and killed her own child in the family garage. She claimed that her Audi had "jumped forward" without her ever putting her foot on the gas pedal. *60 Minutes* bought her story and made a full segment out of it. It destroyed the Audi brand for years to come.

So, what did Audi do to refute or explain their side of the story? Nothing! Well, not nearly enough anyway. Perhaps they thought the charge so ridiculous that they didn't take it seriously. They obviously didn't appreciate the fact

that, at that time, *60 Minutes* was the most-watched show on TV. But the show had made some very drastic charges against Audi cars — they were unsafe and they could kill people — and, sadly for Audi, people believed the story and Audi's sales in the U.S. went into the tank for the next decade. Only in the last few years has Audi reached, and surpassed, the level of sales it enjoyed before the *60 Minutes* story was broadcast.

The manufacturer shot itself in the foot big time when it didn't bother to use the power of public relations to answer the charges and to prove the accusations were completely false.

Reporters and editors all have the same problem: They must fill their pages or their broadcast news airtime with interesting stories each and every day. For this reason they welcome the receipt of a well-written, attention-grabbing publicity release from time to time. It helps them do their jobs. They may not print the story verbatim — instead, they may use your publicity release as a basis for a story they write themselves, after interviewing you for more information. But newspapers always print stories they find worthwhile. Getting "good ink" isn't hard, as long as your subject matter is of interest.

Do not send out a publicity release unless you have something important to say. Make sure the story is interesting, relevant, possibly amusing, always newsworthy, and, above all, not frivolous or boring in its content. You'll make an editor very crabby with a story about the roof of your store leaking during a recent rainstorm. If, on the other hand, the roof of your store caved in and trapped dozens of shoppers, you're going to get all the free publicity (all negative, of course) that you can possibly handle.

When you have something interesting to say (your business has just won an award, for example) and you want to submit a press release, you need to write the release in the form that editors and reporters are used to seeing The standard press release format is a fairly structured one, written in the *journalistic style* (a narrative style in which the most important facts come first) and containing the five *W*s: who, what, when, where, and why. The reader of a press release should be able to grasp all the necessary facts after reading only the first paragraph.

What editors and reporters look for in a press release

I asked a columnist for the _San Jose Mercury News_ what he looks for in a press release, why he prints one story and discards another. His response was succinct: "What's a good press release? Brief, to the point, and promising information no one else has." He then went on to say, "If I were to offer one suggestion to people sending out press releases, it would be to first read the publication the release is going to, and to read the writings of the editor or reporter to whom the release is being sent. That, more than anything else, will increase your chances of being published."

Remember: Sending out a press release is not a guarantee that you will ever see it in print. You may think your story is newsworthy, but the editor may not. Editors will only print news that will interest their readers. And they know what their readers want. Your story could also be killed because you had the unfortunate timing of sending it in just when a major news story erupted. Because space (whether print or broadcast) is finite, your story could get bumped in favor of more important news. Sometimes, it's the luck of the draw.

Your release should include the following information in this order:

- ✔ The sending company's name, address, phone number, fax number, e-mail address, and contact person (that's you)

- ✔ A headline (a straightforward, one-line summary of the story)

- ✔ An introductory paragraph (a slightly more detailed summary of the story)

- ✔ The bulk of the story (containing straightforward, pertinent information)

- ✔ Fluff (information of some interest, but not directly relevant to the story)

- ✔ A photo, drawing, chart, or other graphic element directly related to the story, along with a suggested caption written by you

For example, let's say Jane Smith owns a donut shop called Donut City and has devised an earth-shattering innovation for the making of the fattening little pastries. Her donut shop, and *her* donut shop alone, has introduced donuts with (gasp!) smaller holes. She now wants to get a news story printed that extols the virtues of this most unique donut feature. Although it's a pretty boring story — and I'm sure most editors would think the same — she can spin it around a bit and make it more provocative by being confrontational. She can publicize her smaller donut holes by attacking, with tongue firmly planted in cheek, her competition. Check out Figure 17-1 to see how it's done and the form in which it should be written.

If Jane Smith sends the release in Figure 17-1 to an editor along with a couple dozen donuts as a bribe, the editor, on a slow news day, will probably pick up on this story and call Jane for an interview. Editors are always looking for feel-good stories to offset all the bad news they have to print every day. Most television news programs end with an upbeat, sometimes funny news story to offset the heavy dose of bad news you've just been fed. The Pet Rock publicity was a perfect example of this. I absolutely believe this tongue-in-cheek approach would garner some ink for an otherwise obscure donut shop.

Refer to Figure 17-1, and take a closer look at the elements of the press release form. After Jane Smith's contact information, the first entry is the date of submission and the instructions as to when the story is to be released to the public. In this case, Jane instructs the publication, "For immediate release." The next entry is "Press Release" — this way the editors know what this story is. Next comes the headline. Although some people feel that including a headline on a press release is an insult to the editor of the publication (who may want to write his own headline), I usually add a headline anyway in order to attract the editor's attention and to make the story easily understood. Then comes a subhead of additional information. Then comes the story, written with the copious use of quotes. (Using quotes allows you to impart information that then appears to have been gleaned by a reporter from an actual interview of the person "speaking.") The end of the story should be clearly marked with # # #.

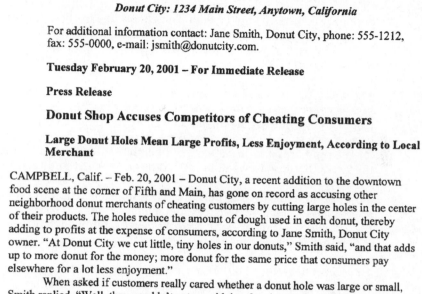

Donut City: 1234 Main Street, Anytown, California

For additional information contact: Jane Smith, Donut City, phone: 555-1212, fax: 555-0000, e-mail: jsmith@donutcity.com.

Tuesday February 20, 2001 – For Immediate Release

Press Release

Donut Shop Accuses Competitors of Cheating Consumers

Large Donut Holes Mean Large Profits, Less Enjoyment, According to Local Merchant

CAMPBELL, Calif. – Feb. 20, 2001 – Donut City, a recent addition to the downtown food scene at the corner of Fifth and Main, has gone on record as accusing other neighborhood donut merchants of cheating customers by cutting large holes in the center of their products. The holes reduce the amount of dough used in each donut, thereby adding to profits at the expense of consumers, according to Jane Smith, Donut City owner. "At Donut City we cut little, tiny holes in our donuts," Smith said, "and that adds up to more donut for the money; more donut for the same price that consumers pay elsewhere for a lot less enjoyment."

When asked if customers really cared whether a donut hole was large or small, Smith replied, "Well, they wouldn't put up with less hamburger for the money at the local greasy spoon. Why should they put up with less donut from the local donut shops? At Donut City, we give them more than their money's worth — and we think our customers appreciate the added sugar, calories, and fat for the same price!"

Other area donut shops did not respond to requests for interviews prior to publication.

Figure 17-1:
A sample press release.

You will also notice that the five *W*s are present in the story:

- **Who:** Jane Smith, owner of Donut City
- **What:** Donut City, the new kids on the block
- **Where:** Downtown at Fifth and Main
- **When:** A recent addition to the downtown food scene, with an immediate problem
- **Why:** Because consumers are being cheated by other donut makers

Getting the story to the media

When you have your press release written, you can either hand-carry, mail, or e-mail the story directly to your local publication. Or if you're eager to get the story published by multiple publications or broadcasters (if the story has national implications, for instance) you can use a professional service such as the Business Wire (www.businesswire.com). The Business Wire is a service that will electronically disseminate your story and photos to a wide variety of national and international media. You choose the list of recipients (specific editors for magazines, radio or television stations, daily newspapers, or all of the above), and you pay for the service based upon the scope of your media choices.

The worst thing you can do with your press release is send it to a post office box or general street address or to the Editor-in-Chief. Your release will get lost in a huge pile of daily mail received by the publication and may never find its way to the proper editor or reporter. Unfortunately, the right person for the right story varies at each publication or broadcast station. It could be the News Director, News Editor, City Editor, Executive Editor, or Senior Editor.

Take the time to call or write the publications and ask who should be addressed for a particular story. Get a name, title, and routing address for this person. Your release will have a much better chance of seeing print if you invest this small amount of effort.

The secret to getting a reporter's attention for your story is salesmanship. You must pursue your target market, in this case the media, with a nicely packaged product (meaning a well-written story or provocative story outline). And your product must be something that the reporter needs or desires, meaning a story about a subject he covers that can be resold to the editor or producer. Like all sales efforts, you need to sell reporters on you, on your product, on your story, and on why they and their audience should care. Tell them how your story adds to any particular point of public discussion or marketplace need. The sell must be timely or must be cultivated over time (serving that reporter as a source of tips and information). The reporter must trust you and be interested in what you have to say.

Unless you see the story as having very broad implications and want to get as much news coverage as possible, limit the number of publications you send it to. If the information is highly technical and specific to your own trade, send it to journals and trade publications within your industry. If the release is more general (you're introducing a new product or you're involved in a community project, for example), send it to your trade journals, plus all area newspapers, magazines, broadcast stations, and publications.

Editors receive piles of press releases each week. They are all read and considered, but they are not all published. Every publication has its own ideas as to what constitutes news. Some releases may result in a phone call, an interview, and a full write-up. Others may get a line or two of copy. If you've sent along a photo, you may see the story but no picture, or visa versa. Or, sadly, none of the above may happen. Don't be too discouraged if your story never gets ink. Try again with another story at some future date.

ANECDOTE

The Adjective Game

One of my first jobs in the advertising business was as a copywriter for a Northern California agency that specialized in homebuilders. This was in the 1960s, when the California housing boom was in full swing, when the fruit orchards in the Santa Clara Valley were being decimated in favor of what Pete Seegar called "Ticky Tacky Houses." It was part of my job to write print ads, brochures, and press releases about the various subdivisions being built by the agency's clients. The press releases were then sent to the same publications in which the agency bought paid advertising space. The agency represented a multitude of homebuilders who were constructing scores of subdivisions comprised of dozens of model homes, all of which looked the same, and all of which were in about the same price range.

Because it was nearly impossible to differentiate between the various houses advertised (and publicized), let alone to find something unique to say about each house in a press release, my fellow writers and I came up with The Adjective Game. This was a series of small boxes filled with adjectives written on scraps of paper. It was designed to help us copywriters retain our collective sanity while writing nearly identical ads and publicity releases day after day. We had a box for every room and exterior in and around the average tract house. When we were writing a new paragraph about a living room, we drew words from the Living Room Box; the dining room, the Dining Room Box; and so forth. These words included *soaring, vaulted,* and *open-beamed* to describe ceilings; *spacious, inviting,* and *fully-carpeted* to describe living rooms; *verdant, oak tree–studded,* and *breathtaking vistas* to describe the surrounding areas. Our sentences, I am embarrassed to report, read something like this: "Nestled in the verdant, green foothills of the oak tree–studded Evergreen Valley, enjoying unmatched vistas, are the breathtaking, spacious homes of Shadowbrook."

Everything we wrote was pure crap, but the local newspapers, eager to fill the pages of the real estate section, printed every word.

TIP

If you don't see your story printed within a reasonable amount of time, you can call the editor to whom you sent the story to innocently ask if she received it. However, your release probably arrived as part of a huge pile of mail, so don't get all bent out of shape because the editor doesn't know what you're talking about. Calling will alert the editor that your story is somewhere on her desk and will likely get her to at least look at it. Remember to be respectful, not confrontational.

Dealing with the news media

When you have a story, keep it simple, clear, brief, and to the point. Here are some tips for dealing with the news media:

✔ **Target media representatives covering your area of business.** Send notes complimenting them about stories they do. Call or write and let them know that you could be a good resource on specific topics. Alert them to things you may know about.

✔ **Provide good photography whenever possible.** Use the photography to help tell your story.

✔ **Develop a point of view.** To the extent possible, make your perspective colorful, entertaining, provocative, confident, and visionary.

Remember: If you know how to work with the news media effectively, you can get all kinds of free publicity for your business — and publicity is a great form of advertising.

Chapter 18

Specialty Advertising: Getting Your Name Out There

> *Americans are the only people in the world known to me whose status anxiety prompts them to advertise their college and university affiliations in the rear window of their automobiles.*
>
> — Paul Fussell

*E*very year around the holidays my barber gives me a little gift. Most recently, he gave me a plastic clip to reseal opened potato chip bags — with the name of his barbershop on it. I was touched. I've also received from him such thoughtful items as a rubber pad to make unscrewing jar lids easier, a small magnetic notebook in which to list phone numbers, a variety of key chains, and, of course, the ubiquitous coffee mugs. I accept these logo-emblazoned "gifts" graciously . . . and usually throw them away. In the world of advertising, these free gifts are called *specialty advertising* (which is stuff on which you print your company logo and slogan) and *premium items* (which are the toys and goodies your kids get when they buy a kid's meal at the fast food emporium). Specialty advertising is quite likely the only advertising my barber does. (He doesn't need to do more — getting an appointment with him is harder than it is with my doctor.)

Radio and television stations are a wonderful source of specialty advertising. I have an antique hat rack in my office that has one purpose: to hold the dozens of embroidered baseball caps I receive each year from various stations in the area. Usually, I hang on to these caps until I have no more room, and then they're taken away once a year to be sold in employees' garage sales. My agency is also the fortunate recipient of an infinite supply of T-shirts, golfing jackets, sweatshirts, umbrellas, letter openers, stadium blankets, bumper stickers, calculators, calendars, coffee mugs, even *Ally McBeal* pajamas and Martin Short shorts — all with station logos, all graciously received, and all passed along by us to friends, clients, or office neighbors who don't mind parading around wearing or displaying advertising.

Despite all the negative things consumers say about advertising, they're increasingly willing to be walking billboards for various brands as they don all sorts of promotional wearables and display everything from logo-covered coffee mugs to candy jars on their desks. Face it: For better or for worse, specialty advertising items are everywhere.

Because I've been on the receiving end of so much specialty advertising for so many years, I have mixed feelings about the worth and effectiveness of it. But it is a big part of the advertising world (all you have to do is walk into a fast food restaurant to see which freebie your kid is being offered this week to see for yourself), and so it deserves a look. In this chapter, I let you know the advantages and disadvantages to using specialty advertising, so you can decide for yourself whether to use it as part of your ad campaign.

Recognizing the Advantages of Specialty Advertising

If you do your homework and pick out a truly useful specialty advertising item to include in a promotion, an item with intrinsic or decorative value that your customers will be glad to receive and certain to use, this form of advertising is worth including in your overall advertising campaign. In the following sections, I cover a few good reasons to add *quality* premiums to your media mix.

Specialty items are relatively inexpensive

If you're advertising on a budget (as my barber obviously is), then specialty advertising items may be just the thing to get your name before the buying public. For the most part, specialty items can be very affordable. Of course, if you were a high roller, you could print your logo onto $1,000 Mont Blanc fountain pens. But assuming you're *not* a high roller, you could print the same logo onto a fairly good ballpoint pen for 50 cents apiece. The plastic clip that reseals opened potato chip bags, the rubber circle that aids in removing jar lids, the razor-blade letter opener — all of these are items that people may use every day, and none of them costs more than a dollar a piece. If you print your logo on them and give them out, the recipients will be continually reminded of your business.

It ain't the fast food, it's the prizes!

In 2000, McDonald's, the premium item and promotional champion of the world, rolled out a holiday promo tied to Disney's *102 Dalmatians* movie, offering 102 different toy premiums inside Happy Meals. This is premium advertising and promotion at its pinnacle, backed by huge advertising budgets and aimed squarely at the prime demo — kids! And when you find kids in a fast-food restaurant, their parents can't be far away. Premium items work for McDonald's (and other fast food chains). Otherwise, why would they continue to spend multimillions of dollars each year on them? But I also suspect that, at this level, premiums have become essential to the fast-food outlets in order to compete. In other words, they've all been doing it for so long that it's expected of them and they're stuck with it.

I'm not convinced brand loyalty enters into the minds of kids when they want the latest fast-food premium giveaway. If Wendy's is putting something into their kids' meals that kids can't live without, then the kids are going to direct their parents to Wendy's instead of other fast-food locations. If McDonald's has what the kids want, goodbye Wendy's. To kids, the food quality has absolutely nothing to do with it. It's who's handing out the best prizes! I doubt I'll ever hear my 8-year-old granddaughter, Emilie, say, "Oh no, we can't go to Burger King regardless of what toys they're giving away; I consider Chicken McNuggets far superior to Chicken Tenders, and I'd prefer to go to McDonald's."

You can pay thousands of dollars for a television package and then hope that a few of your spots run in good viewing times. And although the television station may tell you that thousands of people will be watching, you'd better hope that only a few of them will be visiting the bathroom or refrigerator when your spots run. But for just a few bucks apiece (or less), you can get a whole pile of specialty items printed with your logo and ready to advertise your company on a long-term basis (provided, that is, that you select an item people actually want)

Specialty advertising products are one of the few advertising vehicles that can stand alone. Most other types of advertising need to be supported with more advertising. For instance, you need to buy advertising on mass media in order to direct people to your Web site. But a promotional item, whether mailed to your customer list or handed out at your store, is pretty much self-sufficient in getting your advertising message across to your customers.

A radio station once gave me a really nifty pocket calculator that folds away and takes up no room at all on my desk. I use this item each and every day. And when I do, when I touch the little button that unfolds this clever item, I can't help but see the station's logo, and I am reminded of who gave it to me. This is a specialty advertising item with a purpose, an item I actually use on a daily basis. On the other hand, I have a whole shelf filled with dusty, logo-covered coffee mugs that I never use. You want to be sure to find a premium that people will enjoy and use for years to come — otherwise, you're just wasting your money.

You can imprint anything

Forget the T-shirts, coffee mugs, and key chains. There is a company that will laser-etch your logo onto the shells of live crabs and lobsters so you can send these tasty crustaceans to clients you *really* want to impress. You can have your logo engraved onto solid-gold putters for those golfers you desperately want to do business with. A bakery in my area will, by some high-tech printing process, inkjet (using edible inks) your logo, four-color photo, whatever, onto delicious cakes, which they will then deliver to your clients. And I have personally used a local microbrewery to make up a batch of beer with my own private label, then packed bottles of Gary Dahl Brew into wooden cases that were laser-etched with my logo and sent to clients as holiday gifts. It was a big hit.

If you can look beyond the obvious promotional items, the ones everyone sends out, then you'll truly make an impression.

Multiple impressions are a good thing

When I measure the effectiveness of radio or television buys, I do so in terms of *gross impressions* (the number of audience members delivered by a media schedule without regard to duplication) and *cost-per-thousand* (the cost per 1,000 people or households delivered by a media schedule). With specialty items, using these methods of measurement is impossible, because specialty items — at least the ones that are useful and have actual value to the recipient — have the advantage of scoring repeated impressions without repeated costs. You buy it once, and it sits on a customer's desk forever.

Last Christmas, a radio station sent me beautiful note cards and envelopes with my name richly embossed on top-quality paper. Every time I send a note, I am reminded of that station — a station that had the very good taste to send me something I am proud to use. Multiple impressions are a *very* good thing!

Premiums reinforce your other media efforts

McDonald's and other fast-food giants use premiums to reinforce their mass media efforts, so why shouldn't you? When McDonald's is giving away an item tied to a movie promotion (like *102 Dalmatians*), they call attention to their giveaway items in their TV and radio advertising, saying something like, "Get a Dalmatian puppy cuddly toy with the purchase of a Happy Meal." Likewise, the premium item itself calls attention to their broadcast efforts. Every form of media reinforces every other form of media, thereby making the entire promotion just that much more effective.

If you're giving away a premium or a specialty item with your logo affixed, by all means tell people about it in your other advertising: "Come in today, browse our new selection of fine kitchen cabinets, and be sure to ask for your very own laser-etched lobster." This cross-referencing will go a long way in stretching your advertising dollars.

Premiums are user-friendly

Advertising, by its very nature, is designed to be intrusive. If it weren't intrusive, how would anyone notice it? Specialty advertising items, on the other hand, are not so intrusive that they irritate people — especially items with a purpose. People actually want and appreciate advertising specialties that have utilitarian, intrinsic, or decorative value. What they do *not* want are commercials interrupting their favorite TV shows.

Selecting Specialty Items with a Purpose

Coffee mugs, key chains, baseball caps, and T-shirts are the ubiquitous mainstays of specialty advertising, but there are literally thousands of items onto which your logo or ad slogan can be printed or etched. The trick is to select an item that has real appeal to the consumer; something unusual and interesting; something that will be gratefully accepted and actually used. For example, 20 years ago I received a candy jar with a wooden lid on which a radio station's call letters were etched. It's a tasteful item (in more ways than one) and it still sits, two decades later, on the coffee table in my office, continually filled with a fresh supply of M&M's. The candy jar was a specialty item with a purpose. Over the years, I have tossed out hundreds of caps, T-shirts, and bumper stickers, but I still keep the candy jar.

Over 250,000 premium items and specialty advertising items are on the market today, just waiting for your logo. Look for something that you would be proud to give away and your customers would be happy to receive. In just a quick glance around my office, I see specialty items of every size and shape. Here are my favorites:

 ✔ A very utilitarian folding calculator
 ✔ A candy jar

✔ Embossed personal stationery and note cards

✔ A desktop business card holder

✔ A clever, razor-blade letter opener

I use these items many times throughout the day. Then there are all the rest: mugs, sports bottles, a can insulator, a golfing jacket, baseball caps, magnetic vinyl bumper stickers, key chains, ballpoint pens, and other things that are still lying around the office because no one has bothered to throw them out (or sell them at a garage sale). The neat stuff gets used. The not-so-neat stuff — at least the stuff that won't be used by the people here — just takes up space.

If you are thoughtful in your selection of specialty advertising items, you can then measure their effectiveness in terms of frequency just as you would a radio or TV commercial. Why? Because if the item is used on a daily basis, perhaps multiple times every day, then each time the item is used you have made another impression with the same advertising message. That is called *frequency*. However, in order to attain frequency, you must first select an item that has either a utilitarian or a decorative value and will, therefore, be used or displayed by the recipient. You're not going to get a lot of mileage out of some cheapo T-shirt that is relegated to the bottom of a dresser drawer (especially if it falls apart after just one washing). But you will win friends and influence people with a gift item that solves a problem or fills a need. When my barber gave me a logo-imprinted rubber pad that aids in opening sticky jar lids, I thought he was nuts. What a gigantic waste of money, I huffed. But that was only until I used it once and found out that this goofy item actually works! Hard-to-open jars are no longer a problem (especially important for a guy who loves pickles). It turned out to be a specialty item with legs — its effectiveness is, therefore, measurable on a frequency basis.

An endorsement from the FDA

The Food and Drug Administration (FDA), in ruling against the use of promotional items to encourage tobacco use, inadvertently gave a very strong endorsement to this particular advertising genre. The FDA wrote, "This form of advertising is particularly effective with young people. Young people have relatively little disposable income, so promotions are appealing because they represent getting something for nothing." Then a federal court added, "Printed advertising is customarily quickly read and discarded by typical customers. Utilitarian objects [read: *premium items* or *specialty advertising items*] on the other hand, are retained precisely because they have utility. They may be around for years. And each use of them brings a new reminder of the sponsor and his product." I couldn't have said it better myself.

If you want to get an overview of the incredible array of specialty advertising items that are available, as well as some great promotional ideas and insights, visit the Advertising Specialty Institute Web site at www.promomart.com. You can also check your local Yellow Pages to find specialty advertising salespeople in your area.

Some specialty advertising items can be quite effective. However, choose your items as though you were picking out something for yourself. Ask yourself: "Would I actually use this thing, would I be grateful to receive it?" If you answer *yes,* incorporate it into your overall advertising scheme.

Writing Good Copy for Your Premium Items

No matter what the medium, the success of an ad often comes down to the copy — the words that tell your audience what they need to know. Here are some tips for writing solid copy for premium items, contributed by specialty advertising consultants Dr. Stan Madden and Dr. Marjorie Cooper (reprinted with permission from *Imprint Magazine,* Philadelphia, PA):

- ✔ **Consider the audience.** The most important thing is to connect with the person who receives the product, so put just as much thought into what the copy says as you do in selecting what it's imprinted on.

- ✔ **Create a position statement.** Something simple; a line or two that identifies where you are in your respective field. Examples: "#1 Screen Printer in Philadelphia" or "The Des Moines Area's Leader in Aluminum Siding."

- ✔ **Tell a story.** Whether it's the next day, six weeks later, or five years down the road, your copy should still tell the tale of the promotion.

- ✔ **Make it look good.** Remember that *eye-catching* applies to the copy as well as the product. This combined appeal largely determines how long recipients hold on to a promotional product.

- ✔ **Tie it all together.** Make sure there's continuity with the rest of your promotion. If not, you might confuse your audience. This is where the product/copy combination is critical.

- ✔ **Avoid clutter.** You need to grab people's attention quickly. A product with wall-to-wall copy might turn people off instead of sparking their interest and getting your message across.

- ✔ **Watch those fonts.** Thin fonts are often problematic because they don't print clearly and are difficult to read for some people. Overly decorative fonts can also be difficult to read. Stick to simple styles with the possible exception of initial caps.

✓ **KISS (Keep it simple, stupid).** Copy should be easy to read and under-stood by all ages and educational backgrounds in the target audience. *Remember:* Most newspapers are written at a sixth-grade level. Unless the audience is specialized, the copy on your promotional item should probably be around that level, too.

REMEMBER

It's a premium item, not an encyclopedia

I agree completely with Doctors Stan Madden and Marjorie Cooper, consultants to the spe-cialty advertising industry, that a promotional product isn't an information source; it's an advertisement. Its job is to capture people's attention and help them remember you. If the product does its job, there's often no need for additional information. The phone call or e-mail you'll likely receive will provide that opportunity.

Keep your copy brief and to the point, toss in some selling points or a slogan, and let it go at that. Don't try to include everything you do or a list of your entire store inventory. Stick to the main selling proposition. A logo, phone number, Web site address and perhaps your company slogan are more than enough information to include on a specialty advertising item.

Chapter 19

Promotions and Event Sponsorships

Advertising is salesmanship mass produced. No one would bother to use advertising if he could talk to all his prospects face-to-face. But he can't.

— Morris Hite

Sometimes, getting the world to beat a path to your door requires that you offer a little bribery — an incentive to get the world to even *consider* your door, let alone beat a path to it. Promotions and events are a good way to call attention to yourself, your business, your current sale, your new inventory, or your expanded showrooms. They're also a great way to meet prospective customers face to face. But these advertising forms can add to your bottom line only if you're careful about what you participate in and objective as to whether the promotion or event is truly relevant to your business.

Radio stations are famous for devising promotions to create value-added benefits for their advertisers, and for selling sponsorships designed solely to get more income from their advertisers. Some are good, and some are simply awful. So what makes a good promotion, how do you know it's good, and should you participate? Should you do your own promotion, and will it actually bring customers through your door? I explore these questions and others in this chapter while trying to steer you into well-conceived promotions, events, and sponsorships that stand a good chance of succeeding.

Promotions: Stand Back, Here Come the Prize Pigs

It never ceases to amaze me what people will endure in order to get a free T-shirt. *The San Jose Mercury News,* my area's major daily newspaper, sponsors a charity-based 10K race promotion each year and gets 10,000 runners, walkers, strollers, saunterers, staggerers, whatever — many of whom are only there to get the free T-shirt (which isn't really free because there is a ten buck entry fee). And the radio and TV stations in the Bay Area trot out a nearly infinite variety of promotions each year to attract new listeners and viewers for the stations and new customers for the advertisers, who are willing to pony up extra dollars to buy space at the event and the advertising to tell people about it. What do the folks who attend these promotions receive for their trouble? Yep, you guessed it. Free T-shirts — oh, maybe water bottles, almost certainly CDs specific to that station's formatting, and perhaps a flimsy painter's cap with a cheesy logo, but always a T-shirt!

Promotions are events designed to generate traffic for one reason or another. They are a way to get lots of people together in one place at one time in order to do a sales job on them. Many of the people seen at promotions can be spotted at every promotion. The same faces keep showing up. They are known in the advertising business as the *prize pigs,* which simply means that this particular group of people, who apparently have nothing better to do with their lives, attend each and every promotional event just to get the free stuff. It begs the question: How many T-shirts does one person need?

Once upon a time, car dealers were famous for their weekend promotions that asked that you to "hurry on down" for free hot dogs, soft drinks, and potato chips, and, oh, by the way, to take a test drive in an all-new car while you're at it. The dealerships bought a ton of broadcast time (usually cheap weekend time) to announce free key chains for the men, corsages for the ladies, and balloons for the kiddies if listeners would only "come on down this weekend and bring your wife, your kids, your pink slip, and your checkbook." Consumers aren't that naïve anymore. They no longer respond to this kind of stuff, and the car dealers, tired of cleaning the sales lot of the discarded hot dog wrappers, rarely do that kind of lame promotion in this enlightened day and age. But that same tired old promotion, in various permutations for assorted advertisers, is still done all the time and is, for some businesses, still successful in generating traffic.

Radio: The promotions king

When you buy your radio advertising, there are two kinds of promotions that you can tie in with your radio buy: station promos and sales-drive promos.

No promotion, no media buy

A surprising number of large budget radio advertisers won't even buy a station unless the station develops and includes an exclusive promotion at no extra charge. Amusement parks, water slide parks, ski resorts, and major movie premieres are famous for promotion-driven advertising. Often these entertainment-based advertisers trade tickets to their venues for on-air mentions (that's where all those freebies that your sales rep will be giving to you come from).

If you're convinced that a promotion will help your business, if you want hundreds (okay,

dozens) of prize pigs descending upon your store in search of station bumper stickers, T-shirts, and whatever you've tossed into the pot, then insist upon a promotion as part of your media commitment. The promotion itself should be included at no cost. The merchandise you contribute to the prize pool should be entirely up to you, but do make it interesting and desirable stuff that listeners will actually want.

A *station promotion* is one invented by the station and is often produced on a regular basis. The station then solicits advertisers to provide goods and services to fold into the promotion. For example, one of the radio stations in my area has a promotion called "The Coffee Break." This promotion is designed to encourage people to listen to the station while they're at work. Regular listeners are asked to fax to the radio station their names, the names of their companies, the number of employees, and so on. Then this information is put into a hopper and drawn at random each day or week. The winning company gets a visit from members of the station's promotions department and members of the on-air staff, who bring along gourmet coffee provided by a coffee shop that advertises on the station, donuts or bagels provided by a bakery that advertises on the station, flower arrangements contributed by a florist that advertises on the station, and so forth. In return, each of the station advertisers who donate goods to the coffee break (the coffee shop, the bakery, and the florist) get multiple free mentions throughout their paid broadcast schedules.

If you are an advertiser and have something the station needs in order to produce a station promotion, chances are they will come to you. In case they don't, a good time to get involved is when you buy your media schedule. Ask the sales rep what promotions are available to you as *value-added advertising* (extra stuff, generally free) to help boost your paid media buy. There isn't a radio station in the known universe that doesn't produce a multitude of promotions on a regular basis, and what you're selling will probably fit nicely into at least one of them. If you don't have a food or beverage operation, not to worry. The stations also need a variety of goods and services to use as prizes.

Station remotes: They still work

Many station promotions are tied to *live remotes,* which bring on-air personalities (disc jockeys) to your location. In addition to broadcasting their shows from the remote location, the on-air personalities bring along all kinds of logo-emblazoned specialty items — T-shirts, bumper stickers, coffee mugs, movie tickets — to give away to the lucky people who show up for these events.

These live-remote promotions are usually offered to advertisers as part of their media buy. They're called *value-added,* and they're usually free. Because you're going to have to do a lot of advertising anyway to get people to your location, why not throw a remote into the mix and give listeners an added reason to visit your store? The only additional out-of-pocket expense is a modest talent fee for the on-air personality, which makes these promos an inexpensive way to stretch an ad budget and to publicize a new location, new inventory, new restaurant, the latest model cars, or anything else you can think of. In addition to the 60-second spots you buy, you'll also receive a multitude of 10-second promotional announcements inviting listeners to your store on such and such a date where . . . gasp! . . . they can meet, live and in person, that wacky morning guy.

The beauty of a live remote is that you, the advertiser, don't have to do anything to make it happen (other than make some merchandise available as giveaways). The station does all the work. Your broadcast commercials will, of course, talk about what it is you are trying to sell during the promotion, but the ten-second announcements that the station throws into the pot will drive the traffic to your store on the appointed day and time. And employees of the station's promotions department will be there to make sure that everything runs smoothly. It's pretty much a turnkey deal.

Sales-drive promotions are advertiser-specific — they are invented for the advertiser and are exclusive to that advertiser. Sales-driven promos are always sold in conjunction with a media buy. When you agree to advertise on the station, talk to the sales rep about a sales-driven promotion if you're interested in doing one. The rep will go back to the station and have the promotions department invent something especially for you. You will then be asked to provide some merchandise for prizes, make your store available on a certain day, contract for a non-cancelable media buy, and pay a modest talent fee to any on-air personalities who might show up. In addition to your paid media schedule, you'll get a large number of on-air mentions (10– or 15-second announcements specific to your promotion) for a couple weeks leading up to the event, and, hopefully, a bunch of traffic into your store at the appointed date and time.

So how does a sales-driven promo work? Let's say you own a kitchen store and you want to build a promotion around a celebrity chef doing demonstration cooking in your store. You can simply give this information to the station sales rep, who will conference with his promotions department and come back with multiple ideas. The station will have on-air call-in contests in which their listeners can win a cookbook autographed by your featured chef, or dinner and wine for two at the chef's restaurant. And for your store, they'll put forward everything from rolling-pin tossing to pancake races to pie-eating contests. Your problem will be to sift through all their suggestions to find the ones you can live with. Radio station promotions directors really get into this stuff — they're your best source for ideas.

Not every station promotion brings in hundreds of new customers, so don't set your expectations too high. One of my clients seems satisfied if a promotion brings out a few dozen new faces. *Remember:* The promotion needs to be relevant and interesting to the station's listeners. In other words, don't do a promotion for an antique furniture store on a station with a teenage audience. If a promotion fails miserably, you'll tend to blame the station, not the fact that what you're selling isn't compatible with their listener's tastes — but there's more to it than that. If a promotion fails, you may want to reconsider your media buy on that particular station, because if their listeners won't even come out to your location for free stuff, how can you expect them to respond positively to the selling message in your 60-second spots?

Other promotional opportunities

Radio station promotions aren't the only way you can go. You can come up with your own unique promotion as well. Many other media forms lend themselves to successful promos. Here are just a few promotional ideas:

- ✔ **In-store counter displays.** You can have your customers register to win a contest by having a drawing. Or you can set up a buy-one-get-one-free offer.

- ✔ **Direct mail.** Send your customers coupons as a way to get them into your store. Or mail them a card that they return to register to win a contest. Send out open-house invitations to get them into the store.

- ✔ **Newspaper.** As part of your newspaper ad, you could provide coupons, which serve as promotions to get people in to your store. You could tell readers to present the ad for half off their purchase. You could even offer coloring contests for kids, which is sure to get their parents in to your store.

- ✔ **Printed flyers.** You could have flyers printed, and then place them on parked cars, telling people to bring the flyer in for a discount or advertising a one-day-only sale or a parking-lot sale.

- ✔ **Statement stuffers.** When you send out your monthly statement to your customers, you can put an ad in with the statement, offering loyal customer discounts, coupons, or buy-two-get-one-free offers.

ANECDOTE

A promotion so successful I lost the account

I was once given a make-or-break advertising budget by an underperforming local micro-brewery and restaurant whose owners had decided to take one more shot at success before closing their doors forever. Accepting the challenge was both daunting and invigorating. Their target market was young adults and the brewery/restaurant had been wasting a lot of advertising dollars in newspapers, an advertising vehicle not famously efficient in reaching yuppies. I chose to spend every last dime of their budget on an all-or-nothing radio blitz, selecting stations that had good ratings in the adults 18–34 demographic. I explained the critical nature of the advertising buy to each of the station reps and asked them all to bring me a promotion that they would be willing to toss in to the media buy as value-added advertising. They were all good, as it turned out, but one stands out in my mind.

One of the stations came back to me with a "Beer and Burger" lunchtime promotion. The promotion was invented by the station sales rep, Marnie Doherty, who later became my business partner. The idea was that customers could come in on a certain day and have a great lunch (a giant cheeseburger, fries, and a brewsky) for just five bucks. The promotion was,

of course, tied to a station live remote, which would feature their "morning man" and his sidekick — two guys who were very well known in the market — broadcasting live from the brew-pub. The promo would also feature the ubiquitous station speciality advertising items for the prize pigs and a drawing for a $500 bar and restaurant credit. The cost of the advertising schedule covered eveything — the remote was added as the icing on the cake (or the foam on the beer).

The big day came, the doors opened at 11:00 a.m., and we had to step quickly back to avoid getting trampled. It was a restaurant owner's dream come true. Hundreds of station listeners stampeded through the door until it was standing room only and a two-hour wait for $5 worth of burgers and beer. The promotion had everything going for it — discounted food, free prizes, cheap beer, a famous disc jockey, and a great place in which to eat and drink. The restaurant was "discovered" by hundreds of new customers (many of whom stayed all that day to sip more beers and became long-time regular customers), was able to remain open, eventually prospered, and, when it was back on its feet, fired me because they no longer needed my services! Go figure.

When you're trying to decide which kind of promotional materials to use, think about items of which you've been on the receiving end. Have you ever received a promotional piece that not only caught your attention, but compelled you to respond? What was it about that piece that cut through all the advertising clutter and struck a nerve? Was it the design, the offer, an impossible-to-ignore deal, a clever attachment, or a promise of something free? Chances are, if something works well in grabbing *your* attention, it'll grab your customers' attention as well. Promotional ideas are limited only by your own imagination. I'm sure you can come up with some great ones.

Sponsoring Events

Sponsored events — events that are devised and produced with commercialism and financial gain foremost in mind — are available in many forms. There are tech fairs, which are actually recruiting fairs at which high-tech companies hope to meet future employees. There are home improvement fairs, at which homeowners can find the very latest bells and whistles for their houses. There are campus fairs, where colleges and universities show off their erudite wares to prospective students. An infinite variety of trade shows exist. And, of course, you can find a plethora of chili cook-offs, jazz festivals, blue grass festivals, arts and crafts affairs . . . you name it, and it's out there. All of these events have one thing in common: You can become a sponsor, get your name mentioned on the radio and in the newspaper as being a sponsor, pay for and provide manpower for an on-site booth, and hope that all the expense and work involved will result in some added exposure and new business.

So should you participate in these kinds of events? One of my clients cannot get involved in these events, even though some of them would very likely expose his business to some highly qualified customers, for the simple reason that he can't spare the employees to "work the booth" for the duration of the event. This client has nearly 70 stores, and finding qualified help is his main business headache. He has enough trouble finding people to work in his locations, let alone sending a bunch of them out into the field. The same may be true for you. Can you take the time away from your store to man your own street-fair booth, particularly if the street fair runs multiple days? Do you have trustworthy employees who can represent you at the event if you can't be there yourself? Whether you can participate may come down to logistics.

When deciding whether to participate in a sponsored event, you need to ask yourself: "What's in it for me? Will I really get added exposure to qualified customers?" Be objective. Do a bunch of good old boys and girls who are looking for a bowl of free chili and a paper cup of beer fit the demographic profiles of your customers? If not, then regardless of the number of people the event promoters guarantee will attend, you'll want to avoid the Red Hot Chili Cook-Off. But what if you're in the large appliance business and the big Home Improvement and Remodeling Expo is coming to town? I'd say, jump on it. Pay for the booth, haul your sample refrigerators and ranges to the convention center, and get it on. It's all a matter of relevance.

So how do you find out about these sponsorship opportunities? Because you own a business, you should be on the mailing lists of the Chamber of Commerce, the local convention center, arena, stadium, or any other source of information as to what events are coming to your town. If you aren't being kept up to date on upcoming events and shows either by mail or through your manufacturer's reps, then find a way to do so. You can't participate if you don't know what's happening, and by the time you read about an event in a newspaper ad or hear about it on the radio, it's probably too late to get space.

Let's say that you are the owner of a plant nursery and want to participate in the gigantic, bombastic Annual Flower and Garden Show coming to an arena near you. The event promoters will be more than happy to sell you booth space for, let's say, $1,500 for the three-day show. Believe it or not, you can also buy the same booth from your local radio station for $5,000. But what you are getting from the promoters is the booth to exhibit your stuff in. What you receive from the radio station is the booth, dozens of 10– to 15-second on-air mentions, a *run-of-station spot package* (a group of commercials scheduled throughout the day and night at the sole discretion of the station), and a link to the station's Web site.

You can use the 60-second spots to tell listeners what you are selling and why they should visit your booth. The promotional announcements that mention your store name for two or three weeks leading up to the show aren't going to hurt you a bit. And linking your Web site to theirs just may generate a few extra hits. The station has made an arrangement to sell sponsorships (and additional exhibitor space) in exchange for a large media buy from the promoters of the event. Out of your $5,000 package deal, the station still has to pay the promoters the $1,500 for your booth, but they keep the additional advertising revenue for themselves.

So, if all you want is the booth space to demonstrate your wares, go directly to the event promoter. If you want to preannounce that you'll be there, and you can afford the added expense, or you were going to buy advertising anyway, buy the station's package deal. Pre-show advertising is an important consideration and, in this scenario, well worth the extra $3,500.

The booth, the whole booth, and nothing but the booth

When you participate in a trade show or street fair event, you will be paying for exhibitor space. This is a booth (probably ten feet square) made up of a metal frame holding flimsy cloth panels on three sides to create the illusion of privacy. You get nothing else for your money — no tables, chairs, banners, signs, display backgrounds, nothing. This means that the day before the show opens you will have to arrange to have all these rather important items delivered to the location and set them up yourself; conversely, you can bring your own from home, but that's a pain in the neck. The event sponsors can steer you to their prearranged source for the furniture and other accoutrements you will

need. You will also want to have a sign company create a nice display banner and other signage for your space. *Remember:* All of these extras will cost you extra dough.

When all is ready, you, too, can then spend 15 hours each day standing on a cement floor while handing out brochures and demonstrating your products. Giving away your expensive brochures can become quite discouraging when you see that the people who ask for your printed materials already have entire bags stuffed with printed materials (will they ever read yours?).

Part VI
The Part of Tens

The 5th Wave   By Rich Tennant

In this part . . .

It is a tradition in all *For Dummies* books to include the Part of Tens. You may not choose to read every page of this book, but I strongly urge you to read through the following three chapters. Here you'll find tips for writing effectively for all media and tricks of the trade for money-saving media negotiations. I also help you decide whether your business could use the services of an advertising agency. Plenty of valuable advice in just a few short pages — you won't find more bang for your buck anywhere.

Chapter 20

Ten Secrets for Writing Memorable Advertising

. . . .

In This Chapter

▶ Knowing how to get the consumer's attention

▶ Keeping your message simple so your audience will remember it

▶ Delivering your message with clarity

. . . .

If you are writing about baloney, don't try to make it Cornish hen, because that is the worst kind of baloney there is. Just make it darned good baloney.

— Leo Burnett

*W*hen you're creating ads, your primary goal is to come up with something that will stick in the minds of your target audience. In this chapter, I offer up ten great tips for doing exactly that.

Ignore the Rules of Grammar

Advertising legend David Ogilvy admitted that he didn't know the rules of grammar. In spite of this revelation, he was, unquestionably, one of the greatest advertising copywriters ever to have strolled down Madison Avenue. He said, "If you're trying to persuade people to do something, or buy something, it seems to me you should use their language, the language they use every day, the language in which they think. I try to write in the vernacular." This is wonderful advice from the master — advice that I have always tried to remember when writing ads for my clients, and advice that will work equally well for you when you crank up your own creative machine and begin to write ads for yourself.

You can ignore the rules of grammar at times — even write incomplete sentences — and do whatever it takes to create a hard-hitting sales message. In radio, you have only 60 seconds; in TV, you have just 30. And in print or outdoor ads, you want your message to be quickly understood and acted upon. Those requirements don't always lend themselves to correct sentence structure. In short: Write the way people think.

Make Your Ads Effective

Whether your advertising budget is a million a month or a thousand, you'll be wasting your money if your ads aren't effective. And what makes ads effective is a combination of content and creativity. Your ads need to give the consumer a good reason to act (content), and they have to be unique enough in their design and copy to attract the consumer's attention in the first place (creativity). Consumers are exposed to so much advertising on a daily basis — some of it so subtle they don't even know they're absorbing it — that you need to make sure your ads cut through all that clutter.

Know Why People Buy Your Products

Most retail businesses (and many manufacturers) don't know why people buy their products. They just know that people *do* buy their products, so they're somehow satisfied with their less than in-depth marketing knowledge. Before you begin the creative process of finding your inimitable message, ask yourself a few simple questions:

- What are you selling, and what makes it so unique?
- To whom do you want to sell it?
- Why should people buy it from you as opposed to your competition?

You don't have to create the next big advertising slogan to get people into your store. You just have to use a bit more creativity than the other guys in devising a compelling message so people will choose your store over the competition.

Find a Creative Hook

Because you want your ads to stand head and shoulders above the crowded universe of advertising, you need to work hard at finding a *creative hook* — something that will grab the potential customer (but not necessarily by the neck) and drag him into your store. A creative hook is an emotional trigger that attracts the buyer, something that appeals to the self-image of the buyer, an affirmation that you provide what the buyer is looking for. It may be a slogan, a phrase, a jingle, a single line of copy, or a unique "look" that appears in all your ads. But whatever it is, your creative hook must be yours and yours alone, because you will use it, across all media, to differentiate your business from all the others.

Remember That Creativity Is Hard Work

Advertising agencies, when designing new ad campaigns (or redesigning old ones) often hold what is called a *creative session* — a meeting where all the people who will be working on a particular account gather together to come up with ideas. Owners, creative directors, copywriters, artists, even the account service people contribute. These ideas then beget more and more ideas, which will, eventually, result in the perfect creative answer to the problem at hand. The only rule of these meetings is that no idea will be laughed at or discarded out of hand. No idea is too far-fetched or too stupid. Everything gets tossed onto the table. Even if you're not a part of an agency, you can hold these kinds of brainstorming sessions with your coworkers, your partners, your family, and your friends to come up with ideas for your business's advertising campaign.

Ideas don't just jump up and bite you. You need to search for them very diligently.

Let Your Creative Hook Dictate Your Media Buy

When your great new idea hits you right between the eyes; when the light bulb of creativity suddenly shines brightly, it's time to begin incorporating this message into a full-blown ad campaign — or, at least, as full-blown an ad campaign as you can afford. Assuming you have identified all the reasons you truly do have a unique product and have put your finger on a hard-to-resist reason that people should seek you out in order to buy it, you need to find ways to make this idea fit into various forms of advertising.

Often, your creative hook will dictate what media you will be using — your creative hook will literally drive your campaign. If your hook is visual, then you'll use print, collateral, and television. If your concept is audio-driven, you'll want to use radio. If your clever new idea is a catchy slogan or a headline, you can consider using any variety of media, including billboards and bus cards.

Consider Your Budget

Before you get carried away with all the great things you'd like to do in your ad campaign, you need to think about your budget. You cannot buy a 50-pound ad campaign with a 10-pound budget. So you need to carefully pick and choose your media and adjust your message accordingly.

You don't need to buy every media in town in order to get your message across. You can accomplish your goals with not only a creative message, but also with a creative media buy. So, before you start writing your campaign, and before you get too carried away with your creative hook, come to grips with how your message will translate into various media, and how much of this media you can afford.

Strive for Continuity

Whatever your unique message turns out to be — whether it's a headline, a sentence, a slogan, a graphic, or another creative hook — use that message consistently in all forms of media. You need to apply the *same message* in all the forms of media in order to establish that message as yours and yours alone. Plus, continuity gives the consumer a better chance to remember it.

Don't say one thing in your radio advertising, and another in print. Don't advertise one item in the newspaper and another on TV. Retailers make this mistake over and over again, and it only serves to confuse the consumer and to water down their overall advertising impact (and budget). If your radio commercials are talking about a half-price sale on a specific item, then your newspaper ads should be featuring the same price and sale terms for the same item.

Keep It Simple

Here is the best rule you can use as you work toward creating memorable advertising for today's marketplace: KISS. That simple acronym is something to keep uppermost in your mind as you go through the process of writing and producing your ads. And it stands for "Keep It Simple, Stupid."

Today, consumers are deluged with information at a rate unheard of in kinder, gentler times. The fact that we're even capable of absorbing a tiny percentage of the information available to us is remarkable. And into this cauldron of information, you now must inject quality advertising for your business, and hope that, at the very least, it will be noticed, recalled, and acted upon. And the best way to accomplish that is to keep it simple.

Be Clear in Your Message

Whether you're writing advertising for print, radio, television, direct mail, or any of the myriad forms of media, deliver your message in clear, easy-to-understand terms. That way, the consumer can see at a glance what it is you're selling and make a snap decision as to whether she wants to read or listen further. You want to place your most powerful selling message at the beginning of the radio or TV spot, or in the form of a headline for your printed advertising. Cut right to the chase! Don't get bogged down in details — the consumer doesn't care and won't take the time to decipher too much copy or superfluous information. The consumer needs to read or hear your selling message immediately, and it must be compelling enough to get her to act. If you don't write your advertising in clear, concise terms that can be easily understood, you're wasting your money.

Chapter 21

Ten Ways to Know It's Time to Hire an Agency

If your advertising goes unnoticed, everything else is academic.

—William Bernbach

You don't need a multimillion-dollar advertising budget to seek out the services of an ad agency. Many local, retail-oriented agencies will provide you with all the services offered by the major agencies, but scaled down to fit within your budget and your advertising requirements. If you're thinking about hiring an agency, take a look at the sections in this chapter. If you see yourself in one or more of these ten reasons to hire an agency, give it some thought. Advertising is an extremely important part of your overall marketing plan. Hiring a team of professionals to handle it for you is something you should think about. And, in the case of many local ad agencies, it very likely won't cost you as much as you think — and it may even save you quite a bit of money in the long run.

Your Ad Budget Has Become Substantial

If your advertising budget has grown to major proportions — essentially, when you feel the need to find help in handling it — it's quite likely time to seek out a local ad agency to handle your account. Ask yourself one question: "Am I spending my ad budget as wisely as I could be?" If you think you aren't being as diligent as you could be in allocating your advertising funds; if you're becoming insecure with your media choices; if you've become lazy in your media selections; and if you're ready to admit that you need the services of a team of professionals to advise you in this area, then it may be time to make the call.

You Need the Expertise of a Professional Media Buyer

If a media buyer is diligent and knowledgeable, he will give you the most bang for your buck and stretch your media budget, regardless of its size, as tightly as it can be stretched without breaking. This person will become very important to you because he will field all the phone calls from, take all the meetings with, and gently or firmly (as the case requires) say no to the dozens upon dozens of media sales reps who want a piece of your business. If there is one good reason to hire an ad agency, it is the media buyer. A good one will be fair but firm with the media, insisting upon the correct format, impressive ratings or circulation, and the right audience composition and demographic before committing your hard-earned dollars to a station, newspaper, or magazine. He will also pore over the media invoices to make sure everything he purchased on your behalf is accounted for.

Your Creative Light Bulb Has Burned Out

If you're burned out with the creative process, no longer have the time to devote to it, would rather spend your days running your business, and want a team of creative professionals working behind the scenes to generate fresh, new ideas for your business, there's no better place to find them than in an ad agency. From the agency creative director to the copywriters and artists, everyone will give you their best shot. The highly trained group of specialists employed by most agencies will work on your account with a mutual goal — to grow your business, keep you happy, and retain your account.

You're Overwhelmed by the Demands of Production

If the myriad details of producing and placing your ads has you completely bogged down, you need to think about calling in the pros. When you simply don't have the time, energy, or desire to write and produce your own advertising; when creating and producing your ads has become more of a chore than a pleasure; when you dread sitting down at the computer to create unforgettable prose, start interviewing agencies.

You're Having Trouble Keeping Up with the Bookkeeping

If the bookkeeping process of sorting through multiple media invoices each month has become a major chore, then you may want to begin thinking of a simple way to hand off this responsibility to a professional who sifts through this stuff all day long. If you've come to the conclusion that most media invoices are written in a secret code that you will never learn to crack; if you have reached a point of frustration with trying to determine whether you have received all the spots or column inches you have been billed for; if you are avoiding the invoices until you receive a nasty call from the media's collections department, make a call, get an agency, and relax. Handling this kind of stuff is why the agency gets 15 percent off the top.

You're Leaving Co-Op Funds on the Table

When you've had it with fulfilling all the obligations, rules, and restrictions for collecting your co-op reimbursements; when you're sick and tired of calling the various media to remind them that you need notarized scripts and the proper tear sheets in order to collect your money; when you recognize that you have much more important things to do than assemble a pile of invoices, scripts, tapes, tear sheets, and God-only-knows-what in order to receive a payment from your manufacturer, it's time to call an agency. If you aren't receiving co-op reimbursements because it's just too much trouble, get an agency. Agencies are used to handling co-op funds and, for them, it isn't a big deal.

Your Time Is Being Taken Up by Media Reps

This may be one of the best reasons to hire an agency. Media reps aren't necessarily obnoxious or bothersome — some of my best friends are media reps. But they have a mission, and that mission is to get as large a share of your advertising budget as possible. They will phone you, drop in on you, and send you faxes and e-mails to "simply stay in touch," and then they will drop in on you again. They are extremely tenacious and rarely take *no* for answer. Their sales managers give them a quota and, if they know your business is buying local media, they will target you. In the legitimate process of trying to earn a living, however, they sometimes become a nuisance. An advertising agency will remove these pesky (albeit, well-meaning) people from your life.

You're Running Faster to Stay in the Same Place

You need to spend your limited and very important time productively running your business. Do you really have the time and energy to give full attention to your advertising? When you hire an advertising agency, you will eliminate a lot of daily phone calls and drop-in visits from various reps so you can do just that. You will remove mountains of monthly paperwork from your desk. You will also, in all likelihood, receive a more polished creative product from the agency than you have been producing on your own, because there will be a whole gang of professional writers, designers, and creative directors working for your business. No one knows your business as well as you do (you will become the best source of information for your agency), but unless you want to sell your store and become a full-time ad person you will do well to turn loose a group of specialists who will take an objective view of your advertising needs.

You Realize an Agency Won't Really Cost You Much

Since the dawn of advertising time — and because of some obscure arrangement made between the early founders of the ad agency business and newspapers — an agency generally earns a media commission of 15 percent. This figure has not changed over the ages, even though agencies have been crying about it for eons. The 15 percent is paid to the agency by the media in the form of a discount. If *you* buy a newspaper ad with a space cost of $1,000 directly from the paper, you will receive an invoice for $1,000. If your ad agency buys the same ad, they will receive an invoice for $850. Your agency will invoice you for the full $1,000 and keep the rest (the 15 percent) as its commission. So, in effect, having an agency place your media buy isn't costing you a dime, because you're paying the same amount to buy that ad whether you have an agency handle all the details for you or you do it yourself.

You Want a Bunch of Free Stuff

Break down the doors and rush right out to hire an agency if you want to get all sorts of free lunches; rounds of golf; lift tickets to nearby ski resorts; tickets to rock concerts, sporting events, and movie premieres; even vacation trips to world-class resorts, international cities, and famous vacation destinations around the globe.

Okay, maybe I'm exaggerating a bit here, but your agency will always have a good supply of some of these freebies (which it gets from the media it's buying from). And if the agency is honest about it, it will pass most of the good stuff along to you and its other clients — the people whose advertising budgets earned this stuff in the first place.

You're going to spend your budget anyway. You may as well get something extra for it. This may be the best possible reason to hire an agency. Some of my clients certainly think so.

Chapter 22

Ten Ways to Stretch Your Broadcast Media Budget

In This Chapter

▶ Getting the most for your money

▶ Asking for what you want

▶ Forging relationships with your sales reps

When executing advertising, it's best to think of yourself as an uninvited guest in the living room of a prospect who has the magical power to make you disappear instantly.

—John O'Toole

Whether you are buying radio or television, the drill is the same. The station is going to send a sales rep out to your business, and that person will tenaciously try to get as much of your budget as possible — hopefully, all of it. But don't sign anything until you are certain that you have gotten the best deal possible, and don't be afraid to ask for the moon. You just may get it!

In this chapter, I give you tried-and-true suggestions for lowering your spending through successful media negotiations. These tips are slanted to broadcast media, but they'll work just as well with any other media form.

Ask for a Better Rate

Okay, so this seems obvious. However, many first-time advertisers are reluctant to ask for a better rate. *Remember:* There are many different advertisers on any given station, and they are *not* all paying the same price. So go ahead and ask! The sales rep may want something in return, such as more flexibility, or a larger share of the buy. But there is almost always a better rate available. In fact, your sales rep may already have a better rate "in her pocket" — a rate preapproved by her sales manager, just in case you ask.

Don't Buy the Top-Rated Station

Usually, the highest-rated station in your area will have the highest ad rates. Depending on the disparity between the top station and the rest of the market, you may find that looking at the number two– or three-rated stations is more efficient. Buying the top-rated station may require so much of your ad budget that you're limited to that one station only. Multiple stations will generally yield better results faster. So if you can advertise on number two and three, or three and four, for about the same investment, do it! You will most likely end up with a better market reach and a more well-rounded campaign.

Broaden Your Dayparts

The broader the dayparts you buy, the more flexibility the station has to run your commercial, and therefore the lower the rate. So, if you need to be in morning drive time, consider 5:00 a.m. to 10:00 a.m. rather than 6:00 a.m. to 9:00 a.m. If you don't need to run specifically in drive times, consider 6:00 a.m. to 8:00 p.m. This strategy is especially effective on a station with a strong *at-work listening audience* (people who listen to the radio during the day while they're on the job). If you are buying television, consider buying blocks of similar programming rather than one specific program. Don't broaden your dayparts to the point where you minimize effectiveness, of course. Just broaden them enough to bring the rate down a bit.

Buy Early-Week Times

Virtually all radio and TV stations are busier Wednesday through Saturday than they are Sunday through Tuesday. If the bulk of your business is done on the weekend, you may feel the need to focus your efforts later in the week. But if your business doesn't rely heavily on weekend traffic, you can save a considerable amount of money by running your advertising in the first part of the week, when demand is lower. In addition to lower rates, you will also find less clutter on the air, allowing your message to stand out.

Avoid Peak Advertising Seasons

Try to avoid peak advertising seasons. Again, if you make most of your sales around Christmas, this strategy may not be possible. However, if your business is not seasonal, you can take advantage of slower advertising months, when rates and demand are likely to be lower. January is generally one of the slowest advertising months for broadcast, whereas December and May are likely to be the busiest.

Plan Ahead

Stations are always more likely to discount their rates if you're working well in advance, or even better, if you're planning the entire year at once. If you plan long-term, the station's inventory will be wide open. They will be willing to wheel and deal with you because there is no risk — if they undersell a few commercials to you and the inventory gets tight, they will simply raise the rates for the last-minute advertisers to make up the difference.

Make sure that the station is not going to preempt your schedule if the rates you've paid are too low. Negotiate make-goods up front and get all the assurances you can that your commercials will run.

Create a Slush Fund

A slush fund is a great way to maximize your exposure on a given station. It can work in several ways. The first way is to give the sales rep permission to schedule special opportunities for you, up to a certain dollar amount, as they become available. (This strategy can be risky, however, depending on the reliability of your rep.) The second way is to keep your slush fund a secret, but be sure your sales rep knows to contact you with any special opportunities that come up. For example, let's say your local sports team miraculously makes it to the playoffs. Nobody expected it, so the local station did not sell very many commercials in the playoff game. Now, all of a sudden, they have a lot of commercials to sell, there is tons of interest in the game, and they only have a few days. If you've already spent you entire budget, you're out of luck. But if you have a slush fund, you're in the game.

Develop Strong Relationships with Sales Reps

If you develop strong relationships with your sales reps, they will take good care of you. **Remember:** People like to do business with people they like. If you are close to your reps, they will give you inside information, oversee your commercial rotation to make sure you get the best placement, and give you first crack at special opportunities, among other things. In short, they will take a personal interest in you and your business.

One of my clients has been invited by stations to attend events and even take incentive trips, none of which he qualified for based on his ad spending. They invited him just because he is well liked by the station rep and management.

Ask for Value-Added Opportunities

Most stations offer additional opportunities beyond paid 30– or 60-second commercials, referred to as *value-added*. These opportunities can be anything from sponsorable on-air features, such as traffic and weather, to on-air contests and giveaways, to live remote broadcasts from your business. Whenever possible, be sure your advertising schedule contains value-added opportunities as part of the package. These elements should be included at no additional charge, and although they may be tied to your overall spending (spend this much for paid commercials, get this value-added opportunity tossed into the pot), they should not be in addition to your paid commercials.

Glossary

In this appendix, I provide definitions for *ad-speak* — the insider words, terms, and acronyms used by advertising professionals to confound all of those who are not. This glossary will prove helpful if you're planning and buying media. And, if you will be sanctioning and approving media plans and buys done by others (like your ad agency), it will give you a better understanding of what is being proposed.

Don't try to memorize all the definitions in this glossary. Just refer to it when some hotshot radio rep brings you a proposal filled with unintelligible words, terms, and abbreviations.

:10: A ten-second commercial.

:30: A 30-second commercial.

30-sheet poster: See *poster panel.*

:60: A 60-second commercial.

accordion fold: An advertising pamphlet or brochure that has been folded in an accordion style for binding into a print publication.

accrual: The amount of co-op advertising funds earned over a stated period.

ad/edit ratio: The ratio of advertising pages to editorial pages in a print medium. An ad/edit ration of 70/30 indicates that 70 percent of all pages are advertising and 30 percent are editorial.

add-on rate: A different rate, negotiated at the time the schedule is purchased, for any subsequent additions to the schedule.

addressable: The ability of media such as magazines or television to direct advertising to specific individuals.

adjacent: A television commercial that is scheduled immediately before or after a scheduled program; the opposite of an in-program placement.

advertising contract: A written agreement made between the advertiser and the advertising medium, which states the content, cost, and placement of the advertisement for which both parties are bound.

advertorial: A print advertisement styled to look like editorial content. Most publishers require that advertorials be labeled "advertisement" so that readers are aware that they're reading an ad.

affidavit: A notarized statement from a broadcast station that confirms the actual run time of a commercial or commercials. In order to collect co-op advertising funds, you will be required to get an affidavit from the broadcast station.

afternoon drive: A radio daypart, usually 3:00 to 7:00 p.m.

allotments: The number of outdoor billboards or panels in a showing.

alternate weeks: A method of scheduling advertising for a period of one week, then skipping a week, then running it again for a week, and so forth.

announcement: A broadcast media advertising message, usually 10, 15, 30, or 60 seconds in length. Synonymous with the term *commercial* and generally referred to in the advertising world as a *spot.*

approach: In outdoor media, the distance between the advertising structure and the point where it first becomes visible.

Arbitron Company: A media research company that reports on audience levels of radio stations.

area of dominant influence (ADI): Arbitron Company's definition of a TV market; an unduplicated geographic area in which stations have the highest share of viewing audience.

audience: The number of homes or persons exposed to a media or advertising message.

audience accumulation: The total net number of people (or homes) exposed to a medium during its duration; for example, the number of people, or homes, exposed to a half-hour broadcast program or a single magazine issue.

audience fragmentation: The splintering of mass media's audience into small segments due to the increasing number of media vehicles available to the total audience.

audience guarantee: A representation made to an advertiser by a media vehicle that a certain amount of audience will be exposed to the programs or time slots purchased by that advertiser.

audio: The sound portion of a television or radio commercial or program.

availability: The commercial position in or between a program that is available for purchase by an advertiser. You may hear this referred to as *avails* for short.

average audience: In television or radio, the number of homes (or individuals) tuned to the average minute of a program. In print media, the number of individuals who looked into an average issue of a publication and are considered to be readers.

average hours of viewing: The number of hours (and minutes) a household (or demographic group) views television during a particular time frame (daily, weekly, and so on).

average net paid circulation: The average number of copies of a publication sold per issue, as opposed to copies given free of charge.

average quarter hour (AQH): The time segment in which an average rating is measured. It is the average minute of a 15-minute segment.

average time spent listening (TSL): The time spent listening to a radio station by the average listener.

b/w: Abbreviation for *black and white,* as in a newspaper ad printed with black ink on a white background.

barter: The exchange of goods and services without the use of cash, such as trading media time or space for merchandise. Also known as *trade.*

billboard: In broadcast, (usually) free airtime, two to ten seconds in length, given to an advertiser as part of an advertising package or sponsorship. In outdoor media, an advertising structure. See also *painted bulletin.*

blanket coverage: A media vehicle's total coverage of a given geographical area.

bleed: In print media, to extend the illustration or copy to the edge of the page so there is no white border.

block: A time segment of consecutive hours in a broadcast schedule.

block programming: Scheduling television or radio programs with similar appeal and audiences within a two–, three–, or four-hour time period.

bonus circulation: The circulation of a publication that is above its average circulation. Advertisers are not charged for this extra circulation.

bonus spot: A free television or radio commercial given to an advertiser for a missed spot or to make up for under-delivered audience, or as an inducement to buy additional spots. See also *make good.*

book: To place an order for an advertising schedule.

book ahead: To purchase and approve ads weeks or months in advance of when the schedule will actually run.

bookends: Television spots from one advertiser placed within a commercial pod but separated from each other by other commercials.

brand: An identifying symbol, word, mark, or combination of all, developed to separate one company's product or services from another.

brand awareness: Consumers' awareness of a product's or service's name and its attributes.

bridge: In print, an advertisement that runs across the center margin of two facing pages in a magazine or newspaper. Also called a *double truck.*

broad rotator: In broadcast, a commercial, usually sold at a discounted rate, that will run on an "as available" time and date at the sole discretion of the selling station.

broadcast: Any television program an individual without cable can receive over the air. See also *cable-cast.*

broadcast calendar: An industry-accepted calendar used for developing media schedules, making media buys, and billing. The broadcast calendar week begins on a Monday, and the broadcast calendar month ends on the last Sunday of the month.

broadcast coverage area: The geographic area within which a signal from an originating station can be received.

bulldog edition: The morning edition of a newspaper, usually distributed the night before its issue date.

bump rates: The costs that must be paid by an advertiser to secure a commercial position previously sold to another advertiser. To bump the previous advertiser, the new advertiser must pay an inflated rate.

bus shelter/bus bench: Advertising posters positioned on a freestanding covered structure or bench, often located at a bus stop.

buying service: A company that primarily buys and plans media, as opposed to an advertising agency, which also offers creative development and production services.

buyout: A one-time payment to talent appearing in commercials or advertisements, and to illustrators, designers and photographers, which grants the advertiser unlimited use of the creative material or talent without further payments.

cable-cast: Programming originated by the cable systems and fed directly to cable subscribers. See also *broadcast*.

cable penetration: The percentage of television households that subscribe to cable TV within a given geographical area.

call letters: A television or radio station's identification (for example, KCBS-FM).

campaign: An advertising effort, potentially in several different media, for a product or service over a given period of time.

cancel: To terminate a scheduled media buy.

cancellation date: The last possible date you may terminate a scheduled ad without incurring cancellation charges.

car card: An advertising unit within a transit vehicle, such as a bus or taxicab.

card pack: In direct mail, a cooperative mailing of postage-paid business reply cards paid for by multiple advertisers.

cash discount: A discount granted by the media to an advertiser for payment within a certain amount of time (for example, 2 percent discount for payment within 10 days).

checking copy: A copy of a print ad that is sent to the advertiser as proof that the ad ran as scheduled, and in the position requested.

circulation: In print, the number of copies sold or distributed by a publication; in broadcast, the number of homes owning a television or radio within a station's coverage area; in out-of-home media, the number of people passing an advertisement who have an opportunity to see it.

classified advertising: Advertising that appears (usually) in newspapers and some magazines and is arranged according to specific categories.

closing date: The deadline set by a publication for the receipt of material in order for an advertisement to appear in a forthcoming issue.

clutter: Many different commercials that compete for the viewers' or listeners' attention. In print, many different ads printed within a small amount of space.

column inch: A unit of space used in newspaper ad units — 1 column wide by 1 inch deep.

combination rate: A discounted rate given to an advertiser who advertises in both morning and evening editions of a newspaper.

combined reach: The total reach of more than one media vehicle.

combination (combo): In radio, the purchase of one or more spots on two stations for a single discounted price; in television, the purchase of one or more spots in two time periods or programs for a combined single price.

computer graphics (CG): Computer-generated graphics inserted into television commercials during production.

commercial: See *announcement*.

confirmation: The written or verbal acceptance of a commercial order by a television or radio station.

cooperative (co-op) advertising: Retail advertising of branded merchandise, which is financed wholly or in part by the brand manufacturer or the regional distributor. The participation of two or more advertisers in a single advertisement or commercial featuring products or services of each.

corporate advertising: Advertising that promotes the image of a corporation rather than a product.

cost-per-point (CPP): The cost of an advertising unit (for example, a 60-second radio spot) divided by the average rating of a specific demographic group (for example, women 18–49). A unit that costs $1,000 and delivers a 10 women 18–49 rating has a CPP of $100.

cost-per-thousand (CPM): The cost per 1,000 people (or homes) delivered by a medium or media schedule. A media vehicle that costs $10,000 and has an audience of 500,000 men 18–49 has a CPM of $20.

coverage area: In broadcast, the geographical area reached by a station's signal; in print, the geographical area covered by the publication's circulation.

cumulative audience: The total net unduplicated media audience accumulated over a particular period of time (for example, the total audience of a radio station during morning drive).

cumulative rating: The total cumulative unduplicated audience of a radio or television program or station; the total number of persons tuned in.

dailies: Newspapers that are published at least five times a week; the video or film footage from each day's shoot, which is viewed at the end of each day.

daily rate: The cost of an ad that will appear in the daily (Monday through Friday or Monday through Saturday) edition of a newspaper.

daypart: A broadcast time period or segment. In television, the most common spot media dayparts are:

- **Morning news:** 5:00 a.m.–9:00 a.m.
- **Morning:** 9:00 a.m.–12:00 p.m.
- **Daytime:** 12:00 p.m.–3:00 p.m.
- **Early fringe:** 3:00 p.m.–5:00 p.m.
- **Early news:** 5:00 p.m.–7:00 p.m.
- **Access:** 7:00 p.m.–8:00 p.m.
- **Prime:** 8:00 p.m.–11:00 p.m.
- **Late news:** 11:00 p.m.–11:30 p.m.
- **Late fringe:** 11:30 p.m.–1:00 a.m.

In radio, the most common dayparts are:

- **Morning drive:** 6:00 a.m.–10:00 a.m.
- **Daytime:** 10:00 a.m.–3:00 p.m.
- **Afternoon drive:** 3:00 p.m.–7:00 p.m.
- **Evening:** 7:00 p.m.–midnight
- **Overnight:** Midnight–6:00 a.m.

daytimer: A radio station that broadcasts only during the day (from sunrise to sunset).

diary: A questionnaire that asks the respondent to record his television-viewing or radio-listening habits for a specific period of time.

direct-response advertising: Any form of advertising that requests a consumer to respond directly to the advertiser (for example, by calling a toll-free number to place an order).

display advertising: Newspaper advertising that is not part of the classifieds.

double truck: See *bridge*.

drive time: The morning and afternoon hours of radio broadcasting. Morning drive is usually 6:00 a.m. to 10:00 a.m.; afternoon drive is 3:00 p.m. to 7:00 p.m.

dub: To make one or more copies of a radio or television commercial; a copy of a radio or TV commercial. Also referred to as a *dupe*, short for *duplicate*.

duplicate (dupe): See *dub*.

earned rate: A rate given to an advertiser that reflects the frequency of ads running or the volume of advertising placed over a given period of time.

efficiency: The relative costs of delivering media audiences. See also *cost-per-point* and *cost-per-thousand*.

eight-sheet poster: A 5-x-11-foot outdoor poster panel, also known as a *junior panel*.

electronic tear sheet: Notarized documentation provided by broadcasters on the script itself to certify the number of times a particular script was broadcast and at what cost. Important in collecting co-op funds.

ethnic media: Media targeted to a specific ethnic group.

facing: In outdoor advertising, the direction a billboard faces (for example, a south facing can be seen by northbound traffic).

finished art: See *mechanical*.

fixed position: In print, a position within a publication guaranteed to the advertiser (for example, *Sports section far forward* means that you're guaranteed a spot in the front of the Sports section).

flighting: The scheduling of advertising for a period of time, followed by a hiatus and then another schedule of advertising.

format: In broadcast, the style or content of the material aired on a radio station (classical, country western, and so on) or the style of content of a television program (situation comedy, drama, and so on).

four-color process: The halftone printing process that utilizes four ink colors (black, magenta, cyan, and yellow) to produce a printed image that matches the color of the original image.

free-standing insert: A preprinted advertising message that is inserted into, but not bound into, print media (usually newspapers).

frequency: The number of times people (or homes) are exposed to an advertising message, campaign, or specific media.

frequency discount: A rate discount that is based on the number of ads scheduled within a specific amount of time.

frontload: A scheduling tactic where the bulk of the advertising is scheduled in the beginning days or weeks of a campaign.

full-service agency: An advertising agency that provides multiple services to an advertiser such as creative, market research, media buying, public relations, and so on.

gatefold: A folded advertising page that, when unfolded, is bigger than the regular page.

gross rating points (GRPs): The sum of all ratings delivered by a given list of media vehicles.

gutter: The white space on the inside margin of a printed page within a newspaper; the inside edges of pages facing the bound, or stapled, side of a magazine.

homes using TV (HUT): The percentage of homes tuned in to TV at a particular time.

horizontal half page: A unit size in a magazine or newspaper, positioned either on the bottom or top half of a page.

household audience: A tabulation of the number of households in which at least one member viewed TV during a specified time period. The household member can be anyone aged 2 years and older.

identification (ID): A short, usually ten-second, TV or radio commercial.

illuminated panel: A lighted poster panel or billboard.

impressions: The gross sum of all media exposures (number of people or homes), without regard to duplication.

independent station: A broadcast station not affiliated with a major network.

infomercial: A long-form (30-minute) broadcast commercial that provides much more information than can be supplied in a typical 30– or 60-second commercial. Most infomercials contain a direct-response mechanism, such as a toll-free telephone number.

in-house agency: An advertising agency operating within an advertiser's office and owned by the advertiser.

in-program: A television commercial that is scheduled in the middle of a scheduled program. The opposite of an *adjacent* placement.

insertion order: A form or document sent to a publication or station that contains information relating to an ad's placement or a broadcast schedule.

jargon: A specialized language used by people in a given industry; the reason for this glossary.

junior page: In print, an ad-size unit that is smaller than a full page and is surrounded by editorial content.

junior panel: See *eight-sheet poster.*

junior spread: Two facing junior pages.

keyline: See *mechanical.*

kiosk: A free-standing display on which back-lit advertisements are shown. Usually found in airports, shopping malls, and so on.

late fringe: A television daypart that follows prime time, usually 11:00 p.m. to 1:00 a.m. or later.

late news: A TV news program airing in the late evening, usually between prime and late fringe.

letterpress: Printing from type or plates with a raised surface. See also *lithography, offset,* and *rotogravure.*

liner: A 10– to 20-second mention of an advertised product or service, usually tied to a promotion.

lithography: Printing from a zinc or aluminum plate.

live tag: A short message (usually about five seconds) added to the end of a pre-recorded commercial.

log: A chronological listing created by television or radio stations and networks of programs and commercials showing exact air times of each element.

make good: In broadcast, a commercial offered in lieu of what was, for whatever reason, missed; in print, the free repeat of an advertisement to compensate for the publication's error in the original insertion.

mass media: All advertising media that have general, or mass, appeal.

masthead: The title of a newspaper or magazine displayed at the top of the front page.

mechanical: A camera-ready paste-up of artwork; includes type, photography, line art, and so on, all on one piece of art board or on computer disk. Also known as a *keyline* or *finished art.*

media: The communication vehicles that may or may not contain advertising (television, radio, newspaper, and so on).

media mix: The use of two or more media forms for an advertising campaign.

merchandising: Promotional activities that complement purchased advertising and that are usually provide by the media at no charge.

middle of the road (MOR): A radio programming format that appeals to an older demographic (big band, very soft hits, and so on).

morning drive: A radio daypart, generally 6:00 a.m. to 10:00 a.m.

multimedia: An advertising campaign that uses more than one form of media.

multi-set household: A household with more than one television set.

niche marketing: A marketing effort targeted to a highly selective group of consumers using media directed at this group.

Nielsen, A.C.: A research supplier that reports on audience levels of television stations and networks.

no-charge spots: A free television or radio spot given to an advertiser, usually as part of a paid advertising schedule.

off card: A negotiated advertising rate not listed in a rate card.

offset: Printing on a surface (such as paper) by putting the surface in contact with another surface that has been freshly inked.

on air: The first date of a scheduled television or radio advertising campaign.

open rate: The maximum rate charged by a print media for one insertion.

opening billboard: A brief commercial at the beginning of a television or radio program that identifies a sponsor of the program ("This news update brought to you by . . .").

outdoor advertising: A type of advertising found outdoors in public places. Refers to painted bulletins, posters, billboards, outdoor boards, outdoor panels, and so on.

overnight: Radio spots airing between midnight and 6:00 a.m.; television spots airing between 1:00 a.m. and 6:00 a.m.

overnights: Nielsen reports that provide daily household ratings for selected markets.

package: A group of television or radio spots offered for sale at a lower price than spots that are sold separately.

painted bulletin: An outdoor advertising structure on which advertising is either painted directly or preprinted on special vinyl and affixed to the structure.

penetration: The percentage of people (or homes) within a defined universe that are capable of being exposed to a medium.

people meters: An electronic device connected to a television set by A.C. Nielsen, which allows the measurement of audiences tuned to a specific program.

people using radio (PUR): The percentage of people using (listening to) radio at a particular time.

people using TV (PUT): The percentage of people using (viewing) TV at a particular time.

per inquiry (PI): A figure used to evaluate the relative performance of inquiries received as a result of advertising.

pod: A group of commercials run back to back during a commercial break.

point-of-purchase (POP) display: An advertising display at the point where people purchase goods (for example, a counter card at a retail location).

post analysis: An analysis of a media schedule's success after it has run.

poster panel: An outdoor advertising structure on which a preprinted advertisement is displayed. Also referred to as a *30-sheet poster.*

prime access: A television daypart, generally between 7:00 p.m. and 8:00 p.m., immediately preceding prime time.

prime time: In broadcast, the daypart that attracts the most viewers or listeners. On television, generally 8:00 p.m.–11:00 p.m.; on radio, generally morning and afternoon drive times (6:00 a.m.–10:00 a.m. and 3:00 p.m.–7:00 p.m.).

print media: Refers to all magazines, newspapers, newsletters, brochures, pamphlets, or any publications that contains advertising.

public service announcement (PSA): Community service announcements carried by broadcast stations free of charge.

qualitative research: Research based on the quality, type, or components of a group and applied to advertising audience research in order to determine the quality of audience responses to advertising.

quantitative research: Research based on the measurement of quantity or amount, applied to advertising audience research to develop actual numbers of audience members in order to accurately measure market situations.

quarter-hour cume: The reach of a television or radio station or program during a 15-minute airing segment; the total unduplicated audience during that 15-minute segment.

ranker: A computer-generated report showing a selected demographic audience of each radio station in a market, ranked from the highest to the lowest.

rate card: A printed piece that states the costs for advertising on or in an advertising vehicle, plus other relevant information such as circulation, mechanical requirements, and so on.

rating: The percentage of a given population group consuming a medium at a particular time. Generally used for broadcast media. For instance, to say that a television program has a 10 rating of adults 18–49 is to say that 10 percent of the adult population between the ages of 18 and 49 viewed an average minute of programming.

reach: The number or percentage of a population group exposed to a media schedule within a given period of time. For example, to say that a media schedule will produce a 50 reach is to say that 50 percent of the defined population group will be exposed to one or more advertising messages.

regional edition: An edition of a national magazine that is designed for advertisers in a particular geographic area. Advertising in regional editions costs less than advertising in the full circulation of a publication.

remote: The broadcast of a program (generally radio) from a location other than the station's studio. Used as a promotional device on behalf of an advertiser.

retail rate: A newspaper advertising rate offered to local retailers.

rotation: In broadcast, the running of commercials at different times each day within the time period ordered; in outdoor, moving a bulletin to a different location at stated intervals.

rotator: A broadcast commercial in rotation.

rotogravure: An impression (art, copy, photo) engraved or etched on a cylindrical printing surface (usually copper) whereby the ink is held within the etched crevices. Paper is run through a rotary press that prints both sides of the paper at the same time.

run of station (ROS): A tactic used in broadcast whereby commercials are scheduled throughout the day and night at the discretion of the station, as opposed to time periods designated by the advertiser.

saturating: Scheduling many commercials within a short time period to create maximum impact for an advertising message.

share of audience: The percentage of persons or households tuned to a particular program or station.

short rate: In print media, the dollar penalty an advertiser pays for not fulfilling space requirements that were contracted for.

showing: The number of outdoor boards purchased and the length of time they will be displayed.

skew: A statistical deviation. A radio station that has proportionately more younger than older listeners is said to *skew* to a younger audience.

space discount: A discount earned off the open rate for placing a specified amount of space in print media.

sponsorship: The purchase of multiple commercials within a program, allowing advertisers to receive bonus time via billboards.

spot: See *announcement*.

spot radio: Local radio time set aside for commercials.

spot television: Local television time set aside for commercials.

spot times: The specific times that a commercial airs.

station format: The type of programming carried by a radio station (for example, rock, news, or classical).

sweeps: The period when local market television ratings are studied. Sweeps are issued four times per year in all markets and more frequently in major markets.

tear sheet: The actual ad that ran in a publication sent to the advertiser as proof of running; usually required to collect co-op advertising funds.

teaser: An advertising message, often brief, that is used to tease the audience by containing only bits of information about the product; it may not include the name of the advertiser.

television household: A household that has at least one television set.

tent card: A display ad printed and folded so it is readable on both sides; usually used in restaurants.

test market: A market chosen for the purpose of conducting a media test.

time spent listening (TSL): The time spent listening to a radio station by the average listener.

total audience plan (TAP): A radio term for a schedule of spots airing in multiple time periods meant to accumulate high levels of audience reach on a station.

trade: See *barter.*

traffic department: In broadcast, the department that processes and schedules the creative material (commercials) to be used on the media.

traffic instructions: Written instructions given to a medium on how commercials or print ads are to be inserted into the medium.

transit advertising: Advertising that appears on buses, taxis, subways, commuter trains, and other forms of transit.

two-color (2C): The use of one color in addition to black and white in a print ad.

under-delivery: A situation in which a media schedule or unit generated less audience than originally estimated by the media. Under-delivery usually results in make goods.

unduplicated audience: See *cumulative audience.*

universe: The total population within a defined demographic, geographic, psychographic, or product consumption segment against which media audiences are calculated to determine ratings, coverage, reach, and so on.

vertical half page: A magazine or newspaper advertising unit that divides the page in half vertically as opposed to horizontally.

voice-over: The part of a television commercial that is spoken by an announcer who is heard but not seen on the screen.

zone (or zoned) edition: An edition of a newspaper geared toward and distributed to a particular geographic zone (usually determined by zip codes). You can buy less than a newspaper's full circulation by targeting your advertising to particular zones of the paper's circulation.

Index

Notes

Notes